A Greek Reader

**EERDMANS
LANGUAGE
RESOURCES**

The Eerdmans Language Resources series is a collection of textbooks, readers, reference books, and monographs pertaining to languages commonly used in biblical and theological studies. In these volumes, students and scholars will find indispensable help in understanding and mastering Hebrew, Aramaic, Greek, and other languages.

Other ELR Titles

Jacob N. Cerone and Matthew C. Fischer, *Daily Scriptures: 365 Readings in Hebrew, Greek, and Latin*

N. Clayton Croy, *A Primer of Biblical Greek*

S. R. Driver, *A Treatise on the Use of the Tenses in Hebrew and Some Other Syntactical Questions*

Holger Gzella, *Aramaic: A History of the First World Language*

William L. Holladay, *A Concise Hebrew and Aramaic Lexicon of the Old Testament*

Page H. Kelley and Timothy G. Crawford, *Biblical Hebrew: An Introductory Grammar*, 2nd ed.

Page H. Kelley, Terry L. Burden, and Timothy G. Crawford, *A Handbook to "Biblical Hebrew: An Introductory Grammar,"* 2nd ed.

William Sanford Lasor, *Handbook of Biblical Hebrew*

Rodney A. Whitacre, *A Grammar of New Testament Greek*

A GREEK READER

Companion to *A Primer of Biblical Greek*

MARK JEONG

WILLIAM B. EERDMANS PUBLISHING COMPANY

GRAND RAPIDS, MICHIGAN

Wm. B. Eerdmans Publishing Co.
4035 Park East Court SE, Grand Rapids, Michigan 49546
www.eerdmans.com

28 27 26 25 24 23   2 3 4 5 6 7

ISBN 978-0-8028-7991-2

Library of Congress Cataloging-in-Publication Data

A catalog record for this book is available from the Library of Congress.

τοῖς μαθηταῖς μου τοῖς πρώτοις
To my first students

CONTENTS

While planning to teach my first Greek course, I searched in vain for a resource that would help my students engage with Koine Greek *from the beginning* in a natural and enjoyable way. By natural, I mean the way people learn and use languages outside of academic settings. Having learned several modern languages, I knew that the way to acquire a language is not through rote memorization of grammar rules or through dissecting difficult sentences, but through large amounts of input in the form of reading and listening.

Research into second-language acquisition supports this claim. In recent years, linguists have shown that students need input that is "comprehensible" and "compelling" to acquire a language, but this is sorely lacking when it comes to Koine Greek.* Few resources or textbooks exist that provide simple narratives for first-year students to read from the beginning of their studies. Instead, students must claw their way through beginner textbooks, with only isolated sentences to guide them.

It is my hope that this book can help alleviate the transition between isolated sentences and authentic texts by providing simple narratives written in Koine Greek that mostly use only the vocabulary and grammar studied up to a certain point. Students who use Clayton Croy's *A Primer of Biblical Greek* will especially be able to follow along, since each section is keyed to the vocabulary and grammar of Croy's textbook. Students using other textbooks can also benefit from these stories, since each narrative is accompanied by vocabulary and grammar notes.

Whether these stories are "compelling" is, of course, up to the reader, but I have tried to write a continuous narrative following the adventures of Paul, Philemon, and Onesimus, with some other stories sprinkled throughout. Students should note that I have not aimed at historical accuracy in this retelling, but have simply aimed to write a comprehensible, compelling story that is easy to follow for beginning students.

---

* The terms "compelling" and "comprehensible" are used by Stephen Krashen in Stephen D. Krashen, Sy-Ying Lee, and Christy Lao, *Comprehensible and Compelling: The Causes and Effects of Free Voluntary Reading* (Santa Barbara: Libraries Unlimited, 2018). For a summary of how these principles apply to classical language instruction, see Robert Patrick, "Comprehensible Input and Krashen's Theory," *Journal of Classics Teaching* 20.39 (2019): 37–44.

How to Use This Book

I have used these stories in a variety of ways with my students, including the following:

- Having students translate all or a portion of a narrative
- Having students read the stories without translating, using the notes and English translation as a guide
- Having students listen to the stories to internalize them

Because each lesson of Croy contains a lot of grammar, students are advised to thoroughly read and learn the vocabulary of a chapter before attempting to read that chapter's story. Instructors can assign these stories after they have reviewed the material in a chapter, or they can use the stories themselves to introduce new grammar points.

Some instructors will prefer to ask students to avoid the English translations and continue to meticulously translate each story. I have done this as well, but through trial and error, I have found that my students benefit most from simply reading each story several times, with the notes and English translation as a guide. They should do this until they can read the Greek completely without any help and with full understanding. Since each Greek text is on its own page, students can cover the notes to test themselves. In class, I then assess students' understanding by reading the story to them and asking them comprehension questions (e.g., Why couldn't Philemon find Onesimus?), grammar questions (e.g., Why is the imperfect used here?), or calling on them to translate.

I have erred on the side of providing more help than some may think is necessary, but the vocabulary and grammar notes will keep students focused *on the text*, instead of forcing them to flip through another resource. My goal in all this is to help students *read* the stories *as Greek*, and not as a code for English. This will be difficult at first, but with a bit of practice, this book can serve as a student's first steps toward fluent and enjoyable reading of authentic Greek texts.

1p	first-person plural	inf.	infinitive
1s	first-person singular	lit.	literally
2p	second-person plural	masc.	masculine
2s	second-person singular	mid.	middle
3p	third-person plural	neut.	neuter
3s	third-person singular	nom.	nominative
acc.	accusative	opt.	optative
act.	active	pass.	passive
adj.	adjective	perf.	perfect
adv.	adverb	pl.	plural
aor.	aorist	pluperf.	pluperfect
compar.	comparative	pres.	present
dat.	dative	pron.	pronoun
fem.	feminine	ptcpl.	participle
fut.	future	rel.	relative
gen.	genitive	sing.	singular
impf.	imperfect	subj.	subjunctive
impv.	imperative	usu.	usually
ind.	indicative	voc.	vocative
indef.	indefinite		

GREEK STORIES

1   *(Lesson 1 of Croy covers the alphabet and pronunciation, so students can use this story to familiarize themselves with the Greek letters and to learn vocabulary for future dialogues and stories)*

5   Ἰάκωβος, "Χαῖρε! ἐγώ εἰμι Ἰάκωβος."

Δαυίδ, "Χαῖρε! ἐγώ εἰμι Δαυίδ."

(Again)

10 Ἰάκωβος, "Χαῖρε! τίς εἶ σύ;"

Δαυίδ, "Ἐγώ εἰμι Δαυίδ. τίς εἶ σύ;"

15 Ἰάκωβος, "Ἐγώ εἰμι Ἰάκωβος."

(Mary, who knows David, joins the group)

Μαρία, "Χαῖρε! Τίς ἐστιν αὐτός;"

20 Δαυίδ, "Αὐτός ἐστιν Ἰάκωβος."

Ἰάκωβος (to David), "Τίς ἐστιν αὐτή;"

25 Δαυίδ, "Αὐτή ἐστιν Μαρία."

(ὁ διδάσκαλος says hello to everyone)

Μάρκος, "Χαίρετε!"

30 Δαυίδ, "Χαῖρε!"

Μαρία, "Χαῖρε! τίς εἶ σύ;"

35 Μάρκος, "Ἐγώ εἰμι ὁ διδάσκαλος."

Δαυίδ, "Τί;"

αὐτή, she

αὐτός, he

Δαυίδ, ὁ, David

διδάσκαλος, ου, ὁ, teacher

ἐγώ, I

εἶ, you (sing.) are

εἰμί, I am

ἐστίν, he/she/it is

Ἰάκωβος, ου, ὁ, Jacob
  (or James in the NT)

Μαρία, ας, ἡ, Mary

Μάρκος, ου, ὁ, Mark

ὄνομα, ὀνόματος, τό, name

σύ, you

τί, what?

τίς, who?

χαῖρε, hello (a greeting to one
  person; lit. rejoice!)

χαίρετε, hello (to more than
  one person)

5 χαῖρε – the most common way to greet someone in Greek. It literally
   means "rejoice!" as a command. When addressing more than one person,
   χαίρετε is used.

19 αὐτός – personal pronouns such as αὐτός, αὐτή, and ἐγώ are introduced
   later (Croy lesson 7), but are used throughout these earlier stories.

1   Μάρκος, "Ἐγώ εἰμι ὁ διδάσκαλος."

Ἰάκωβος, "Τί ὄνομά σοι;"

5   Μάρκος, "Ἐγώ εἰμι Μάρκος! τί ὄνομά σοι;"

Ἰάκωβος, "Ἐγώ εἰμι Ἰάκωβος."

Μάρκος, "Τί ὄνομα αὐτῇ;"

10

Ἰάκωβος, "Ὄνομα αὐτῇ Μαρία."

διδάσκαλος, ου, ὁ, teacher
ἐγώ, I
εἰμί, I am
Ἰάκωβος, ου, ὁ, Jacob (or James in the NT)

Μαρία, ας, ἡ, Mary
Μάρκος, ου, ὁ, Mark
ὄνομα, ὀνόματος, τό, name
τί, what?

3   **Τί ὄνομά σοι;** – an idiomatic way of asking, "what is your name?" σοι is a form of the personal pronoun. Likewise, Τί ὄνομα αὐτῇ; asks, "what is her name?"

11   **Ὄνομα αὐτῇ Μαρία** – "her name is Mary."

1 Ἰάκωβος, "Χαῖρε! ἐγώ εἰμι Ἰάκωβος. τίς εἶ σύ;"

Δαυίδ, "Χαῖρε! ἐγώ εἰμι Δαυίδ. τί γράφεις;"

5 Ἰάκωβος, "Ἐγὼ γράφω βιβλίον."

(Mary joins them)

Μαρία, "Χαῖρε!"

10 Δαυίδ, "Χαῖρε! βλέπεις ὅτι Ἰάκωβος γράφει;"

Μαρία, "Βλέπω ὅτι ὁ Ἰάκωβος γράφει. τί γράφει ὁ Ἰάκωβος;"

15 Δαυίδ, "Βιβλίον γράφει ὁ Ἰάκωβος."

Μαρία, "Καὶ ἐγὼ θέλω γράφειν βιβλίον."

Μαρία καὶ Ἰάκωβος γράφουσιν.

20 Δαυὶδ οὐ γράφει. Δαυὶδ οὐ θέλει γράφειν. Δαυὶδ θέλει λύειν τὸ βιβλίον.

Μάρκος βλέπει ὅτι Μαρία καὶ Ἰάκωβος γράφουσιν.

25 Μάρκος, "Τί γράφετε; θέλω βλέπειν καὶ ἀκούειν."

Ἰάκωβος καὶ Μαρία, "Γράφομεν βιβλίον. θέλεις γράφειν;"

30 Μάρκος, "Οὐ θέλω γράφειν. θέλω διδάσκειν."

Δαυίδ, "Καὶ ἐγὼ θέλω διδάσκειν . . ."

Δαυὶδ λύει τὸ βιβλίον! Ἰάκωβος καὶ Μαρία οὐ γράφουσιν.

35 Μαρία λέγει, "Τί ποιεῖς;"

Δαυὶδ λέγει, "Διδάσκω!"

ἀκούω, I hear

βιβλίον, ου, τό, book

βλέπω, I see

γράφω, I write

διδάσκω, I teach

ἐγώ, I

εἶ, you (sing.) are

εἰμί, I am

θέλω, I wish, will, desire

καί, and

λέγω, I say, speak, tell

λύω, I destroy, loosen

ὅτι, that, because

οὐ, οὐκ, οὐχ, not, no

ποιεῖς, you are doing, you do

σύ, you (sing.)

τί, what?

τίς, who?

χαῖρε, hello (a greeting to one
  person; lit. rejoice!)

5 Ἐγὼ γράφω βιβλίον – the pronoun "ἐγώ" is not strictly necessary, since
   it is implied by the first-person singular verb γράφω, but its inclusion
   adds emphasis.

13 ὁ Ἰάκωβος – the definite articles "ὁ" and "τό" (line 21) are introduced later
   in lesson 4. Proper names often take the definite article.

17 Καὶ ἐγὼ θέλω . . . – καί can be used adverbially to mean "also." See also
   line 32, "Καὶ ἐγὼ θέλω διδάσκειν . . ."

36 Τί ποιεῖς; – "What are you doing?" The conjugation of the verb ποιέω is
   slightly different from the verbs learned in lesson 2. For now, focus on the
   meaning of the verb. Such verbs are fully introduced in lesson 21.

1 Ἰάκωβος λέγει, "Οὐ διδάσκεις! σὺ λύεις τὸ βιβλίον!"

Μαρία καὶ Ἰάκωβος λέγουσιν, "Οὐ πιστεύομεν ὅτι λύεις τὸ βιβλίον. διὰ τί λύεις τὸ βιβλίον; θέλομεν γινώσκειν!"

5 Δαυὶδ λέγει, "Λύω τὸ βιβλίον ὅτι οὐ θέλω γράφειν!"

Μαρία κλαίει. Ἰάκωβος κλαίει. Μαρία καὶ Ἰάκωβος κλαίουσιν.

10 Μάρκος ἀκούει ὅτι Μαρία καὶ Ἰάκωβος κλαίουσιν.

Μάρκος λέγει, "Διὰ τί κλαίετε;"

Μαρία καὶ Ἰάκωβος, "Κλαίομεν ὅτι Δαυὶδ λύει τὸ βιβλίον!"

15 Μάρκος λέγει, "Ὦ, Δαυίδ! διὰ τί λύεις τὸ βιβλίον;"

Δαυὶδ λέγει, "Λύω τὸ βιβλίον ὅτι θέλω διδάσκειν αὐτοὺς ὅτι οὐ θέλω γράφειν."

20 Μάρκος λέγει, "Τί; οὐ γινώσκεις ὅτι ἐγώ εἰμι ὁ διδάσκαλος;"

Δαυὶδ λέγει, "Τί ἐστιν διδάσκαλος;"

25 Μάρκος λέγει, "Διδάσκαλος διδάσκει."

αὐτούς, them
βιβλίον, ου, τό, book
γινώσκω, I know
διὰ τί, For what reason? Why?
διδάσκαλος, ου, ὁ, teacher

ἐστίν, he/she/it is
κλαίω, I cry
πιστεύω, I believe
τί, what?
ὦ, oh! (an exclamation)

1   σὺ λύεις τὸ βιβλίον! – Like "ἐγώ" above, the pronoun "σύ" is not neces-
    sary, since it is implied by the second-person singular verb λύεις, but its
    inclusion adds emphasis.

1 **Story A**

Πρίσκα, "Ἡ ἀδελφή μου λέγει ὅτι Ἰησοῦς ἔχει βασιλείαν."

5 Σαῦλος, "Τί ἐστιν ἡ βασιλεία; οὐ βλέπω καὶ οὐ πιστεύω. ἡ ἀδελφή σου οὐ λέγει τὴν ἀλήθειαν."

Πρίσκα, "Λέγει καὶ ἡ ἐκκλησία ὅτι Ἰησοῦς ἔχει βασιλείαν. οὐ πιστεύεις;"

10 Βαρναβᾶς, "Ἐγὼ ἀκούω ὅτι Ἰησοῦς θέλει ἔχειν τὴν βασιλείαν τῆς γῆς."

Πρίσκα, "Οὐ λέγεις τὴν ἀλήθειαν. οὐ γινώσκεις ὅτι Ἰησοῦς βλέπει

15 τὴν καρδίαν;"

Σαῦλος καὶ Βαρναβᾶς οὐ πιστεύουσιν ὅτι Ἰησοῦς ἔχει βασιλείαν.

20 (Jesus appears before them)

Ἰησοῦς, "Τί λέγετε;"

Πρίσκα, "Σαῦλος καὶ Βαρναβᾶς οὐ πιστεύουσιν ὅτι ἔχεις

25 βασιλείαν."

Σαῦλος καὶ Βαρναβᾶς, "Οὐ πιστεύομεν ὅτι οὐ βλέπομεν!"

Ἰησοῦς, "Λέγω τὴν ἀλήθειαν καὶ οὐ πιστεύετε. βλέπω ὅτι οὐ

30 γινώσκετε τὴν ἀλήθειαν."

Πρίσκα καὶ Σαῦλος καὶ Βαρναβᾶς, "Τί ἐστιν ἀλήθεια; θέλομεν γινώσκειν."

35 Ἰησοῦς, "Ἐγώ εἰμι ἡ ἀλήθεια καὶ ἡ ζωή. ἔχω βασιλείαν. οὐ πιστεύετε ὅτι οὐ βλέπετε; οὐκ ἔστιν ὥρα βλέπειν. ὥρα ἐστὶν πιστεύειν!"

ἀδελφή, ῆς, ἡ, sister
ἀλήθεια, ας, ἡ, truth
Βαρναβᾶς, ᾶ, ὁ, Barnabas
βασιλεία, ας, ἡ, kingdom, reign, rule
γῆ, γῆς, ἡ, earth, soil, land
δόξα, ης, ἡ, glory, honor
εἰμί, I am
ἐκκλησία, ας, ἡ, assembly, church
ἐστίν, he/she/it is
ἔχω, I have
ζωή, ῆς, ἡ, life

Ἰησοῦς, οῦ, ὁ, Jesus (Joshua in the OT)
καρδία, ας, ἡ, heart
μου, my, of me
Πρίσκα, ης, ἡ, Prisca
Σαῦλος, ου, ὁ, Saul
σου, your, of you (sing.)
τήν, the (acc. fem. sing. definite article)
τῆς, the (gen. fem. sing. definite article)
τί, what?
ὥρα, ας, ἡ, hour, time

3 ἡ ἀδελφή μου – "my sister." μου is the gen. sing. form of the personal pronoun ἐγώ.

8 καὶ ἡ ἐκκλησία – καί can be used adverbially to mean "also."

36 οὐκ ἔστιν ὥρα βλέπειν – "it is not time to see." Ἐστίν means "is" and can either link two nouns (e.g., "The earth **is** my kingdom") or be used in an impersonal sense (e.g., "**It is** time to believe") as here.

FORMS OF THE DEFINITE ARTICLE

	Singular			Plural		
	Masc.	Fem.	Neut.	Masc.	Fem.	Neut.
Nom.	ὁ	ἡ	τό	οἱ	αἱ	τά
Gen.	τοῦ	τῆς	τοῦ	τῶν	τῶν	τῶν
Dat.	τῷ	τῇ	τῷ	τοῖς	ταῖς	τοῖς
Acc.	τόν	τήν	τό	τούς	τάς	τά

1   *Story B*

(Ποσειδῶν, the god of the sea, and Γαῖα, the goddess of the earth, are having a friendly chat)

5

Ποσειδῶν, "Ἐγὼ ἔχω βασιλείαν."

Γαῖα, "Τί ἐστιν ἡ βασιλεία σου;"

10   Ποσειδῶν, "Ἡ βασιλεία μου ἡ θάλασσά ἐστιν."

Γαῖα, "Οὐ πιστεύω! οὐκ ἔχεις βασιλείαν! θέλω βλέπειν."

Ποσειδῶν, "θέλεις βλέπειν; Οὐκ ἔστιν ὥρα βλέπειν. ὥρα ἐστὶν
15   ἀκούειν καὶ πιστεύειν."

Γαῖα, "Οὐ λέγεις τὴν ἀλήθειαν. ἐγὼ λέγω τὴν ἀλήθειαν καὶ ἔχω βασιλείαν. θέλεις βλέπειν;"

20   Ποσειδῶν, "Τί ἐστιν ἡ βασιλεία σου;"

Γαῖα, "Βλέπεις τὴν γῆν; ἡ γῆ ἐστιν ἡ βασιλεία μου. βλέπεις τὴν δόξαν τῆς γῆς;"

25   Ποσειδῶν, "Βλέπω τὴν γῆν, ἀλλὰ δόξαν οὐκ ἔχει ἡ γῆ."

Γαῖα, "Καὶ ἡ θάλασσα οὐκ ἔχει δόξαν . . ."

30   *Story C*

(John receives a vision from an angel and begins to write a letter to the church)

35   Ἰωάννης γράφει. ὁ ἄγγελος λέγει ὅτι ἡ ἐκκλησία οὐκ ἔχει ζωὴν ὅτι οὐ πιστεύει καὶ οὐκ ἀκούει.

Ἡ ἐκκλησία θέλει ἔχειν δόξαν καὶ οὐ θέλει ἔχειν ζωήν. Ἰωάννης

ἄγγελος, ου, ὁ, angel
ἀλλά, but
Γαῖα, Γαίας, ἡ, Gaia
δόξα, ης, ἡ, glory, honor
ἐστίν, he/she/it is
θάλασσα, ης, ἡ, sea, lake

Ἰωάννης, ου, ὁ, John
μου, my, of me
Ποσειδῶν, Ποσειδῶνος, ὁ, Poseidon
σου, your, of you (sing.)
τί, what?

22 τὴν δόξαν τῆς γῆς – "the glory of the earth." Τῆς is the fem. gen. sing. form of the definite article.

25 δόξαν οὐκ ἔχει ἡ γῆ – "the earth does not have glory." Greek word order is very flexible, unlike English. The cases of the nouns determine their function in a sentence. The object of a verb can come first (as here) for emphasis.

1   γράφει ὅτι ἡ ἐκκλησία οὐ γινώσκει τὴν ἀλήθειαν καὶ τὴν ὥραν. τί
    ὥρα ἐστίν; ὥρα ἐστὶν πιστεύειν!

5   *Story D*

(Satan meets Jesus in the desert)

Σατανᾶς, "Ὦ, Ἰησοῦ, τί θέλεις ἔχειν;"

10

Ἰησοῦς, ". . ."

Σατανᾶς, "Οὐ θέλεις ἔχειν τὴν βασιλείαν τῆς γῆς;"

15 Ἰησοῦς, "Οὐ θέλω ἔχειν τὴν βασιλείαν τῆς γῆς."

Σατανᾶς, "Οὐ βλέπεις τὴν βασιλείαν τῆς γῆς; οὐ βλέπεις τὴν
δόξαν τῆς βασιλείας;"

20 Ἰησοῦς, "Οὐ βλέπω τὴν δόξαν τῆς βασιλείας τῆς γῆς. αἱ βασιλείαι
    τῆς γῆς οὐκ ἔχουσιν δόξαν."

Σατανᾶς, "Τίς ἔχει δόξαν;"

25 Ἰησοῦς, "Αἱ ἐκκλησίαι ἔχουσιν δόξαν ὅτι αἱ ἐκκλησίαι ἀκούουσιν
    τῆς φωνῆς μου."

Σατανᾶς, "Αἱ ἐκκλησίαι ἔχουσιν δόξαν; οὐ βλέπω τὴν δόξαν τῶν
ἐκκλησιῶν."

30

Story E

(Paul is writing to the churches)

35

Παῦλος γράφει τῇ ἐκκλησίᾳ τῆς Γαλατίας καὶ τῇ ἐκκλησίᾳ
τῆς Κορίνθου. τί γράφει; Παῦλος γράφει ὅτι αἱ ἐκκλησίαι οὐκ

Γαλατίας, of Galatia
ἐστίν, he/she/it is
Κορίνθου, of Corinth
μου, my, of me
Παῦλος, ου, ὁ, Paul

Σατανᾶς, ᾶ, ὁ, Satan
τῇ, the (dat. fem. sing. definite article)
τί, what?
τίς, who?

25 ἀκούουσιν τῆς φωνῆς – the verb ἀκούω most often takes a gen. object.

1   ἀκούουσιν τῆς φωνῆς τῆς ἀληθείας καὶ οὐ πιστεύουσιν τῇ
ἀληθείᾳ. Παῦλος γινώσκει ὅτι αἱ ἐκκλησίαι θέλουσιν ἔχειν δόξαν,
ἀλλὰ οὐ θέλουσιν ἔχειν ζωήν.

5   Παῦλος θέλει λέγειν ταῖς ἐκκλησίαις ὅτι αἱ δόξαι τῆς γῆς λύουσιν
τὰς καρδίας τῶν ἐκκλησιῶν. Παῦλος γράφει ὅτι αἱ ἐκκλησίαι οὐ
γινώσκουσιν τὴν ἀλήθειαν.

τί ποιοῦσιν αἱ ἐκκλησίαι; ἀκούουσιν αἱ ἐκκλησίαι τῆς φωνῆς
10   τῆς ἀληθείας; πιστεύουσιν τῇ ἀληθείᾳ; οὐκ ἀκούουσιν καὶ οὐ
πιστεύουσιν!

Story F

15

(Adapted from Acts 1 before Jesus is about to depart)

Πέτρος καὶ Ἰάκωβος καὶ Ἰωάννης, "Ὥρα ἐστὶν βλέπειν τὴν
βασιλείαν; γινώσκομεν ὅτι ἔχεις βασιλείαν. θέλομεν βλέπειν
20   τὴν βασιλείαν."

Ἰησοῦς, "Θέλετε βλέπειν τὴν βασιλείαν μου; θέλετε βλέπειν τὰς
δόξας τῆς βασιλείας;"

25   Πέτρος καὶ Ἰάκωβος καὶ Ἰωάννης, "Ναί! θέλομεν βλέπειν!"

Ἰησοῦς, "Οὐκ ἔστιν ἡ ἡμέρα τῆς δόξης. ὥρα ἐστὶν πιστεύειν τῇ
φωνῇ μου καὶ τῇ ἀληθείᾳ. πιστεύετε;"

30   Πέτρος καὶ Ἰάκωβος καὶ Ἰωάννης, "Πιστεύομεν!"

ἐστίν, he/she/it is

ἡμέρα, ας, ἡ, day

ναί, yes

Πέτρος, ου, ὁ, Peter

ποιοῦσιν, they do, are doing

τάς, the (acc. fem. pl. definite article)

τί, what?

φωνή, ῆς, ἡ, voice, sound

1 **οὐ πιστεύουσιν τῇ ἀληθείᾳ** – the verb πιστεύω takes a dat. object when used without a preposition.

23 **δόξας τῆς βασιλείας** – though the endings of these fem. nouns are the same, δόξα is a "mixed" first declension noun, while βασιλεία is a "pure alpha" first declension noun (Croy p. 14).

1 *Λογος Α*

Ἄνθρωπός τις ἔχει δοῦλον. ὁ δὲ δοῦλος ἔχει τέκνον καὶ τὸ τέκνον
ὁ υἱὸς τοῦ δούλου ἐστίν. ὁ δὲ ἄνθρωπος κύριος τοῦ δούλου ἐστίν.
5 τί ὄνομα δούλῳ; ὄνομα δούλῳ Εὔτυχος. τί ὄνομα τῷ υἱῷ τοῦ
δούλου; ὄνομα Τέρτιος.

τί λέγει ὁ υἱός; λέγει ὅτι θέλει ἔχειν οἶκον.

10 Τέρτιος, "Πάτερ, διὰ τί οὐκ ἔχομεν οἶκον;"

Εὔτυχος, "Ὅτι δοῦλος εἶ."

κύριος τοῦ δούλου, "Ναί. δοῦλος οὐκ ἔχει οἶκον, ἀλλὰ ὁ κύριος
15 ἔχει οἴκους. οὐ γινώσκετε ὅτι ὁ κύριός εἰμι;"

Τέρτιος καὶ Εὔτυχος, "γινώσκομεν . . ."

Τέρτιος ἔχει ἀδελφόν. ὁ δὲ ἀδελφὸς τοῦ Τερτίου ἐστὶν Ὀνήσιμος.
20 Ὀνήσιμος ἔχει ἔργον, ἀλλὰ οὐ θέλει ποιεῖν τὰ ἔργα.

Ὀνήσιμος, "Τὸ ἔργον τοῦ δούλου θάνατός ἐστιν."

Τέρτιος, "Στ! οὐ γινώσκεις ὅτι ὁ κύριος ἀκούει;"
25

ὁ κύριος οὐκ ἀκούει, ἀλλὰ ἔχει υἱόν. ὄνομα τῷ υἱῷ Φιλήμων.
ἀκούει ὁ Φιλήμων τῶν φωνῶν τῶν δούλων; οὐκ ἀκούει, ἀλλὰ
ἀκούει ὁ Φιλήμων τῆς φωνῆς ἀνθρώπου. τίς ἐστιν ὁ ἄνθρωπος;
Παῦλός ἐστιν.

ἀδελφός, οῦ, ὁ, brother

ἀλλά, but

ἄνθρωπος, ου, ὁ, human being, person, man

δέ, but, and

διὰ τί; why?

δοῦλος, ου, ὁ, slave, servant

εἶ, you (sing.) are

εἰμί, I am

ἔργον, ου, τό, work, deed

ἐστίν, he/she/it is

Εὔτυχος, ου, ὁ, Eutychus

θάνατος, ου, ὁ, death

κύριος, ου, ὁ, Lord, master, owner

λόγος, ου, ὁ, word

ναί, yes

οἶκος, ου, ὁ, house

Ὀνήσιμος, ου, ὁ, Onesimus

ὄνομα, ὀνόματος, τό, name

πάτερ, father (voc. of πατήρ)

Παῦλος, ου, ὁ, Paul

ποιεῖν, to do

στ! Shh!

τέκνον, ου, τό, child

Τέρτιος, ου, ὁ, Tertius

τί, what?

τίς, who?

τις, a certain . . .

υἱός, οῦ, ὁ, son

Φιλήμων, Φιλήμονος, ὁ, Philemon

1   Λογος Α – "Story A." λόγος means "word" in the sense of "message," and can also refer to a narrative or story.

3   Ἄνθρωπός τις – "a certain person." τις is an indefinite pronoun, which is covered later in lesson 27.

5   τί ὄνομα δούλῳ; – "what is the slave's name?" (In the construction "the name of A is B," A is in the dative.)

5   ὄνομα δούλῳ Εὔτυχος – "the slave's name is Eutychus."

1 *Λογος Β*

Ἀκούει ὁ Φιλήμων τῆς φωνῆς ἀνθρώπου. τίς ἐστιν ὁ ἄνθρωπος;
Παῦλός ἐστιν. ὁ Φιλήμων ἀκούει τῶν λόγων τοῦ Παύλου.

5

ὁ Φιλήμων βλέπει τὸν ἄνθρωπον καὶ λέγει τῷ ἀνθρώπῳ.

Φιλήμων, "Τί λέγεις;"

10 Παῦλος, "Λέγω τὸν λόγον τοῦ θεοῦ. θέλεις γινώσκειν τὸν λόγον
τῆς ἀληθείας;"

Φιλήμων, "Τί ἐστιν ἀλήθεια; τί ἔχεις λέγειν; ἐγὼ καὶ ὁ κύριος τῶν
δούλων, ἔχομεν οἴκους καὶ δούλους καὶ τέκνα. βλέπεις τὴν δόξαν
15 τοῦ οἴκου ἡμῶν;"

Παῦλος, "Ὦ, ἄνθρωπε! ὁ οἶκός σου οὐκ ἔχει δόξαν, ἀλλὰ ὁ θεὸς
τῆς ζωῆς καὶ τῆς ἀληθείας ἔχει δόξαν."

20 Φιλήμων, "Τί; τίς ἐστιν ὁ θεός; ἔχομεν θεοὺς τῆς γῆς καὶ τῆς
θαλάσσης καὶ τοῦ θανάτου, ἀλλὰ οὐ γινώσκομεν τὸν θεὸν τῆς
ζωῆς καὶ τῆς ἀληθείας."

Παῦλος, "Οἱ θεοί σου οὐκ εἰσὶν θεοί, ἀλλὰ ἔργα ἀνθρώπων.
25 ὁ λόγος τοῦ θεοῦ λέγει ὅτι ὁ θεὸς θέλει ἔχειν τὰς καρδίας
τῶν ἀνθρώπων."

Φιλήμων, "Οὐ πιστεύω τοῖς λόγοις σου! θέλω βλέπειν τὸν θεόν
σου."

30

Παῦλος, "Οὐκ ἔστιν ὥρα βλέπειν, ἀλλὰ πιστεύειν."

εἰσίν, they are
ἡμῶν, of us, our
θεός, οῦ, ὁ, God, god

σου, your (sing.)
τί, what?
τίς, who?

10   τὸν λόγον τῆς ἀληθείας – "the word of truth." Greek definite articles are
not always translated into English.

13   τί ἔχεις λέγειν – question words such as τί can act as the object of a verb,
as it does here.

1   *Λογος Α*

Ἀκούει ὁ Φιλήμων τῆς καλῆς φωνῆς ἀνθρώπου. τίς ἐστιν ὁ
ἄνθρωπος; Παῦλός ἐστιν. ὁ δὲ Φιλήμων βλέπει τὸν ἅγιον
5   ἄνθρωπον καὶ ἀκούει τῶν λόγων τῶν ἀγαθῶν καὶ λέγει τῷ
ἀνθρώπῳ, θέλει γὰρ γινώσκειν τί λέγει.

Φιλήμων, "Τί λέγεις;"

10   Παῦλος, "Λέγω τὸν λόγον τοῦ ἀγαθοῦ θεοῦ. θέλεις γινώσκειν τὸν
λόγον τῆς ἀληθείας;"

Φιλήμων, "Τί ἐστιν ἀλήθεια; τί ἔχεις λέγειν; ἐγὼ καὶ ὁ κύριος τῶν
δούλων, ἔχομεν οἴκους καὶ δούλους καὶ τέκνα. βλέπεις τὸν καλὸν
15   οἶκον ἡμῶν;"

Παῦλος, "Ὦ, ἄνθρωπε! ὁ οἶκός σου οὐ καλός, ἀλλὰ ὁ θεὸς τῆς
ζωῆς καὶ τῆς ἀληθείας καλός."

20   Φιλήμων, "Τί; τίς ἐστιν ὁ θεὸς ὁ καλός; ἔχομεν θεοὺς τῆς γῆς καὶ
τῆς θαλάσσης καὶ τοῦ θανάτου, ἀλλὰ οὐ γινώσκομεν τὸν θεὸν τῆς
ζωῆς καὶ τῆς ἀληθείας."

Παῦλος, "Οἱ θεοί σου οὐκ εἰσὶν θεοί, ἀλλὰ ἔργα τῶν πονηρῶν
25   ἀνθρώπων. οἱ θεοί σου πονηροί, ἀλλὰ ὁ θεός μου δίκαιος, ὁ γὰρ
θεός μου θέλει ἔχειν τὰς καρδίας τῶν ἀνθρώπων."

Φιλήμων, "Οὐ λαμβάνω τὸν λόγον σου! λέγεις κακοὺς λόγους!
θέλω βλέπειν τὸν θεόν σου."

30
Παῦλος, "Οὐκ ἔστιν ὥρα βλέπειν, ἀλλὰ πιστεύειν τῇ καλῇ
ἀληθείᾳ."

ἀγαθός, ή, όν, good, noble
ἅγιος, α, ον, holy, consecrated
γάρ, for
δίκαιος, α, ον, righteous, just
εἰσίν, they are
ἐστίν, he/she/it is
ἡμῶν, of us, our
κακός, ή, όν, bad, evil

καλός, ή, όν, good, beautiful
λαμβάνω, I take, receive
μικρός, ά, όν, small, little
μου, my, of me
πονηρός, ά, όν, wicked, evil
σου, your (sing.)
τί, what?
τίς, who?

3 τῆς καλῆς φωνῆς – adjective in the attributive position.
5 τῶν λόγων τῶν ἀγαθῶν – adjective in the attributive position.
6 γινώσκειν τί λέγει – τί is a question word that can also be used in indirect questions ("to know what he is saying").
17 ὁ οἶκός . . . οὐ καλός – adjective in predicate position.

1 *Λόγος Β*

Ἄνθρωπός τις ἔχει δοῦλον. ὁ δὲ δοῦλος ἔχει τέκνον καὶ τὸ τέκνον
ὁ υἱὸς τοῦ δούλου ἐστίν. ὁ δὲ ἄνθρωπος κύριος τοῦ δούλου ἐστίν.

5 τί ὄνομα δούλῳ; ὄνομα δούλῳ Εὔτυχος. τί ὄνομα τῷ υἱῷ τοῦ
δούλου; ὄνομα Τέρτιος. Τέρτιος ἀγαθὸς δοῦλός ἐστιν καὶ ἔχει
ἀδελφόν. ὁ δὲ ἀδελφὸς τοῦ Τερτίου ἐστὶν Ὀνήσιμος. ἀγαθὸς δέ
ἐστιν Ὀνήσιμος; Ὀνήσιμος ἔχει ἔργον, ἀλλὰ οὐ θέλει ποιεῖν τὰ
ἔργα. κακὸς δοῦλός ἐστιν.

10 Ὀνήσιμος, "Τὸ ἔργον τοῦ δούλου θάνατός ἐστιν. τὸ ἔργον κακόν,
ὁ γὰρ κύριος πονηρός."

Τέρτιος, "Στ! οὐ γινώσκεις ὅτι ὁ κύριος ἀκούει;"

15

Λόγος Γ

(Ποσειδῶν, ὁ θεὸς τῆς θαλάσσης καὶ Γαῖα, ἡ θεὰ τῆς γῆς,
20 λέγουσιν)

Ποσειδῶν, "Ἔχω βασιλείαν καλὴν καὶ ἀγαθήν."

Γαῖα, "Τί ἐστιν ἡ βασιλεία σου;"

25 Ποσειδῶν, "Ἡ βασιλεία μου ἡ θάλασσά ἐστιν."

Γαῖα, "Οὐ πιστεύω! ἡ θάλασσα οὐκ ἔστιν ἡ βασιλεία σου! γινώσκω
ὅτι ἡ θάλασσα καλὴ καὶ ἀγαθή, ἀλλὰ ἡ βασιλεία σου κακὴ καὶ
30 μικρά. ἐγὼ ἔχω βασιλείαν. θέλεις βλέπειν;"

Ποσειδῶν, "Τί ἐστιν ἡ βασιλεία σου;"

Γαῖα, "Βλέπεις τὴν γῆν τὴν καλήν; ἡ γῆ ἐστιν ἡ βασιλεία μου."

35 Ποσειδῶν, "Βλέπω τὴν γῆν, ἀλλὰ οὐ καλὴ ἡ γῆ ὅτι ἔχει πονηροὺς
ἀνθρώπους. οἱ πονηροὶ λύουσιν τὴν γῆν τὴν καλήν."

Γαῖα, "Τὴν ἀλήθειαν λέγεις . . . οἱ ἄνθρωποι κακοὶ καὶ πονηροί!"

ἐστίν, he/she/it is
ἔσχατος, η, ον, last
θεά, ᾶς, ἡ, goddess
μου, my, of me

ποιεῖν, to do
σου, your (sing.)
τί, what?
τις, a certain . . .

37 οἱ πονηροί – substantive adjective.

1   *Λογος Α*

Ἰωνᾶς προφήτης θεοῦ ἐστιν. οἱ δὲ ἄνθρωποι τῆς Νινευὴ πονηροί,
ἀλλὰ ὁ θεὸς θέλει διδάσκειν τοὺς ἀνθρώπους τῆς Νινευὴ τὸν
5   λόγον τὸν τῆς ἀληθείας. Ἰωνᾶς δὲ οὐ θέλει, γινώσκει γὰρ ὅτι κακοὶ
καὶ πονηροὶ οἱ ἄνθρωποι.

ὁ θεὸς πέμπει Ἰωνᾶν εἰς τὴν Νινευὴ ὅτι θέλει λαμβάνειν τοὺς
πονηροὺς ἀνθρώπους τῆς Νινευή. ἀλλὰ ἀκούει Ἰωνᾶς τῆς τοῦ
10   θεοῦ φωνῆς; οὐκ ἀκούει.

ὁ δὲ θεὸς βάλλει τὴν θάλασσαν πρὸς τὸν Ἰωνᾶν, ὁ γὰρ θεὸς θέλει
διδάσκειν Ἰωνᾶν ὅτι καὶ τοὺς ἀνθρώπους τοὺς κακοὺς θέλει
λαμβάνειν. νῦν δὲ ἀκούει Ἰωνᾶς καὶ πιστεύουσιν οἱ ἄνθρωποι τῆς
15   Νινευὴ εἰς τὸν θεόν.

Λογος Β

20   Παῦλος διδάσκει Φιλήμονα τὸν λόγον ἀπὸ θεοῦ. Φιλήμων δὲ
πιστεύει ὅτι ἄγγελος ἐξ οὐρανοῦ ἐστιν ὁ Παῦλος.

λέγει Φιλήμων, "Ἄγγελος εἶ τοῦ θεοῦ!"

25   Παῦλος, "Οὐκ εἰμὶ ἄγγελος ἀλλὰ προφήτης θεοῦ, λέγω γὰρ τὸν
λόγον ἀπὸ θεοῦ. θεὸς πέμπει με εἰς τὰς βασιλείας τοῦ κόσμου ὅτι
θέλει λαμβάνειν τὰς καρδίας τῶν ἀνθρώπων. πιστεύεις τῷ θεῷ;
πιστεύεις ὅτι ἄνρθωπος οὐκ ἐξ ἔργων νόμου ἔχει ζωήν;"

30   Φιλήμων, "Νῦν πιστεύω εἰς τὸν θεόν σου!"

νῦν πιστεύει Φιλήμων εἰς τὸν θεόν. νῦν γινώσκει τὴν ὁδὸν
τῆς ἀληθείας. νῦν ἐν Χριστῷ ἐστιν. νῦν μαθητής ἐστιν. καὶ
Ὀνήσιμος ἀκούει τῶν λόγων τοῦ Παύλου καὶ τοῦ Φιλήμονος
35   ἀλλὰ οὐ γινώσκει τί λέγουσιν. θέλει γινώσκειν, ἀλλὰ οὐκ
ἔχει διδάσκαλον.

ἄγγελος, ου, ὁ, angel, messenger
ἀπό, (+ gen.) from
βάλλω, I throw, put, place
διδάσκαλος, ου, ὁ, teacher
εἶ, you (sing.) are
εἰμί, I am
εἰς, (+ acc.) into, to, against
ἐκ, ἐξ, (+ gen.) out of, by
ἐν, (+ dat.) in
ἐστίν, he/she/it is
Ἰωνᾶς, ᾶ, ὁ, Jonah
μαθητής, οῦ, ὁ, disciple, student
με, me (acc.)
Νινευή, ἡ, Nineveh (indeclinable)

νόμος, ου, ὁ, law
νῦν, now
ὁδός, οῦ, ἡ, way, road, path
οὐρανός, οῦ, ὁ, heaven, sky
πέμπω, I send
πρός, (+ acc.) to, toward, with
προφήτης, ου, ὁ, prophet
σου, your
τί, what?
ὑμῶν, you, of you (gen. pl. pron.)
Φιλήμονα, Philemon (acc.)
Φιλήμονος, Philemon (gen.)
Χριστός, οῦ, ὁ, the Christ, Messiah

3   τῆς Νινευή – nouns such as Νινευή, which come from other lan-
    guages, are often indeclinable. Their cases can be discerned from the
    definite article.

9   τῆς τοῦ θεοῦ φωνῆς = τῆς φωνῆς τοῦ θεοῦ.

13 καὶ τοὺς ἀνθρώπους – As seen above, καί can function as an adverb to
    mean "also" or "even." So also in line 33 (καὶ Ὀνήσιμος).

1 *Λογος Γ*

λέγει ὁ Ἰησοῦς, "Καλόν ἐστιν πιστεύειν εἰς τὸν θεὸν καὶ εἰς τὸν
Χριστόν. ὁ γὰρ θεός μου ἔχει οἴκους ἐν οὐρανῷ καὶ λαμβάνετε
5 τοὺς καλοὺς οἴκους ἀπὸ θεοῦ. κακὴν ὁδὸν βλέπετε ἐν τῷ κόσμῳ,
ἀλλὰ τὴν ὁδὸν τὴν ἀγαθὴν γινώσκετε."

λέγει Θωμᾶς, "Κύριε, οὐ γινώσκομεν τί λέγεις. οὐ γινώσκομεν τὴν
ἀγαθὴν ὁδὸν καὶ οὐ βλέπομεν τοὺς οἴκους τοὺς ἀπὸ θεοῦ. τί ἐστιν
10 ἡ ἀγαθὴ ὁδός;"

λέγει ὁ Ἰησοῦς, "Ἐγώ εἰμι ἡ ὁδὸς καὶ ἡ ἀλήθεια καὶ ἡ ζωή· τὸν θεὸν
γινώσκετε ὅτι γινώσκετέ με. τὸν θεὸν βλέπετε ὅτι βλέπετέ με."

15 Λέγει Φίλιππος, "Κύριε, θέλομεν βλέπειν τὸν θεόν."

λέγει ὁ Ἰησοῦς, "Ἐγώ εἰμι μεθ' ὑμῶν καὶ οὐ γινώσκεις με, Φίλιππε;
βλέπεις τὸν θεὸν ὅτι βλέπεις με. ἀλλὰ λέγεις ὅτι θέλεις βλέπειν
τὸν θεόν; οὐ πιστεύεις ὅτι ἐγὼ ἐν τῷ θεῷ καὶ ὁ θεὸς ἐν ἐμοί ἐστιν;
20 οἱ λόγοι μου ἀπὸ θεοῦ εἰσιν, ὁ δὲ θεὸς μένει ἐν ἐμοὶ καὶ ποιεῖ τὰ
ἔργα αὐτοῦ. πιστεύετε ὅτι ἐγὼ ἐν τῷ θεῷ καὶ ὁ θεὸς ἐν ἐμοί; διὰ τὰ
ἔργα πιστεύετε."

25 *Λογος Δ*

(Adapted from Galatians 1:1–13)

Παῦλος, ἀπόστολος οὐκ ἀπ' ἀνθρώπων καὶ οὐ δι' ἀνθρώπου,
30 ἀλλὰ διὰ Ἰησοῦ Χριστοῦ καὶ θεοῦ, καὶ οἱ ἀδελφοὶ οἱ μεθ' ἡμῶν
ταῖς ἐκκλησίαις τῆς Γαλατίας. ἔχετε χάριν καὶ εἰρήνην ἀπὸ θεοῦ
καὶ κυρίου Ἰησοῦ Χριστοῦ, ὁ γὰρ θεὸς θέλει λαμβάνειν τοὺς
ἀνθρώπους ἐκ τοῦ πονηροῦ κόσμου. ἡ δόξα τῷ θεῷ!

35 ἀκούω περὶ ὑμῶν ὅτι νῦν οὐ πιστεύετε εἰς τὸν πρῶτον λόγον
τὸν ἀπὸ Χριστοῦ, ἀλλὰ πιστεύετε εἰς τὸν πονηρὸν λόγον. οἱ γὰρ
πονηροὶ ἄνθρωποι θέλουσιν διδάσκειν τὸν λόγον τὸν πονηρὸν καὶ
ἀκούετε τῶν πονηρῶν φωνῶν.

ἀπόστολος, ου, ὁ, an apostle

αὐτοῦ, his (gen. pron.)

Γαλατία, ας, ἡ, Galatia

διά, (+ gen.) through; (+ acc.) for the sake of, because of

ἐγώ, I (nom. pron.)

εἰμί, I am

εἰρήνη, ης, ἡ, peace

εἰσίν, they are

ἐμοί, me (dat. pron.)

ἔρημος, ου, ἡ, desert, wilderness

ἐστίν, he/she/it is

ἡμῶν, us, of us (gen. pl. pron.)

Θωμᾶς, ᾶ, ὁ, Thomas

Ἰουδαϊσμός, οῦ, ὁ, Judaism

Ἰωάννης, ου, ὁ, John

κόσμος, ου, ὁ, world

με, me (acc.)

μένω, I remain, stay, abide (in John)

μετά, (+ gen.) with; (+ acc.) after, behind

μου, my (gen. sing. pron.)

νῦν, now

περί, (+ gen.) about, concerning

ποιεῖ, he/she/it does

πρῶτος, η, ον, first

τί, what?

ὑμῶν, you, of you (gen. pl. pron.)

Φίλιππος, ου, ὁ, Philip

χάρις, χάριτος, ἡ, grace

Χριστός, οῦ, ὁ, the Christ, Messiah

3   καλόν ἐστιν + infinitive – "it is good to . . ." καλόν is neut. sing. nom., because it is describing the action of the infinitive (πιστεύειν here). Cf. Mark 9:5.

29   Παῦλος, ἀπόστολος . . . – Like most of his letters, Galatians begins without an explicit verb.

1 ἀλλ' ἐγὼ καὶ ἄγγελος ἐξ οὐρανοῦ τὸν λόγον τὸν πονηρὸν
οὐ διδάσκομεν, ἀλλὰ τὸν καλόν. διὰ τί οὐ πιστεύετε τῷ λόγῳ
τῆς ἀληθείας;

5 γινώσκετε τὸν λόγον περὶ τῆς ἀληθείας. ἐγὼ οὐκ ἀπὸ τῶν
πονηρῶν ἀνθρώπων λαμβάνω τὸν λόγον, ἀλλὰ διὰ τοῦ κυρίου
Ἰησοῦ Χριστοῦ. γινώσκετε περὶ τῆς ζωῆς μου ἐν τῷ Ἰουδαϊσμῷ,
ἀλλὰ νῦν οὐ μένω ἐν τῇ ζωῇ τῇ πρώτῃ, ἀλλὰ ἐν Χριστῷ. βλέπετε
τὴν ἐν Χριστῷ ζωήν μου; θέλετε ἔχειν τὴν ἐν Χριστῷ ζωήν; οὐκ
10 ἔχετε ὅτι οὐ πιστεύετε εἰς τὸν Χριστόν!

Λόγος Ε

15 Ἰωάννης ὁ βαπτιστὴς ἔχει μικρὸν οἶκον ἐν τῇ ἐρήμῳ, ἀλλὰ θέλει
βλέπειν τοὺς ἐν Ἰερουσαλὴμ οἴκους τοὺς καλούς.

Ἰωάννης δὲ τρέχει πρὸς τοὺς καλοὺς οἴκους, ἀλλ' οἱ ἄνθρωποι οἱ
ἐν τοῖς οἴκοις οὐ θέλουσιν βλέπειν Ἰωάννην.
20

λίθους βάλλουσιν πρὸς τὸν Ἰωάννην, ὅτι οὐ θέλουσιν ἀκούειν
τῶν λόγων αὐτοῦ. Ἰωάννης τρέχει ἐκ τῆς Ἰερουσαλὴμ καὶ διὰ τῆς
ἐρήμου καὶ εἰς τὸν οἶκον αὐτοῦ. οἶκον καλὸν οὐκ ἔχει Ἰωάννης ἐν
Ἰερουσαλήμ, βασιλείαν δὲ ἀγαθὴν ἔχει ἐν οὐρανῷ.

βαπτιστής, οῦ, ὁ, Baptist, Baptizer
διὰ τί, why? on account of what?
ἐγώ, I (nom. pron.)
ἔρημος, ου, ἡ, desert, wilderness
Ἰερουσαλήμ, ἡ, Jerusalem
  (indeclinable)

Ἰουδαϊσμός, οῦ, ὁ, Judaism
Ἰωάννης, ου, ὁ, John
λίθος, ου, ὁ, stone
μου, my (gen. sing. pron.)
νῦν, now
τρέχω, I run

1 ἐγὼ καὶ ἄγγελος . . . οὐ διδάσκομεν – Greek word order is very flexible; the subject can come at the beginning and the verb at the end of a sentence (or vice versa).

1 *Λογος Α*

Παῦλος καὶ Φιλήμων λέγουσιν περὶ τῆς ἀληθείας καὶ τῆς
βασιλείας καὶ τοῦ υἱοῦ τοῦ θεοῦ. νῦν γὰρ μαθητής ἐστιν Φιλήμων,
5 αὐτὸς γὰρ πιστεύει εἰς τὸν Χριστόν, ἀλλ᾽ οὐ πιστεύουσιν ἡ ἀδελφὴ
αὐτοῦ καὶ ὁ ἀδελφός. Φιλήμων δὲ θέλει διδάσκειν αὐτοὺς περὶ τοῦ
Χριστοῦ. ἀκούουσιν δὲ αὐτοί;

Φιλήμων, "Νῦν μαθητής εἰμι τοῦ Χριστοῦ! νῦν ἔχω ζωὴν μετὰ θεοῦ
10 ἐν οὐρανῷ!"

ὁ ἀδελφὸς αὐτοῦ, "Τί λέγεις; ἡμεῖς ἐσμεν ἄνθρωποι Ἑλληνικοί.
οὐκ ἐσμὲν μαθηταὶ τοῦ θεοῦ τοῦ Παύλου."

15 ἡ ἀδελφὴ αὐτοῦ, "Ναί, Φιλήμων, ὁ ἀδελφός σου λέγει τὴν
ἀλήθειαν."

Φιλήμων, "Ἀλλὰ κατὰ τὸν λόγον τοῦ θεοῦ, ἡμεῖς ἐσμεν πονηροὶ
ἄνθρωποι, οἱ γὰρ θεοὶ ἡμῶν οὐκ εἰσὶν θεοί, ἀλλὰ ἔργα ἀνθρώπων.
20 ὁ δὲ ἅγιος θεὸς ὁ ἐν τῷ οὐρανῷ θέλει σῴζειν ἡμᾶς ἀπὸ τῆς
ἁμαρτίας καὶ τοῦ θανάτου διὰ τῆς ἀγάπης αὐτοῦ."

ὁ ἀδελφὸς αὐτοῦ, "Ὦ κακὲ ἄνθρωπε! τί λέγεις ἡμῖν; οὐκ ἀκούεις
ἡμῶν; ἄνθρωπος Ἑλληνικὸς εἶ σύ! τίς ἐστιν Παῦλος; βάρβαρός
25 ἐστιν! οὐκ ἔστιν Παῦλος ὁ ἄνθρωπος ὁ ἀπὸ Ἰερουσαλήμ; λέγει
σοι Παῦλος λόγους πονηροὺς κατὰ τῶν θεῶν ἡμῶν. θέλω βάλλειν
αὐτὸν ἀπὸ τοῦ οἴκου ἡμῶν εἰς τὴν ἔρημον!"

νῦν ὄχλοι εἰσὶν περὶ τὸν Φιλήμονα. ὁ δὲ ἀδελφὸς αὐτοῦ καὶ ἡ
30 ἀδελφὴ λέγουσιν αὐτοῖς ὅτι Φιλήμων οὐ πιστεύει εἰς τοὺς θεοὺς
αὐτῶν καὶ λέγει κατὰ τοῦ Καίσαρος. οἱ δὲ ὄχλοι βάλλουσιν λίθους
πρὸς τὸν Φιλήμονα.

τί δὲ ποιεῖ Φιλήμων; ὁ μαθητὴς τοῦ Χριστοῦ βλέπει εἰς τὸν
35 οὐρανὸν καὶ λέγει, "*Πάτερ ἡμῶν, ὁ ἐν τοῖς οὐρανοῖς. . . . σοῦ ἐστιν
ἡ βασιλεία καὶ ἡ δύναμις καὶ ἡ δόξα! Ἀμήν.*"

ἀγάπη, ης, ἡ, love
ἀμήν, Amen
ἄρτος, ου, ὁ, bread, loaf
αὐτός, ή, ό, he, she, it
βάρβαρος, ον, (adj.) non-Greek, "barbarian"
δύναμις, δυνάμεως, ἡ, power
δῶρον, ου, τό, gift
εἰμί, I am
Ἑλληνικός, ή, όν, (adj.) Greek
ἐσθίω, I eat
Ἰερουσαλήμ, ἡ, Jerusalem (indeclinable)
Καίσαρος, masc. gen. sing. of Καῖσαρ, Caesar

κατά, (+ gen.) against; (+ acc.) according to
μητέρα, mother (acc. of μήτηρ)
ναί, yes
νῦν, now
ὄχλος, ου, ὁ, crowd, multitude
Πάτερ, father (voc. of πατήρ)
πατέρα, father (acc. of πατήρ)
περί, (+ gen.) about; (+ acc.) around
ποιεῖ, he/she/it does (from ποιέω, I do)
σύ, you (sing.)
σῴζω, I save
τί, what?
τίς, who?

5 ἡ ἀδελφὴ αὐτοῦ καὶ ὁ ἀδελφός – αὐτοῦ modifies both nouns and does not need to be repeated.

21 τοῦ θανάτου – object of the preposition ἀπό. The preposition does not need to be repeated.

25 οὐκ ἔστιν Παῦλος . . . – a question, "Isn't Paul . . ."

29 ὄχλοι εἰσίν – the third person singular and plural forms of εἰμί can be used in an impersonal sense (i.e., "there is," "there are").

35 σοῦ ἐστιν ἡ βασιλεία καὶ ἡ δύναμις καὶ ἡ δόξα! Ἀμήν – a line from the long version of the Lord's prayer in Matthew, "Yours is the kingdom . . ."

PRESENT INDICATIVE OF εἰμί

	Singular		Plural	
1	εἰμί	I am	ἐσμέν	we are
2	εἶ	you (sing.) are	ἐστέ	you (pl.) are
3	ἐστί(ν)	he, she, it is	εἰσί(ν)	they are

1 *Λογος Β*

(Adapted from John 6:22–42)

5 ὁ Ἰησοῦς ὁ ἐν τῷ πλοίῳ διδάσκει τοὺς ὄχλους τοὺς περὶ τὴν θάλασσαν περὶ τοῦ ἄρτου ἐκ τοῦ οὐρανοῦ.

λέγει αὐτοῖς ὁ Ἰησοῦς, "Ὁ ἄρτος τοῦ θεοῦ ἐστιν ἐκ τοῦ οὐρανοῦ καὶ δῶρόν ἐστιν τῷ κόσμῳ ἀπὸ θεοῦ."

10

λέγουσιν αὐτῷ οἱ ὄχλοι, "Δὸς ἡμῖν τὸν ἄρτον τοῦ θεοῦ!"

λέγει αὐτοῖς ὁ Ἰησοῦς, "Ἐγώ εἰμι ὁ ἄρτος τῆς ζωῆς. οἱ ἅγιοι ἐσθίουσιν τὸν ἄρτον τῆς ζωῆς ὅτι πιστεύουσιν εἰς ἐμέ."

15

οἱ ὄχλοι λέγουσιν περὶ αὐτοῦ, "Οὐκ ἔστιν αὐτὸς ὁ υἱὸς τοῦ Ἰωσήφ; γινώσκομεν τὸν πατέρα καὶ τὴν μητέρα αὐτοῦ! διὰ τί λέγει ἡμῖν ὅτι ἄρτος ἐκ θεοῦ ἐστιν;"

20 οἱ ὄχλοι οὐ βλέπουσιν τὸν θεὸν ὅτι οὐ πιστεύουσιν εἰς τὸν Ἰησοῦν τὸν ἄρτον ἐκ τοῦ θεοῦ.

ἁμαρτία, ας, ἡ, sin
διὰ τί, why? on account of what?
δός, give!
δῶρον, ου, τό, gift
ἐσθίω, I eat

Ἰωσήφ, ὁ, Joseph (indeclinable)
μητέρα, mother (acc. of μήτηρ)
πατέρα, father (acc. of πατήρ)
πλοῖον, ου, τό, boat

5   περὶ τὴν θάλασσαν – pay attention to the case of the object of the preposition, which can change the meaning of the preposition.

8   ἐκ τοῦ οὐρανοῦ – ἐκ can mean both "out of" or "from," as it does here.

11 Δὸς ἡμῖν – "give to us!" Δός is a second-person singular imperative of δίδωμι (I give), introduced in lesson 28. For now, focus on its meaning ("give!") and not its form.

1 *Λογος Α*

Ἰωάννης λέγει περὶ οἴκων.

5 Ἰωάννης, "Βλέπω οἴκους καλοὺς ἐν Ἰερουσαλήμ, ἀλλὰ ὁ οἶκός μου οὗτος οὐ καλός, ἀλλὰ κακὸς καὶ μικρός! θέλω οὖν ἔχειν τοὺς οἴκους ἐκείνους ἐν Ἰερουσαλήμ! ἐν γὰρ τοῖς οἴκοις ἐκείνοις ἐστὶν ἄρτος ἀγαθός. ἐγὼ δὲ οὐκ ἔχω ἄρτον ἀγαθὸν ἐν τῷ οἴκῳ μου τούτῳ."

10

Ἰωάννης οὖν τρέχει πρὸς τοὺς οἴκους ἐκείνους ἐν Ἰερουσαλήμ. οἱ δὲ ἄνθρωποι ἐν τοῖς οἴκοις ἐκείνοις βλέπουσιν Ἰωάννην καὶ λέγουσιν περὶ τοῦ ἀνθρώπου τούτου Ἰωάννου.

15 οἱ ἄνθρωποι, "Τίς ἐστιν ὁ ἄνθρωπος ἐκεῖνος; οὐκ ἔστιν ὁ ἄνθρωπος ὁ ἀπὸ τῆς ἐρήμου ἐκείνης; ἀκούομεν ὅτι ἐκεῖνος ὁ ἄνθρωπος θέλει ἔχειν τοὺς οἴκους ἡμῶν τούτους! ὁ ἄνθρωπος ἐκεῖνος θέλει ἐσθίειν τὸν ἀγαθὸν ἄρτον ἡμῶν τοῦτον!"

20 Ἰωάννης δὲ βλέπει τοὺς ἀνθρώπους ἐκείνους τοὺς ἐν τοῖς οἴκοις ἐκείνοις, ἀλλ᾽ οὐ θέλουσιν βλέπειν Ἰωάννην οἱ ἄνθρωποι ἐκεῖνοι. οἱ οὖν ἄνθρωποι λέγουσιν πρὸς αὐτόν.

οἱ ἄνθρωποι, "Τί θέλεις; βλέπεις ὅτι ἔχομεν τοὺς οἴκους τούτους· 25 θέλεις οὖν ἔχειν αὐτούς;"

Ἰωάννης, "Ναί! βλέπω ὅτι ἔχετε καλοὺς οἴκους, ἐγὼ δὲ οὐκ ἔχω. θέλω οὖν ἔχειν τοὺς καλοὺς οἴκους ἐκείνους καὶ τὸν ἀγαθὸν ἄρτον ἐκεῖνον."

30

οἱ ἄνθρωποι, "Τῶν λόγων σου τούτων καὶ τῆς φωνῆς σου ταύτης οὐ θέλομεν ἀκούειν! θέλομεν δὲ βάλλειν σε εἰς τὴν ἔρημον ἐκείνην! οὐκ ἔχεις οἶκον ἐν τῇ ἐρήμῳ ἐκείνῃ; ἡμῶν εἰσιν οἱ οἶκοι οὗτοι. διὰ τοῦτο, θέλομεν ἀποστέλλειν σε ἀπὸ τῶν 35 οἴκων τούτων."

οἱ ἄνθρωποι βάλλουσιν λίθους πρὸς τὸν Ἰωάννην καὶ

ἀποστέλλω, I send
αὐτός, ή, ό, same, -self
ἐκεῖνος, η, ο, that
Ἰερουσαλήμ, ἡ, Jerusalem
  (indeclinable)
Ἰωάννης, ου, ὁ, John
ναί, yes

οὖν, therefore, consequently
  (postpositive)
οὗτος, αὕτη, τοῦτο, this
τί, what?
τίς, who?
τρέχω, I run

11 Ἰωάννης οὖν τρέχει – while οὖν is commonly translated as "therefore,"
    it often functions simply to resume or continue a subject or narrative, in
    which case it may be left untranslated.
34 διὰ τοῦτο – the neut. demonstrative τοῦτο can refer to any inanimate
    object or "thing" referenced in the narrative.

FORMS OF THE DEMONSTRATIVES

	Singular			Plural		
Nom.	οὗτος	αὕτη	τοῦτο	οὗτοι	αὗται	ταῦτα
Gen.	τούτου	ταύτης	τούτου	τούτων	τούτων	τούτων
Dat.	τούτῳ	ταύτῃ	τούτῳ	τούτοις	ταύταις	τούτοις
Acc.	τοῦτον	ταύτην	τοῦτο	τούτους	ταύτας	ταῦτα

	Singular			Plural		
Nom.	ἐκεῖνος	ἐκείνη	ἐκεῖνο	ἐκεῖνοι	ἐκεῖναι	ἐκεῖνα
Gen.	ἐκείνου	ἐκείνης	ἐκείνου	ἐκείνων	ἐκείνων	ἐκείνων
Dat.	ἐκείνῳ	ἐκείνῃ	ἐκείνῳ	ἐκείνοις	ἐκείναις	ἐκείνοις
Acc.	ἐκεῖνον	ἐκείνην	ἐκεῖνο	ἐκείνους	ἐκείνας	ἐκεῖνα

1 ἀποστέλλουσιν αὐτὸν ἀπὸ τῶν οἴκων αὐτῶν. καὶ μετὰ ταῦτα,
ὁ Ἰωάννης τρέχει εἰς τὸν οἶκον αὐτοῦ καὶ φωνῆς ἀκούει
ἀπὸ οὐρανοῦ.

5 ἡ φωνή, "Ὦ Ἰωάννε! διὰ τί θέλεις ἔχειν τοὺς οἴκους ἐκείνους;
οὐ γινώσκεις ὅτι ὁ οἶκός σου οὗτος ἀγαθός ἐστιν; οὐκ ἔχεις τὸν
ἀγαθὸν ἄρτον ἐκεῖνον, ἀλλὰ ἔχεις τὸν ἄρτον τοῦτον ἀπ' οὐρανοῦ
καὶ τὴν βασιλείαν ταύτην ἐν οὐρανῷ."

10

Λογος Β

Φιλήμων μαθητὴς τοῦ Χριστοῦ ἐστιν, ὅτι πιστεύει εἰς τὸν θεόν.
Παῦλος οὖν βαπτίζει αὐτὸν ἐν τῇ θαλάσσῃ τῇ ἐν Κολοσσαῖς. οἱ δὲ
15 ἅγιοι ἐν Κολοσσαῖς περὶ τὸν Φιλήμονά εἰσιν καὶ ἀκούουσιν τῶν
λόγων αὐτοῦ.

Φιλήμων, "Ἐγὼ αὐτός εἰμι ἄνθρωπος Ἑλληνικός. ἔχω οὖν ἐν τῷ
οἴκῳ μου ἐκείνῳ θεοὺς τοῦ λίθου, ἀλλὰ νῦν γινώσκω ὅτι ἐκεῖνοι
20 οὐκ εἰσὶν θεοὶ ἀλλὰ ἔργα ἀνθρώπων. θέλω οὖν μένειν μεθ'
ὑμῶν ἐν τῇ ἐκκλησίᾳ ταύτῃ ἐν Κολοσσαῖς. διὰ τῆς ἀγάπης τοῦ
Παύλου τούτου ἔχω τὴν ζωὴν ταύτην. Παῦλος οὖν αὐτὸς βαπτίζει
με, ἐγὼ γὰρ αὐτός εἰμι ὁ υἱὸς αὐτοῦ, καὶ ὑμεῖς αὐτοί ἐστε οἱ
ἀδελφοί μου!"

βαπτίζω, I baptize
διὰ τί, why? on account of what?
Ἑλληνικός, ή, όν, (adj.) Greek

Κολοσσαῖς, Colossae (dat. of
  Κολοσσαί)
νῦν, now
τρέχω, I run

1   μετὰ ταῦτα – same as above. The plural neut. demonstrative ταῦτα refers to the preceding events (i.e., "after these things").

18   Ἐγὼ αὐτός – an example of the intensive use of αὐτός ("I myself").

1 *Λογος Α*

(Based on the story of Philip and the eunuch in Acts 8:26–40)

5 ὁ Φίλιππος πορεύεται ἐν τῇ ὁδῷ πρὸς Ἱεροσόλυμα. ἄγγελος δὲ κυρίου βλέπει αὐτὸν καὶ λέγει, "Ὁ κύριος θέλει σε πορεύεσθαι ἐν τῇ ὁδῷ τῇ ἀπὸ Ἱερουσαλὴμ καὶ πρὸς Γάζαν, αὕτη ἡ ὁδός ἐστιν ἔρημος."

ὁ οὖν Φίλιππος ἐγείρεται καὶ πορεύεται καὶ βλέπει ἄνθρωπον. ὁ δὲ
10 ἄνθρωπος ἔρχεται ἀπὸ Ἱερουσαλὴμ εἰς τὴν γῆν τῶν Αἰθιόπων. ὁ δὲ θεὸς λέγει τῷ Φιλίππῳ, "Θέλω σε ἔρχεσθαι πρὸς τὸν ἄνθρωπον τοῦτον καὶ λέγειν μετ᾽ αὐτοῦ."

ὁ δὲ Φίλιππος ἀκούει τοῦ ἀνθρώπου τούτου. τί λέγει ὁ ἄνθρωπος
15 οὗτος; λέγει τοὺς λόγους τοὺς τοῦ προφήτου Ἠσαΐου. λέγει Φίλιππος τῷ ἀνθρώπῳ τούτῳ, "Γινώσκεις τί λέγεις;" ἀποκρίνεται δὲ ὁ ἄνθρωπος καὶ λέγει, "Οὐ δύναμαι γινώσκειν ὅτι οὐκ ἔχω διδάσκαλον."

20 ὁ οὖν Φίλιππος ἄρχεται λέγειν περὶ τοῦ προφήτου καὶ τοῦ Χριστοῦ καὶ τῆς ἁμαρτίας καὶ τῆς ζωῆς. ὁ δὲ ἄνθρωπος νῦν γινώσκει ὅτι ἁμαρτωλός ἐστιν, ὁ γὰρ Φίλιππος διδάσκει αὐτόν. ὁ οὖν ἄνθρωπος λέγει, "Δόξα τῷ θεῷ σου! θέλω γίνεσθαι μαθητὴς τοῦ Χριστοῦ!" ὁ δὲ Φίλιππος ἀποκρίνεται καὶ λέγει, "Βλέπω
25 θάλασσαν. δύναμαι οὖν βαπτίζειν σε ἐν τῇ θαλάσσῃ ἐκείνῃ."

ὁ οὖν ἄνθρωπος καὶ ὁ Φίλιππος ἔρχονται πρὸς τὴν θάλασσαν καὶ ὁ ἄνθρωπος βαπτίζεται ὑπὸ τοῦ Φιλίππου. ὁ δὲ ἄνθρωπος ἐγείρεται ἐκ τῆς θαλάσσης καὶ μαθητὴς γίνεται τοῦ Χριστοῦ, ἀλλὰ
30 οὐκ ἀκούει οὐδὲ βλέπει τὸν Φίλιππον, ὁ γὰρ θεὸς λαμβάνει τὸν Φίλιππον καὶ ἀποστέλλει αὐτὸν εἰς Ἄζωτον.

Ἄζωτος, ου, ἡ, Azotus (a city in
  Palestine)
Αἰθιόπων, of the Ethiopians (gen.
  pl. of Αἰθίοψ)
ἁμαρτωλός, οῦ, ὁ, sinner
ἀποκρίνομαι, I answer (+ dat.)
ἄρχομαι, I begin
ἄρχω, I rule (+ gen.)
Γάζα, ης, ἡ, Gaza
γίνομαι, become, be, happen, arise
διδάσκαλος, ου, ὁ, teacher
δύναμαι, I can, am able
ἐγείρομαι, I rise up, I am raised
ἐγείρω, I raise up
ἔρχομαι, I come, I go

Ἡσαΐας, ου, ὁ, Isaiah
Ἱεροσόλυμα, ἡ, Jerusalem
Ἱερουσαλήμ, ἡ, Jerusalem
  (indeclinable)
λαός, οῦ, ὁ, people
Μωϋσῆς, Μωϋσέως, ὁ, Moses
νῦν, now
οὐδέ, and not, nor, not even
πατρός, father (gen. of πατήρ)
πορεύομαι, I go, walk, travel
σύν, (+ dat.) with
τί, what?
τίς, who?
ὑπό, (+ gen.) by; (+ acc.) under
Φαραώ, ὁ, Pharaoh (indeclinable)

5   Ἱεροσόλυμα – the city of Jerusalem has both an indeclinable and a declin-
    able form, as seen here.
6   θέλει σε πορεύεσθαι – σε is the subject of the infinitive πορεύεσθαι ("he
    wants you to go").

1   *Λογος Β*

(Adapted from Exodus 3–4)

5   ὁ θεὸς λέγει τῷ Μωϋσῇ, "Ἐγώ εἰμι ὁ θεὸς τοῦ πατρός σου, θεὸς
Ἀβραὰμ καὶ θεὸς Ἰσαὰκ καὶ θεὸς Ἰακώβ." ὁ δὲ Μωϋσῆς οὐ θέλει
βλέπειν τὸ πρόσωπον τοῦ θεοῦ. καὶ λέγει αὐτῷ ὁ θεός, "Βλέπω
τὸ κακὸν τοῦ Φαραὼ κατὰ τοῦ λαοῦ μου τοῦ ἐν Αἰγύπτῳ καὶ
αἱ φωναὶ αὐτῶν ἀκούονται ὑπ' ἐμοῦ. θέλω οὖν σῴζειν αὐτούς,
10 γινώσκω γὰρ ὅτι δοῦλοί εἰσιν τοῦ Φαραώ. ἀποστέλλω οὖν σε πρὸς
Φαραώ, θέλω γάρ σε λέγειν αὐτῷ ὅτι ὁ θεός σου δύναται λύειν τὴν
βασιλείαν αὐτοῦ."

ἀκούει δὲ ὁ Μωϋσῆς; ἀποκρίνεται δὲ Μωϋσῆς τῷ θεῷ, "Κύριε, τίς
15 εἰμι; οὐ δύναμαι λέγειν τῷ Φαραώ, ὅτι ἡ φωνή μου κακή ἐστιν." ὁ
δὲ θεὸς ἀποκρίνεται αὐτῷ, "Ἀκούω σου, θέλω οὖν ἀποστέλλειν
ἄλλον ἄνθρωπον." τίς ἀποστέλλεται ὑπὸ θεοῦ; Ἀαρὼν ὁ ἀδελφὸς
τοῦ Μωϋσέως ἀποστέλλεται ὑπὸ θεοῦ σὺν Μωϋσῇ.

20 καὶ εἰσέρχονται εἰς γῆν Αἰγύπτου. οἱ δὲ ἀδελφοὶ βλέπουσιν τὸν
Φαραὼ καὶ ἔρχονται πρὸς αὐτόν. ὁ δὲ Ἀαρὼν ἄρχεται λέγειν
περὶ θεοῦ καὶ περὶ τοῦ λαοῦ θεοῦ. ἀκούει δὲ ὁ Φαραὼ τῶν
λόγων αὐτοῦ;

Ἀαρών, ὁ, Aaron (indeclinable)
Αἴγυπτος, ου, ἡ, Egypt
ἄλλος, η, ο, other
εἰσέρχομαι, I go in, I enter
λαός, οῦ, ὁ, people

Μωϋσῆς, Μωϋσέως, ὁ, Moses
πρόσωπον, ου, τό, face
σύν, (+ dat.) with
τίς, who?
Φαραώ, ὁ, Pharaoh (indeclinable)

8   τὸ κακόν – neut. adjectives with the neut. definite article can be used
    to signify inanimate objects or abstract ideas. Here, God sees "the evil
    [thing]" or "evil [deed]," or even just "the evil" of Pharaoh.

1 *Λογος Α (Περὶ Μωϋσέως καὶ Ἀαρών)*

Καὶ μετὰ ταῦτα, εἰσέρχονται Μωϋσῆς καὶ Ἀαρὼν πρὸς Φαραὼ καὶ
λέγουσιν αὐτῷ, "Οὕτως λέγει Κύριος ὁ θεὸς Ἰσραήλ· θέλω σῴζειν
5 τὸν λαόν μου. ὀφείλεις οὖν ἀποστέλλειν αὐτοὺς ἀπὸ τῆς βασιλείας
σου καὶ εἰς τὴν ἔρημον." καὶ λέγει Φαραώ, "Τίς ἐστιν ὁ θεός σου
ὅτι ὀφείλω ἀκούειν τῆς φωνῆς αὐτοῦ; οὐ γινώσκω τὸν κύριον, καὶ
τὸν Ἰσραὴλ οὐκ ἀποστέλλω." καὶ λέγουσιν αὐτῷ, "Κατὰ τὸν λόγον
τοῦ θεοῦ, ὀφείλομεν ἀπέρχεσθαι εἰς τὴν ἔρημον." καὶ λέγει αὐτοῖς
10 ὁ Φαραώ, "Διὰ τί, Μωϋσῆ καὶ Ἀαρών, θέλετε αἴρειν τὸν λαὸν ἀπὸ
τῶν ἔργων; κακοὶ δοῦλοί εἰσιν ὅτι οὐ θέλουσιν ποιεῖν τὰ ἔργα! διὰ
τοῦτο, ὀφείλω καταβαίνειν καὶ συνάγειν αὐτοὺς καὶ ἀποκτείνειν
τοὺς κακοὺς δούλους!"

15 Μωϋσῆς δὲ καὶ Ἀαρὼν λέγουσιν αὐτῷ, "Μέλλει ὁ θεὸς
ἀποστέλλειν τοὺς ἀγγέλους αὐτοῦ κατὰ τῆς βασιλείας σου."
Φαραὼ δὲ ἀποκρίνεται αὐτοῖς, "Βλέπετε τὸ καλὸν ἱερὸν παρὰ τῇ
θαλάσσῃ; δῶρόν ἐστιν ἀπὸ τῶν δούλων μου. δύναμαι γὰρ ἔχειν τὰ
καλὰ δῶρα ταῦτα ὅτι δούλους ἔχω. οὐ δύναμαι οὖν ἀποστέλλειν
20 τὸν λαὸν εἰς τὴν ἔρημον."

μετὰ ταῦτα, ἄγγελοι θεοῦ ἀποστέλλονται ὑπὲρ τοῦ υἱοῦ αὐτοῦ
Ἰσραὴλ κατὰ τοῦ Φαραὼ καὶ τῆς βασιλείας αὐτοῦ. ὁ οὖν Φαραὼ
ἔρχεται πρὸς τὸν Μωϋσῆν καὶ Ἀαρὼν καὶ λέγει, "Διὰ τί γίνεται τὰ
25 κακὰ ταῦτα ἐν τῇ βασιλείᾳ μου;" Μωϋσῆς ἀποκρίνεται, "Ἔλεγόν
σοι ἐχθὲς ὅτι ὁ θεὸς θέλει σῴζειν τὸν λαὸν αὐτοῦ, ἀλλὰ οὐκ
ἤκουες ἡμῶν. νῦν δὲ ὀφείλεις ἀκούειν. οὐ γὰρ δύνασαι ἄρχειν
τοῦ λαοῦ τοῦ θεοῦ." ὁ δὲ Φαραὼ οὐκ ἀκούει αὐτῶν καὶ λέγει,
"Μέλλετε ἀποθνήσκειν τῇ ἐξουσίᾳ μου, ὑμεῖς καὶ ὁ λαὸς ὑμῶν!
30 ἐξουσίαν γὰρ ἔχω κρίνειν καὶ ἀποκτείνειν!"

μετὰ ταῦτα, ἀπέρχονται Μωϋσῆς καὶ Ἀαρὼν ἀπὸ τοῦ προσώπου
τοῦ Φαραώ. ἀποστέλλει δὲ ὁ θεὸς τὸν ἄγγελον τοῦ θανάτου
πρὸς τὸν Φαραὼ καὶ τὸν οἶκον αὐτοῦ. ἀποθνήσκει οὖν ὁ υἱὸς
35 τοῦ Φαραώ.

θέλει οὖν νῦν ὁ Φαραὼ ἀποστέλλειν τὸν λαὸν τοῦ θεοῦ εἰς
τὴν ἔρημον. ὁ δὲ Φαραὼ λέγει τῷ Μωϋσῇ, "Διὰ τί μένετε ἐν

αἴρω, I take up, take away, lift up

ἀπέρχομαι, I depart, go away, go

ἀποθνῄσκω, I die

ἀποκτείνω, I kill

ἐξουσία, ας, ἡ, authority

ἐχθές, yesterday

ἱερόν, τοῦ, τό, temple

Ἰησοῦς, οῦ, ὁ, Joshua

καταβαίνω, I go down

κρίνω, I judge

μέλλω, I am about to, am going to

νῦν, now

ὀφείλω, I owe, ought, must

οὕτως, thus, so, in this way

παρά, (+ gen.) from; (+ dat.) beside, with, among; (+ acc.) by, along

ποιεῖν, to do (from ποιέω, I do)

συνάγω, I gather together

τί, what?

τίς, who?

ὑπέρ, (+ gen.) in behalf of; (+ acc.) above

22 ἄγγελοι θεοῦ ἀποστέλλονται – the "messengers" that are sent are, of course, the plagues.

24 γίνεται τὰ κακὰ ταῦτα – neut. plural nouns often take singular verbs.

27 δύνασαι – an alternative form of the second-person singular δύνῃ.

29 τῇ ἐξουσίᾳ – impersonal dative of means.

IMPERFECT ACTIVE INDICATIVE OF λύω

	Singular		Plural	
1	ἔλυον	*I was loosening*	ἐλύομεν	*we were loosening*
2	ἔλυες	*you (sing.) were loosening*	ἐλύετε	*you (pl.) were loosening*
3	ἔλυε(ν)	*he, she, it was loosening*	ἔλυον	*they were loosening*

1 τῇ βασιλείᾳ μου; ὀφείλετε ἐξέρχεσθαι ἐκ τῆς γῆς Αἰγύπτου."
Μωϋσῆς ἀποκρίνεται, "Ἔλεγες ὅτι σὺ ἔχεις ἐξουσίαν κρίνειν καὶ
ἀποκτείνειν, ἀλλὰ νῦν γινώσκεις ὅτι ὁ θεὸς τοῦ λαοῦ ἡμῶν ἔχει τὴν
ἐξουσίαν ταύτην." μετὰ δὲ ταῦτα, Μωϋσῆς καὶ Ἀαρὼν συνάγουσιν
5 τὸν λαὸν θεοῦ καὶ εἰς τὴν ἔρημον ἀπέρχονται σὺν αὐτοῖς.

μετὰ ταῦτα, Μωϋσῆς παρὰ τῇ γῇ Χανάαν ἐστὶν μετὰ τοῦ λαοῦ
καὶ συνάγει αὐτοὺς περὶ αὐτὸν καὶ λέγει αὐτοῖς περὶ τῶν κακῶν
ἡμερῶν ἐν Αἰγύπτῳ.

10
Μωϋσῆς, "Ἀπεθνήσκομεν ὑπὸ τὴν ἐξουσίαν τοῦ Φαραώ, ἀλλὰ
ἤθελεν ὁ θεὸς σῴζειν ἡμᾶς. νῦν μέλλετε εἰσέρχεσθαι εἰς τὴν γῆν
Χανάαν, ἀλλὰ ἐγὼ μέλλω ἀποθνήσκειν. ὀφείλετε οὖν ἀκούειν τῆς
φωνῆς μου καὶ τῶν λόγων τοῦ θεοῦ! ὀφείλετε πιστεύειν εἰς τὸν
15 θεὸν καὶ εἰς τὸν Ἰησοῦν. ὁ γὰρ Ἰησοῦς μέλλει ἄγειν ὑμᾶς εἰς τὴν
γῆν Χανάαν."

ἀλλὰ ἀκούει ὁ λαὸς τῶν λόγων θεοῦ καὶ τοῦ Ἰησοῦ;

20
Λογος Β (περὶ Φιλήμονος καὶ Ὀνησίμου)

Ἦν ποτε ὁ Φιλήμων κύριος κακὸς τῶν δούλων, ὅτι συνῆγεν τοὺς
δούλους καὶ ἔλεγεν αὐτοῖς λόγους κακούς. καὶ εἶχεν Φιλήμων ἐν
25 ταῖς ἡμέραις ἐκείναις ἀδελφὸν καὶ ἀδελφήν, ἀλλὰ νῦν θέλουσιν
αὐτοὶ ἀποκτείνειν αὐτόν. ἀλλὰ ἀποθνήσκουσιν ὅτι ἔχουσιν
ἁμαρτίαν ἐν ταῖς καρδίαις αὐτῶν. ἔχει δὲ Φιλήμων ζωὴν καὶ
ἄλλους ἀδελφοὺς καὶ ἀδελφὰς ἐν τῇ ἐκκλησίᾳ τῇ ἐν Κολοσσαῖς.
κακὸς κύριος ἦν ποτε ὁ Φιλήμων, ἀλλὰ νῦν δοῦλός ἐστιν
30 τοῦ Χριστοῦ.

καὶ σήμερον συνάγονται ἐν τῇ ἐκκλησίᾳ οἱ ἀδελφοὶ ὅτι θέλουσιν
ἀκούειν τοῦ Φιλήμονος. τί λέγει αὐτοῖς; λέγει περὶ τῆς πρώτης
ζωῆς αὐτοῦ τῆς ἐν τῷ οἴκῳ αὐτοῦ. Φιλήμων λέγει, "Ἐν τῇ πρώτῃ
35 ζωῇ μου εἶχον θεοὺς τοῦ λίθου καὶ ἀνέβαινον εἰς τὰ ἱερὰ τῶν θεῶν
μου. νῦν δὲ οὐκ ἀναβαίνω εἰς τὰ ἱερὰ ἐκεῖνα, ἀλλὰ ἔρχομαι εἰς τὴν
ἐκκλησίαν ταύτην. καί ποτε εἶχον ἀδελφὸν καὶ ἀδελφήν. θέλουσιν
δὲ αὐτοὶ ἄγειν με εἰς τὴν ἄλλην ἐκκλησίαν τὴν ἐν Κολοσσαῖς,

ἄγω, I lead
ἀναβαίνω, I go up
ἀπέρχομαι, I depart, go away, go
ἀποθνῄσκω, I die
ἀποκτείνω, I kill
ἐξέρχομαι, I go out
Ἰησοῦς, οῦ, ὁ, Joshua
ἐξουσία, ας, ἡ, authority
ἱερόν, οῦ, τό, temple
Κολοσσαῖς, Colossae (dat. of
   Κολοσσαί)
κρίνω, I judge
μέλλω, I am about to, am going to
μετά, (+ gen.) with; (+ acc.) after,
   behind

νῦν, now
ὀφείλω, I owe, ought, must
παρά, (+ gen.) from; (+ dat.)
   beside, with, among; (+ acc.) by,
   along
ποτέ, before, once
σήμερον, today
συνάγω, I gather together
τί, what?
ὑπό, (+ gen.) by; (+ acc.) under
Φιλήμονος, gen. of Φιλήμων,
   Philemon
Χαναάν, ἡ, Canaan (indeclinable)

23 συνήγεν, ἔλεγεν, εἶχεν – the imperfect tense here highlights the progres-
    sive, habitual nature of these activities in the past.
38 τὴν ἄλλην ἐκκλησίαν – Outside of Christian contexts, an ἐκκλησία was
    the Greek word for a city assembly, where the citizens would gather to
    make judgments.

IMPERFECT INDICATIVE OF εἰμί

	Singular		Plural	
1	ἤμην	I was	ἦμεν	we were
2	ἦς	you (sing.) were	ἦτε	you (pl.) were
3	ἦν	he, she, it was	ἦσαν	they were

1 θέλουσιν γὰρ κρίνειν καὶ ἀποκτείνειν με, ὅτι μαθητής εἰμι τοῦ
Χριστοῦ. τί ὀφείλω λέγειν αὐτοῖς; τί δύναμαι λέγειν;"

οἱ ἅγιοι τῆς ἐκκλησίας ἀποκρίνονται, "Οὐ δύνῃ αὐτὸς σῴζειν τὴν
5 ψυχήν σου, ὁ δὲ θεὸς δύναται. ὀφείλεις οὖν πιστεύειν αὐτῷ καὶ
μένειν ἐν τῇ ἐκκλησίᾳ ταύτῃ." Φιλήμων δὲ ἀποκρίνεται, "Ἤμην
πονηρὸς κύριος ἐν τῷ οἴκῳ μου. ὀφείλω οὖν ἔρχεσθαι πρὸς τὸν
οἶκόν μου καὶ λέγειν μετὰ τῶν ἀδελφῶν καὶ τῶν δούλων περὶ τῆς
ζωῆς μου, θέλω γὰρ αὐτοὺς λαμβάνειν τὴν ἀγάπην τοῦ θεοῦ." ὁ
10 οὖν Φιλήμων οὐ μένει ἐν τῇ ἐκκλησίᾳ, ἔχει γὰρ ἔργα ἐν τῷ οἴκῳ
αὐτοῦ. ἀπέρχεται οὖν ἀπὸ τῆς ἐκκλησίας πρὸς τὸν οἶκον αὐτοῦ.

καὶ ἐν τῇ αὐτῇ ἡμέρᾳ, Ὀνήσιμος ἐν τῷ οἴκῳ ἐστίν, ἀλλὰ οὐ βλέπει
οὐδὲ ἀκούει τοῦ κυρίου αὐτοῦ. θέλει οὖν πορεύεσθαι ἐν τῇ ὁδῷ
15 παρὰ τοῦ οἴκου τοῦ κακοῦ κυρίου πρὸς ἄλλην γῆν. ἀλλὰ ἐν τῇ
αὐτῇ ὥρᾳ, εἰσέρχεται ὁ Φιλήμων εἰς τὸν οἶκον. Ὀνήσιμος οὖν
εὑρίσκει λίθον οὐ μικρὸν καὶ μένει μετ' αὐτόν. Φιλήμων οὖν οὐ
δύναται εὑρίσκειν αὐτόν. ἄλλοι οὖν δοῦλοι ἀποστέλλονται ὑπὸ
Φιλήμονος εὑρίσκειν Ὀνήσιμον. Ὀνήσιμος δὲ αἴρει ἄρτον καὶ
20 ἀπέρχεται ἐκ τοῦ οἴκου.

οἱ δὲ δοῦλοι τοῦ Φιλήμονος λέγουσιν, "Οὐ δυνάμεθα εὑρίσκειν
αὐτὸν ἐν τῷ οἴκῳ οὐδὲ ἐν τῇ ὁδῷ τῇ περὶ τὸν οἶκον οὐδὲ παρὰ τῇ
θαλάσσῃ τῇ μετὰ τὸν οἶκον. τί οὖν ὀφείλομεν ποιεῖν;"

25
μετὰ ταῦτα, Ὀνήσιμος διέρχεται δι' ἐρήμων καὶ ἔρχεται εἰς ἄλλην
γῆν. καὶ Ὀνήσιμος λέγει, "Ἤμην δοῦλος, ἀλλὰ νῦν δοῦλος οὐκ
εἰμί, ὅτι οὐκ ἔχω κύριον!" Ὀνήσιμος οὖν ἄρχεται ἐσθίειν τὸν ἄρτον
τοῦ κυρίου αὐτοῦ καὶ οὐ βλέπει τὸν ὄχλον περὶ αὐτόν. ὁ δὲ ὄχλος
30 ἄρχεται λέγειν περὶ αὐτοῦ.

ὁ ὄχλος λέγει, "Τίς ἐστιν ὁ ἄνθρωπος οὗτος; οὐκ ἦν ποτε οὗτος
ἐν τῇ γῇ ἡμῶν. γινώσκομεν οὖν ὅτι παρ' ἄλλης γῆς ἔρχεται.
ὀφείλομεν αἴρειν καὶ ἄγειν αὐτὸν εἰς τὴν ἐκκλησίαν. ἡ ἐκκλησία
35 γὰρ ἔχει ἐξουσίαν κρίνειν καὶ ἀποκτείνειν!" ὁ οὖν ὄχλος αἴρει
τὸν ἄρτον καὶ ἄγει Ὀνήσιμον εἰς τὴν ἐκκλησίαν. ὁ δὲ Ὀνήσιμος
ἤμελλεν ἐσθίειν, ἀλλὰ νῦν οὐ δύναται ἐσθίειν ὅτι ὁ ἄρτος αἴρεται
ἀπ' αὐτοῦ. τί μέλλει γίνεσθαι; μέλλει Ὀνήσιμος ἀποκτείνεσθαι;

αἴρω, I take up, take away, lift up
εὑρίσκω, I find
ποιεῖν, to do (from ποιέω, I do)

τίς, who?
ψυχή, ῆς, ἡ, soul, life

13 ἐν τῇ αὐτῇ ἡμέρᾳ – the identical use of αὐτός.

17 λίθον οὐ μικρόν – an example of litotes, where a negative is used to affirm a positive (e.g., "not bad").

17 μένει μετ᾽ αὐτόν – note the case of the object of the preposition μετά.

1 (οὗτος ὁ λόγος περὶ τοῦ λαοῦ τοῦ Ἰσραὴλ ἐστιν)

μετὰ τὸν τοῦ Μωϋσέως θάνατον, οἱ ἄνθρωποι τοῦ Ἰσραὴλ ἦσαν
παρὰ τῇ γῇ Χανάαν, οὐ γὰρ ἔτι ἐν τῷ Χανάαν ἦσαν, ἀλλὰ ἤμελλον
5 εἰσέρχεσθαι εἰς τὸν τόπον ἐκεῖνον. ὁ δὲ Ἰησοῦς ὁ δοῦλος τοῦ θεοῦ
ἔλεγεν αὐτοῖς,

"Ἰδού! ἀμὴν ἀμὴν λέγω ὑμῖν ὅτι ὁ Μωϋσῆς ἔλεγεν τοῖς
ἀνθρώποις τοὺς λόγους ἀπὸ θεοῦ, ἀλλ᾽ οὐκ ἤκουον αὐτοῦ. οὐ
10 γὰρ ἐλαμβάνοντο οἱ λόγοι τε καὶ τὰ ἔργα τοῦ Μωϋσέως. καὶ
ἡμεῖς ἐσμεν τὰ τέκνα τῶν ἐκείνων. οἱ δὲ πατέρες ἡμῶν ἔβλεπον
τὰ ἔργα τοῦ θεοῦ καὶ ἐν τῷ Αἰγύπτῳ καὶ ἐν τῇ ἐρήμῳ, ἀλλ᾽ ἔτι
οὐκ ἐπίστευον οὔτε τῷ Μωϋσῇ οὔτε τῷ θεῷ καὶ οὔτε ἐμοί. ὑμεῖς
δὲ οὐκ ἐδύνασθε πιστεύειν, ὅτι μικροὶ ἦτε. ἀλλὰ νῦν οὐ μικροὶ
15 ἐστε. μέλλετε δὲ βλέπειν τε καὶ ἔχειν τὴν ἁγίαν γῆν. οὐ θέλω οὖν
ὑμᾶς ἀπέρχεσθαι ἀπὸ τῆς ἀγάπης θεοῦ. μένειν δὲ θέλω ὑμᾶς ἐν τῇ
δικαίᾳ ὁδῷ. γινώσκετε γὰρ ὅτι Μωϋσῆς ἦν μεθ᾽ ἡμῶν ἐν Αἰγύπτῳ
καὶ ἐν τῇ ἐρήμῳ, ἀλλὰ νῦν οὐκ ἔστιν. διὰ τοῦτο, λέγω ὑμῖν ὅτι
ὀφείλετε πιστεύειν εἰς ἐμέ, ἔλεγεν γὰρ θεὸς καὶ σὺν ἐμοί.
20
ὁ θεὸς ἔλεγέν μοι· ὦ Ἰησοῦ! ἰδού! ἐπορεύου σὺ ἐν τῇ ἐρήμῳ σὺν
Μωϋσῇ καὶ ἐγὼ ἐπορευόμην μεθ᾽ ὑμῶν. ἀλλὰ νῦν οὐ πορεύεται
Μωϋσῆς μεθ᾽ ὑμῶν. ἐγὼ δὲ ἔτι μεθ᾽ ὑμῶν εἰμι. λαμβάνειν οὖν
θέλω ὑμᾶς τοὺς λόγους τοὺς ἐν τῷ βιβλίῳ τοῦ νόμου. καὶ οὐ θέλω
25 τὸ βιβλίον τοῦ νόμου τούτου ἀπέρχεσθαι ἀπὸ τῶν καρδιῶν τοῦ
λαοῦ μου.

οὕτως ἔλεγεν ὁ θεὸς μετ᾽ ἐμοῦ. ἰδού! ἀπὸ τοῦ τόπου τούτου
δυνάμεθα βλέπειν τὴν γῆν Χανάαν! βλέπετε αὐτήν; καλὴ ἡ γῆ
30 ἐκείνη! ὁ θεὸς ἄρχεται ἄγειν ἡμᾶς εἰς τὴν γῆν τὴν ἀγαθήν."

οἱ δὲ ἄνθρωποι ἤκουον τοῦ λόγου τοῦ Ἰησοῦ, ἀλλ᾽ οἱ ὀφθαλμοὶ
τῶν καρδιῶν αὐτῶν πάλιν ἔβλεπον εἰς τὴν πονηρὰν ὁδόν. ἔμελλον
γὰρ δέχεσθαι τὴν γῆν ταύτην, ἀλλὰ αἱ καρδίαι αὐτῶν ἔτι ἤθελον
35 ἄλλα δῶρα. καὶ τὰ τέκνα οὖν τῶν ἐκείνων πρώτων ἀνθρώπων
πονηρὰ ἦσαν, ὅτι δῶρα μὲν ἐδέχοντο τοῦ θεοῦ, θεὸν αὐτὸν
δὲ οὔ.

Αἰγύπτῳ, Egypt (dat.)

ἀμήν, amen, truly

βιβλίον, ου, τό, book

δέχομαι, I receive, accept

δίκαιος, α, ον, righteous, just

ἔτι, yet, still

ἤθελον, impf. act. ind. 3p of θέλω

ἤμελλον, impf. act. ind. 3p of
    μέλλω

ἰδού, behold! see!

Ἰησοῦ, voc. of Ἰησοῦς, Joshua

Ἰησοῦς, οῦ, ὁ, Joshua

μέν . . . δέ, on the one hand . . .

on the other hand, (or leave μέν
    untranslated) . . . but . . .

νῦν, now

οὔτε, neither, nor

οὕτως, (adv.) thus, in this way

ὀφθαλμός, οῦ, ὁ, eye

πάλιν, again

πατέρες, fathers (nom. pl. of
    πατήρ)

τέ, and (a weak postpositive
    conjunction)

τόπος, ου, ὁ, place

9 οὐ γὰρ ἐλαμβάνοντο οἱ λόγοι τε καὶ τὰ ἔργα τοῦ Μωϋσέως = οἱ λόγοι τε
    καὶ τὰ ἔργα τοῦ Μωϋσέως οὐκ ἐλαμβάνοντο.

10 . . . τε καὶ . . . – both . . . and . . .

12 καὶ . . . καὶ . . . – both . . . and . . .

14 ὅτι μικροὶ ἦτε – the adj. μικρός ("little, small") can be used of age.

19 καὶ σὺν ἐμοί – adverbial use of καί; even, also.

23 λαμβάνειν οὖν θέλω ὑμᾶς = θέλω οὖν ὑμᾶς λαμβάνειν.

35 καὶ τὰ τέκνα – adv. καί here; "even."

36 δῶρα . . . ἐδέχοντο τοῦ θεοῦ = ἐδέχοντο δῶρα τοῦ θεοῦ.

36 θεὸν αὐτὸν δὲ οὔ – the verb ἐδέχοντο is implied here after οὐ.

Λογος Α (Ἰησοῦς θεραπεύει τέκνον)

Ἰησοῦς ἦν σὺν τοῖς μαθηταῖς ἐν πλοίῳ μικρῷ ἐπὶ τῆς θαλάσσης. ἤρχοντο οὖν ὄχλοι εἰς τὴν θάλασσαν καὶ ἤκουον τοῦ Ἰησοῦ ἀπὸ τοῦ τόπου τούτου, ὅτι οὐκ ἦν τόπος αὐτοῖς ἐν τῷ πλοίῳ.

τότε λέγει ἄνθρωπός τις ἀπὸ τοῦ ὄχλου, "Κύριε! δύνῃ ἀκούειν μου; ἔχω τέκνον καὶ τὸ τέκνον ἔχει δαιμόνιον. διὰ τοῦτο λέγω σοι, γινώσκω γὰρ ὅτι ἔχεις ἐξουσίαν θεραπεύειν καὶ σῴζειν. εἰ θέλεις, δύναμαι ἄγειν σε πρὸς αὐτήν. εἰ δὲ θεραπεύσεις αὐτήν, τότε πιστεύσω σοί τε καὶ τοῖς μαθηταῖς σου."

ἀκούει δὲ Ἰησοῦς τῆς φωνῆς τοῦ ἀνθρώπου τούτου, ἀλλὰ μένει ἐν τῷ πλοίῳ. λέγει δὲ οὕτως, "Εἰ πορεύομαι σὺν σοὶ καὶ θεραπεύω τὸ τέκνον, θαυμάσεις; δοξάσεις τὸν θεόν; εἰρήνην ἕξεις; βλέπω τὴν καρδίαν σου· εἰ βλέπεις, πιστεύσεις. οὐκ ἔστιν ὥρα βλέπειν ἀλλὰ πιστεύειν."

ὁ ἄνθρωπος οὖν ἀπέρχεται καὶ φέρει τὸ τέκνον πρὸς Ἰησοῦν. ὁ δὲ ἄνθρωπος λέγει, "Διδάσκαλε! τοῦτο τὸ τέκνον ἐστίν!" μετὰ τοῦτο, ὁ ἄνθρωπος βάλλει τὸ τέκνον εἰς τὴν θάλασσαν! τὸ δὲ τέκνον μέλλει ἀποθνήσκειν, οὐ γὰρ δύναται ἀναβαίνειν ἀπὸ τῆς θαλάσσης. ὁ οὖν Ἰησοῦς πορεύεται ἐπὶ τῆς θαλάσσης καὶ ἐγείρει αὐτὴν ἐκ τῆς θαλάσσης. οἱ δὲ μαθηταὶ καὶ οἱ ὄχλοι θαυμάζουσιν. ὁ δὲ Ἰησοῦς λέγει τῷ δαιμονίῳ τῷ ἐν τῷ τέκνῳ, "Οὐχ ἕξεις οἶκον οὔτε ἐν τῷ τέκνῳ οὔτε ἐν τῇ θαλάσσῃ, ἀποστέλλω γάρ σε εἰς τὴν ἔρημον."

τότε τὸ δαιμόνιον λέγει, "Κύριε! πορεύσομαι εἰς τὴν ἔρημον."

ὁ δὲ πατὴρ τοῦ τέκνου λέγει, "Νῦν πιστεύω σοι, διδάσκαλε!" ὁ δὲ Ἰησοῦς ἀποκρίνεται, "Οὐχ ὑπὲρ σοῦ θεραπεύω τὸ τέκνον, ἀλλ᾽ ὑπὲρ τῆς δόξης θεοῦ."

οἱ δὲ ὄχλοι οὐκ ἐδέχοντο τὸ ἀγαθὸν τοῦτο ὅτι τὸ σάββατον ἦν. διδάσκαλοι μὲν γὰρ ἦσαν τοῦ νόμου, τὸν νόμον δὲ οὐκ εἶχον ἐν ταῖς καρδίαις αὐτῶν.

ἄνθρωπός τις, a certain person
δαιμόνιον, ου, τό, demon
διδάσκαλος, ου, ὁ, teacher
δοξάζω, I glorify
εἰ, if
εἰρήνη, ης, ἡ, peace
ἕξω, I will have (fut. of ἔχω)

θαυμάζω, I marvel, wonder
θεραπεύω, I heal, serve
πατήρ, πατρός, ὁ, father
σάββατον, ου, τό, Sabbath
τότε, then
φέρω, I bring, bear, carry

5 οὐκ ἦν τόπος αὐτοῖς – ἦν used here in an impersonal sense, "there was
   not a place for them" (cf. Luke 2:7).

9 εἰ θέλεις – we've seen θέλω used with infinitives. On its own, it can mean
   "I want" or "I am willing" with an infinitive implied from the context.

1 *Λογος Β (Ὀνήσιμος ἀκούει Παύλου)*

"Τίς εἶ σύ; εἰ ἔχεις τι λέγειν, ἀκούσομεν! εἰ δοῦλος εἶ, οἴσομέν σε εἰς φυλακὴν ὅτι ὁ κύριός σου οὐκ ἔστιν μετὰ σοῦ."

5 θαυμάζουσιν οἱ ὄχλοι ἐν τῇ ἐκκλησίᾳ ταύτῃ ὅτι οὕτως ἐδύνατο ὁ Ὀνήσιμος ἀπέρχεσθαί τε ἀπὸ Κολοσσῶν καὶ πορεύεσθαι εἰς Φιλίππους. ὁ δὲ Ὀνήσιμος οὐκ ἀποκρίνεται τῇ ἐκκλησίᾳ, ὅτι οὐ θέλει τὴν ἀλήθειαν λέγειν. λέγει δὲ ἑαυτῷ,

10 "Δοῦλος μὲν ἤμην ἐγὼ ἐν τῷ οἴκῳ τοῦ κυρίου μου, νῦν δὲ οὐκ εἰμί. ἀλλ᾽ εἰ τὴν ἀλήθειαν λέγω, πάλιν ἔσομαι δοῦλος τοῦ κακοῦ κυρίου ἐκείνου. ἐλεύσεται γὰρ ὁ κύριος καὶ λήμψεταί με. τότε ἔξω ἔργα ἐν τῷ οἴκῳ αὐτοῦ. τί οὖν ὀφείλω λέγειν τοῖς ἀνθρώποις 15 τούτοις; τὴν ἀλήθειαν; θέλουσιν γὰρ φέρειν με εἰς φυλακήν. τότε δυνήσομαι σῴζειν τὴν ψυχήν μου; οὐ δυνήσομαι . . ."

ἡ δὲ ἐκκλησία λέγει, "Διὰ τί οὐκ ἀποκρίνῃ; ὅτι οὐκ ἀποκρίνῃ, γινώσκομεν τὴν ἀλήθειαν· δοῦλος κακὸς εἶ! γινώσκομεν γὰρ ὅτι 20 ἀπὸ Κολοσσῶν εἶ."

ὁ δὲ Ὀνήσιμος ἀποκρίνεται, "Οὐκ εἰμὶ δοῦλος, κύριον γὰρ οὐκ ἔχω! βλέπετε τὸν κύριόν μου; οὐ βλέπετε."

25 ἄνθρωπός τις ἐκ τοῦ ὄχλου ἀποκρίνεται, "Δοῦλος ἦς καὶ δοῦλος εἶ καὶ δοῦλος ἔσῃ! ὦ Φίλιπποι! διὰ τί ἔτι λέγομεν τῷ κακῷ δούλῳ τούτῳ; ὀφείλομεν ἄγειν αὐτὸν εἰς φυλακὴν σὺν τοῖς ἄλλοις! γινώσκετε γὰρ ὅτι οἱ ἄλλοι ἄνθρωποι ἐκεῖνοι ἐκήρυσσον περὶ τοῦ θεοῦ αὐτῶν. νῦν δὲ τόπος ἐστὶν ἔτι ἐν τῇ φυλακῇ."

30 τότε ἀνοίγει ὁ ὄχλος τὴν φυλακὴν καὶ βάλλει αὐτὸν εἰς αὐτήν. ὁ δὲ Ὀνήσιμος νῦν λέγει, "Οὐκ ὤφειλον ἀπέρχεσθαι ἀπὸ τοῦ κυρίου μου. δοῦλος μὲν ἤμην, ἄρτον δὲ εἶχον ἐσθίειν. ἀλλὰ τί φάγομαι νῦν ἐν τῷ τόπῳ τούτῳ; τίς οἴσει ἄρτον ὑπὲρ ἐμοῦ; ἐλεύσεται ὁ κύριός 35 μου; εἰ οὐκ ἐλεύσεται, γενήσομαι δοῦλος τοῦ ἄλλου κυρίου; τότε κακαὶ ἔσονται αἱ ἡμέραι μου. προσεύξομαι οὖν τοῖς θεοῖς μου, σώσουσιν γάρ με."

ἄνθρωπός τις, a certain person
ἀνοίγω, I open
γενήσομαι, I will become (fut. of γίνομαι)
δυνήσομαι, I will be able (fut. of δύναμαι)
ἑαυτῷ, to himself (dat. of ἑαυτοῦ)
εἰ, if
ἐλεύσομαι, I will come (fut. of ἔρχομαι)
ἔσομαι, I will be (fut. of εἰμί)
κηρύσσω, I preach, proclaim
Κολοσσῶν, Colossae (gen. of Κολοσσαί)

λήμψομαι, I will take, receive (fut. of λαμβάνω)
οἴσω, I will bring (fut. of φέρω)
προσεύχομαι, I pray
τί, what?
τι, something (neut. sing. acc.)
τίς, who? (nom. sing.)
τότε, then
φάγομαι, I will eat (fut. of ἐσθίω)
Φίλιπποι, Philippians! (voc. of Φίλιπποι)
Φιλίππους, Philippi (acc. of Φίλιπποι)
φυλακή, ῆς, ἡ, prison

6   ἐν τῇ ἐκκλησίᾳ ταύτῃ – not the church, but the civic assembly of Philippi.

29 τόπος ἐστίν – as in p. 52, line 5, ἐστίν is used in an impersonal sense here ("there is a place" or "there is room/space").

32 οὐκ ὤφειλον ἀπέρχεσθαι – difficult to render this imperfect in English. "I ought not to have departed" or "I should not have departed."

36 κακαὶ ἔσονται αἱ ἡμέραι – in sentences with a predicate nominative, usually the noun with the definite article is the subject (αἱ ἡμέραι).

1 ἀκούει δὲ Ὀνήσιμος φωνῶν ἀνθρώπων, ἀλλ᾽ οὐ δύναται βλέπειν
τὰ πρόσωπα αὐτῶν, ἡμέρα γὰρ οὐκ ἦν. λέγουσιν δὲ οἱ ἄνθρωποι
περὶ ἀληθείας τε καὶ ἀγάπης, εἰρήνης τε καὶ ζωῆς. Ὀνήσιμος δὲ
γινώσκει τὴν φωνὴν τὴν τοῦ ἀνθρώπου τούτου! Ὀνήσιμος οὖν
5 λέγει, "Τίνες ἐστέ;"

ὁ δὲ ἄνθρωπος ἀποκρίνεται, "Παῦλός εἰμι καὶ οὗτός ἐστιν Σιλᾶς.
ἀλλὰ τίς εἶ; διὰ τί εἶ ἐν φυλακῇ;"

10 τὸ πρόσωπον μὲν οὐ βλέπει Ὀνήσιμος, φωνὴν δὲ γινώσκει!
ἀποκρίνεται οὖν καὶ λέγει, "Γινώσκω σέ! ἤκουον γὰρ σοῦ ἐν τῷ
οἴκῳ τοῦ κυρίου μου τῷ ἐν Κολοσσαῖς. οὐκ ἔλεγες σὺν Φιλήμονι
ἐν Κολοσσαῖς; Ὀνήσιμός εἰμι, ὁ δοῦλος αὐτοῦ."

15 ὁ δὲ Παῦλος ἀποκρίνεται, "Χαῖρε, Ὀνήσιμε! Φιλήμων ὁ ἀδελφός
μού ἐστιν, ἔχομεν γὰρ τὸν αὐτὸν πατέρα ἐν οὐρανῷ."

Ὀνήσιμος δὲ ἀποκρίνεται, "Ὁ ἀδελφός σου; τὸν αὐτὸν πατέρα
ἔχετε; τί λέγεις;"
20
ὁ οὖν Παῦλός τε καὶ Σιλᾶς ἄρχονται διδάσκειν Ὀνήσιμον περὶ
τοῦ πατρὸς αὐτῶν.

Κολοσσαῖς, Colossae (dat. of
   Κολοσσαί)
πατέρα, father (acc. of πατήρ)
πατήρ, πατρός, ὁ, father
Σιλᾶς, ᾶ, ὁ, Silas

τίνες, who? (nom. pl.)
Φιλήμονι, Philemon (dat. of
   Φιλήμων)
χαῖρε, hello!

2   ἡμέρα γὰρ οὐκ ἦν – "for it was not day," an impersonal sense to ἦν here,
     as elsewhere with ἐστίν.

3   Ὀνήσιμος δὲ γινώσκει τὴν φωνήν – γινώσκω can have the sense of "rec-
     ognize," as it does here.

11 ἐν τῷ οἴκω τοῦ κυρίου μου τῷ ἐν Κολοσσαῖς = ἐν τῷ οἴκῳ . . . τῷ ἐν
     Κολοσσαῖς.

18 τὸν αὐτὸν πατέρα – identical use of αὐτός.

1   πιστεύεις τῷ θεῷ; γινώσκεις ὅτι ὁ θεὸς ἀγάπη ἐστίν; ἐγὼ γινώσκω,
    ἔχω γὰρ τοὺς ἁγίους λόγους αὐτοῦ ἐν τῷ βιβλίῳ τῷ ἁγίῳ.

    τὸ δὲ βιβλίον λέγει, "Ἔπεμψεν ὁ θεὸς τὸν ἴδιον υἱὸν αὐτοῦ
5   σῶσαι καὶ τοὺς πονηροὺς καὶ τοὺς δικαίους. ὅλον γὰρ τὸν
    κόσμον ἤθελεν σῶσαι. ὁ θεὸς οὖν ἔπεμψεν τοὺς αὐτοῦ προφήτας
    κηρύσσειν τὴν ἀλήθειαν τῷ κόσμῳ."

    τότε οἱ προφηταὶ ἐκήρυσσον ἐν ταῖς ἡμέραις ἐκείναις, ἀλλ᾽ οὐκ
10 ἐδέχοντο αὐτοὺς οἱ πονηροὶ ἄνθρωποι τοῦ κόσμου. ἔλεγον γὰρ οἱ
    προφηταί, "Ἐλεύσεται πάλιν ὁ κύριος! πέμψει τὸν ἔσχατον αὐτοῦ
    προφήτην! θέλει οὖν ὑμᾶς ἐπιστρέψαι πρὸς αὐτόν! ἔπεμψεν οὖν
    ἡμᾶς διδάσκειν περὶ τῆς δικαιοσύνης αὐτοῦ. δεῖ οὖν ἑτοιμάζειν τὰς
    καρδίας ὑμῶν, ἄρχεται γὰρ ὁ θεὸς ἑτοιμάζειν τὴν αὐτοῦ βασιλείαν
15 ὑπὲρ ὑμῶν."

    οἱ οὖν προφηταὶ ἔπειθον τοὺς ἀνθρώπους, ἀλλ᾽ ἤκουσαν αὐτῶν
    οἱ ἄνθρωποι τοῦ κόσμου; οὐκ ἤκουσαν. ὁ θεὸς οὖν ἔπεμψεν τὸν
    ἔσχατον προφήτην, τὸν ἴδιον υἱὸν αὐτοῦ.
20
    τότε ἔπεμψεν ὁ θεὸς τὸν υἱὸν αὐτοῦ ἀπολῦσαι τοὺς ἀνθρώπους
    ἀπὸ τῆς ἁμαρτίας τε καὶ τῶν δαιμονίων. μετὰ τοῦτο, ὁ υἱὸς αὐτοῦ
    ἤρχετο διὰ τῆς γῆς εὑρίσκειν μαθητὰς ἀγαθούς. ὁ δὲ Πέτρος
    ἐπορεύετο ἐν τῇ ὁδῷ ὅτε ἤκουσεν Ἰησοῦ. ὁ δὲ Ἰησοῦς ἔρχεται πρὸς
25 αὐτὸν καὶ λέγει, "Δεῖ σε πορεύεσθαι μετ᾽ ἐμοῦ."

    ὁ δὲ Πέτρος ἀποκρίνεται, "Ἔχεις οἶκον;" ὁ δὲ Ἰησοῦς λέγει, "Οἶκον
    οὐκ ἔχω ὅτι ὁ υἱὸς τοῦ ἀνθρώπου οὐκ ἔχει τόπον τῇ κεφαλῇ αὐτοῦ.
    οἶκον μὲν οὖν οὐκ ἔχω, θρόνον δὲ ἔχω ἐν οὐρανῷ. εἰ πορεύῃ μετ᾽
30 ἐμοῦ, ἀνοίξω τοὺς ὀφθαλμούς σου βλέπειν ταῦτα."

    οὕτως οὖν ἔπεισεν ὁ Ἰησοῦς τὸν Πέτρον. ὁ δὲ Πέτρος ἀποκρίνεται,
    "Ἐκεῖ ἐπὶ τὴν θρόνον σοῦ ἀναβαίνομεν; ἴδιον θρόνον ἔχεις; ὑπὲρ
    ἐμοῦ ἡτοίμασας ἐκεῖνον;"
35
    ὁ δὲ Ἰησοῦς λέγει, "Ἤδη ὥρα ἐστὶν βλέπειν ταῦτα. εἰ οὖν πορεύῃ
    σὺν ἐμοί, διδάξω σε περὶ τῆς δικαιοσύνης τε καὶ τῆς βασιλείας
    τοῦ θεοῦ. τότε ἕξεις τὸν θρόνον τοῦτον ἐν οὐρανῷ μετὰ τὸν
    θάνατόν σου."

ἀπολύω, I release, dismiss

δεῖ, it is necessary (+ inf.)

δικαιοσύνη, ης, ἡ, righteousness

ἐκεῖ, there, to that place

ἐπιστρέφω, I turn, return

ἐπιστρέψαι, aor. act. inf. of
  ἐπιστρέφω (I turn, return)

ἑτοιμάζω, I prepare

ἤδη, already

θρόνος, ου, ὁ, throne

ἴδιος, α, ον, one's own

κεφαλή, ῆς, ἡ, head

ὅλος, η, ον, whole (predicate
  position)

ὅτε, when

πείθω, I persuade

σῶσαι, aor. act. inf. of σῴζω
  (I save)

5 **ὅλον γὰρ τὸν κόσμον ἤθελεν σῶσαι** = ἤθελεν γὰρ σῶσαι ὅλον τὸν κόσμον. ὅλος is an adjective that stands in the predicate position.

17 **ἔπειθον** – impf. act. ind. 3p, the sense here is that they were trying to persuade. The imperfect can have this sense.

25 **δεῖ σε πορεύεσθαι μετ᾽ ἐμοῦ** – δεῖ goes with an infinitive, and σε (acc.) here acts as the subject of the infinitve.

32 **ἔπεισεν** – from πείθω. Remember that for verb stems that end in certain consonants, changes occur when the aorist suffix σα is added.

AORIST ACTIVE INDICATIVE OF λύω

	Singular		Plural	
1	ἔλυσα	*I loosened*	ἐλύσαμεν	*we loosened*
2	ἔλυσας	*you (sing.) loosened*	ἐλύσατε	*you (pl.) loosened*
3	ἔλυσε(ν)	*he, she, it loosened*	ἔλυσαν	*they loosened*

Λογος Α (πάλιν περὶ Μωϋσέως καὶ Ἀαρών)

ὁ θεὸς εἶπεν τῷ Μωϋσῇ, "Ἐγώ εἰμι ὁ θεὸς τοῦ πατρός σου, θεὸς
Ἀβραὰμ καὶ θεὸς Ἰσαὰκ καὶ θεὸς Ἰακώβ." ὁ δὲ Μωϋσῆς οὐκ ἤθελεν
ἰδεῖν τὸ πρόσωπον τοῦ θεοῦ. καὶ εἶπεν αὐτῷ ὁ θεός, "Βλέπω τὸ
κακὸν τοῦ Φαραὼ κατὰ τοῦ λαοῦ μου τοῦ ἐν Αἰγύπτῳ καὶ αἱ
φωναὶ αὐτῶν ἀναβαίνουσιν εἰς τὸν οὐρανόν. θέλω οὖν σῶσαι
αὐτούς. γινώσκω γὰρ ὅτι δοῦλοί εἰσιν τοῦ Φαραώ. νῦν ἔσῃ
ἄγγελός μου, ἀποστέλλω γάρ σε πρὸς Φαραώ. δεῖ γάρ σε εἰπεῖν
αὐτῷ ὅτι ὁ θεός σου δύναται λῦσαι τὴν βασιλείαν αὐτοῦ."

Μωϋσῆς δὲ εἶπεν τῷ θεῷ, "Κύριε, τίς εἰμι; οὐ δύναμαι ἐλθεῖν τε
καὶ εἰπεῖν τῷ Φαραώ, ὅτι ἡ φωνή μου κακή ἐστιν." ὁ δὲ θεὸς εἶπεν
αὐτῷ, "Ἀκούω σου, πέμψω οὖν τὸν ἀδελφόν σου, Ἀαρών. καὶ
οὗτος ἔσται ἄγγελός μου." καὶ εἰσῆλθον εἰς γῆν Αἰγύπτου. οἱ δὲ
ἀδελφοὶ εἶδον τὸν Φαραὼ καὶ ἦλθον πρὸς αὐτόν. ὁ δὲ Ἀαρὼν
ἤρξατο λέγειν περὶ θεοῦ καὶ περὶ τοῦ λαοῦ θεοῦ. ὁ δὲ Φαραὼ οὐκ
ἤκουεν αὐτοῦ.

Καὶ μετὰ ταῦτα, εἰσῆλθον πάλιν Μωϋσῆς καὶ Ἀαρὼν πρὸς Φαραὼ
καὶ εἶπον αὐτῷ, "Οὕτως λέγει Κύριος ὁ θεὸς Ἰσραήλ· θέλω σῶσαι
τὸν λαόν μου, ὀφείλεις οὖν ἀποστέλλειν αὐτοὺς ἀπὸ τῆς βασιλείας
σου καὶ εἰς τὴν ἔρημον." καὶ εἶπεν Φαραώ, "Τίς ἐστιν ὁ θεός σου
ὅτι ὀφείλω ἀκοῦσαι τῆς φωνῆς αὐτοῦ; οὐ γινώσκω τὸν κύριον, καὶ
τὸν Ἰσραὴλ οὐ πέμψω." καὶ εἶπον αὐτῷ, "Κατὰ τὸν λόγον τοῦ θεοῦ,
δεῖ ἡμᾶς ἐλθεῖν εἰς τὴν ἔρημον προσφέρειν δῶρα τῷ θεῷ." καὶ
εἶπεν αὐτοῖς ὁ Φαραώ, "Διὰ τί, Μωϋσῆ καὶ Ἀαρών, θέλετε λαβεῖν
τὸν λαόν μου ἀπὸ τῶν ἔργων; οὐκ ἔχουσιν ἤδη ἄρτον φαγεῖν; οὐκ
ἔχουσιν οἶνον πιεῖν; τί ἔξουσιν ἐν τῇ ἐρήμῳ; ἀλλ᾽ ἔτι θέλουσιν οἱ
δοῦλοι φυγεῖν; οὐ φεύξονται οἱ δοῦλοι οὐδὲ πίονται οἶνον οὐδὲ
φάγονται ἄρτον! ὄψεσθε δὲ κακὰς ἡμέρας ἐν τῇ βασιλείᾳ μου!"
Μωϋσῆς δὲ καὶ Ἀαρὼν εἶπον αὐτῷ, "Εἰ οὐ πέμψεις ἡμᾶς εἰς τὴν
ἔρημον, ὄψῃ σημεῖα ἀπὸ οὐρανοῦ. τὰ δὲ σημεῖα ταῦτα λύσουσιν
τὴν βασιλείαν σου! θέλεις ἀποθανεῖν; ὁ θεὸς ἡμῶν ἔχει ἐξουσίαν
κρίνειν καὶ ἀποκτείνειν!" ὁ δὲ Μωϋσῆς καὶ Ἀαρὼν ἔπειθον Φαραώ,
ἀλλ᾽ οὐκ ἤκουσεν αὐτῶν οὐδὲ ἔπεμψεν τὸν λαὸν εἰς τὴν ἔρημον.
ὁ θεὸς οὖν ἤνοιξεν τοὺς οὐρανοὺς καὶ ἦλθεν σημεῖα τοῦ θανάτου
ἐπὶ τὴν γῆν. τὰ σημεῖα οὖν ἔπεσεν ἐπὶ τοὺς Αἰγύπτους καὶ ἐπὶ τὸν
υἱὸν τοῦ Φαραώ. ὁ υἱὸς οὖν ἀπέθανεν τοῦ Φαραώ.

ἀπέθανον, I died (2nd aor. act. ind. 1s of ἀποθνῄσκω, I die)

ἀποθανεῖν, to die (2nd aor. inf. of ἀποθνῄσκω, I die)

εἶδον, I saw (2nd aor. of ὁράω, I see)

εἶπον, I said (2nd aor. of λέγω, I say)

εἰσῆλθον, they went in (2nd aor. of εἰσέρχομαι, I go in)

ἐλθεῖν, to go/come (2nd aor. inf. of ἔρχομαι, I go, come)

ἦλθον, I came, went (2nd aor. of ἔρχομαι, I go, come)

ἰδεῖν, to see (2nd aor. inf. of ὁράω, I see)

λαβεῖν, to take (2nd aor. inf. of λαμβάνω, I take)

οἶνος, ου, ὁ, wine

ὄψομαι, I will see (fut. of ὁράω, I see)

πατρός, father (gen. of πατήρ)

πιεῖν, to drink (2nd aor. inf. of πίνω, I drink)

πίνω, πίομαι, ἔπιον, I drink, I will drink, I drank

πίπτω, ἔπεσον, I fall, I fell

προσφέρω, I offer, present

σημεῖον, ου, τό, sign, miracle, portent

σῶσαι, to save (aor. inf. of σῴζω, I save)

φαγεῖν, to eat (2nd aor. inf. of ἐσθίω, I eat)

φεύγω, φεύξομαι, ἔφυγον, I flee, I will flee, I fled

φυγεῖν, to flee (2nd aor. inf. of φεύγω, I flee)

---

9 δεῖ γάρ σε εἰπεῖν – δεῖ is an impersonal verb that requires an infinitive. The subject of the infinitive is in the acc. case (σε).

39 ὁ υἱὸς οὖν ἀπέθανεν τοῦ Φαραώ – it's common in Greek for a noun (υἱός) and its gen. modifier (τοῦ Φαραώ) to be separated.

1 τότε ὁ Φαραὼ ἦλθεν πρὸς Μωϋσῆν καὶ Ἀαρὼν καὶ εἶπεν, "Διὰ τί
ἐγένετο ταῦτα κακὰ ἐν τῇ βασιλείᾳ μου; ἰδού! ἤνεγκα τὸν υἱόν μου
πρὸς ὑμᾶς! νῦν νεκρός ἐστιν! εἰ πέμπω ὑμᾶς ἐκεῖ εἰς τὴν ἔρημον,
δυνήσεται ὁ θεός σου ἐγείρειν τὸν υἱόν μου; ὄψομαι αὐτὸν πάλιν;"
5 Μωϋσῆς δὲ εἶπεν αὐτῷ, "Εἰ προσεύχῃ αὐτῷ, δύναται ὁ θεὸς σῶσαι
τὸν υἱόν σου." μετὰ ταῦτα, Μωϋσῆς καὶ Ἀαρὼν συνήγαγον τὸν
λαὸν θεοῦ καὶ ἤγαγον τοὺς ἀνθρώπους εἰς τὴν ἔρημον.

καὶ μετὰ ταῦτα, Μωϋσῆς παρὰ τὴν γῆν Χανάαν ἦν μετὰ τοῦ
10 λαοῦ καὶ συνήγαγεν αὐτοὺς περὶ αὐτὸν καὶ εἶπεν αὐτοῖς περὶ τῶν
κακῶν ἡμερῶν ἐν Αἰγύπτῳ. Μωϋσῆς εἶπεν, "Ἀπεθνήσκομεν ὑπὸ
τὴν ἐξουσίαν τοῦ Φαραώ, ἀλλ᾽ ἔσωσεν ἡμᾶς ὁ θεός. νῦν μέλλετε
εἰσελθεῖν εἰς τὴν γῆν Χανάαν, ἀλλ᾽ ἐγὼ μέλλω ἀποθανεῖν. δεῖ οὖν
ὑμᾶς ἀκοῦσαι τῆς φωνῆς μου καὶ τῶν λόγων τοῦ θεοῦ! ὀφείλετε
15 πιστεῦσαι εἰς τὸν θεὸν καὶ εἰς τὸν Ἰησοῦν. ὁ γὰρ Ἰησοῦς μέλλει
ἄγειν ὑμᾶς εἰς τὴν γῆν Χανάαν."

Λογος Β (Ὀνήσιμος σὺν Παύλῳ ἐν φυλακῇ)

20
Παῦλος καὶ Σιλᾶς καὶ Ὀνήσιμος ἦσαν ἐν τῇ φυλακῇ τῇ ἐν
Φιλίπποις. ὁ δὲ Παῦλος καὶ Σιλᾶς ἐδίδασκον Ὀνήσιμον περὶ τῆς
δικαιοσύνης θεοῦ καὶ τοῦ Χριστοῦ, ἀλλ᾽ ἔτι οὐκ ἐπίστευεν αὐτοῖς
ὅτι οὐκ ἔπεισαν αὐτόν. μαθητὴς οὖν οὐκ ἐγένετο τοῦ Χριστοῦ.

25
ὁ θεὸς δὲ ἤθελεν ἀπολῦσαι αὐτοὺς ἀπὸ φυλακῆς. ἐγένετο οὖν
σημεῖον ἀπὸ οὐρανοῦ. τί δὲ ἦν τὸ σημεῖον; σεισμὸς ἐγένετο οὐ
μικρὸς ἐν αὐτῇ τῇ ὥρᾳ καὶ ἤνοιξεν ὁ θεὸς τὴν φυλακήν. Ὀνήσιμος
οὖν ἔφυγεν ἀπὸ τῆς φυλακῆς ὅτι οὐκ ἤθελεν μένειν τε ἐν φυλακῇ
30 καὶ γενέσθαι δοῦλος πάλιν τοῦ ἄλλου κυρίου. ὁ δὲ Παῦλός τε καὶ
Σιλᾶς οὐκ ἔφυγον.

τότε ὁ δεσμοφύλαξ εἰσῆλθεν καὶ οὐκ εἶδεν τοὺς ἀνθρώπους.
ἤμελλεν οὖν ἀποκτείνειν ἑαυτόν. ὁ δὲ Παῦλος ἔκραξεν, "Ἡμεῖς
35 ἐσμεν ἔτι ἐν τῇ φυλακῇ! οὐ δεῖ σε ἀποθανεῖν!"

ὁ δὲ δεσμοφύλαξ ἐθαύμασεν καὶ εἶπεν τῷ Παύλῳ καὶ τῷ Σιλᾷ,
"Τί δεῖ με ποιεῖν; δύναται ὁ θεός σου σῶσαί με;" ὁ δὲ Παῦλος καὶ

ἀποθανεῖν, to die (2nd aor. inf. of ἀποθνήσκω, I die)

ἀπολῦσαι, to release (aor. inf. of ἀπολύω, I release)

δεσμοφύλαξ, δεσμοφύλακος, ὁ, jailer

ἑαυτόν, himself (acc.)

ἐγένετο, 2nd aor. mid. ind. 3s of γίνομαι (I become, occur, happen)

εἶδεν, 2nd aor. act. ind. 3s of ὁράω (I see)

εἶπαν, 2nd aor. act. ind. 3p of λέγω (I say; often, the 3p in 2nd aor. can end in -αν instead of -ον)

ἔκραξεν, aor. act. ind. 3s of κράζω (I cry out, call out)

ἔπεισαν, aor. act. ind. 3p of πείθω (I persuade)

ἔφυγεν, 2nd aor. act. ind. 3s of φεύγω (I flee)

ἤγαγον, they led (2nd aor. act. ind. 3p of ἄγω, I lead)

ἤνεγκα, I brought, bore, carried (2nd aor. of φέρω, I bring, bear, carry)

ἤνοιξεν, aor. act. ind. 3s of ἀνοίγω (I open)

νεκρός, ά, όν, dead

ποιεῖν, to do

σεισμός, οῦ, ὁ, earthquake

συνήγαγον, they gathered (2nd aor. act. ind. 3p of συνάγω, I gather)

τί, what?

Φιλίπποις, dat. of Φίλιπποι, Philippi

φυλακή, ῆς, ἡ, prison

24 μαθητὴς οὖν οὐκ ἐγένετο τοῦ Χριστοῦ = οὐκ ἐγένετο οὖν μαθητὴς τοῦ Χριστοῦ.

28 ἐν αὐτῇ τῇ ὥρᾳ – intensive use of αὐτός (Croy p. 43) in predicate position, "in that very hour."

1 Σιλᾶς εἶπαν, "Εἰ πιστεύεις εἰς τὸν κύριον Ἰησοῦν, σώσει σε καὶ τὸν
οἶκόν σου."

τότε ἐπίστευσαν εἰς τὸν κύριον Ἰησοῦν ὁ δεσμοφύλαξ τε καὶ ὁ
5 οἶκος αὐτοῦ. καὶ ἐβάπτισεν αὐτοὺς ὁ Παῦλος, καὶ ὁ δεσμοφύλαξ
ἤγαγεν τὸν Παῦλον καὶ τὸν Σιλᾶν εἰς τὸν ἴδιον οἶκον αὐτοῦ.

ἐν δὲ τῷ οἴκῳ αὐτοῦ ἡτοίμασεν ἄρτον φαγεῖν καὶ οἶνον πιεῖν.
τότε ἤσθιόν τε ἄρτον καὶ ἔπινον οἶνον, καὶ ἔλεγον περὶ θεοῦ
10 καὶ ἀληθείας καὶ ζωῆς. καὶ αἱ φωναὶ αὐτῶν ἀνέβαινον εἰς
τὸν οὐρανόν.

μετὰ ταῦτα, ὁ δεσμοφύλαξ ἤνεγκεν Παῦλον καὶ Σιλᾶν πρὸς
τὴν φυλακήν. καὶ οἱ ἄνθρωποι τῶν Φιλίππων ἦλθον ἀπολῦσαι
15 αὐτούς. ὁ οὖν Παῦλος καὶ Σιλᾶς ἀπῆλθον καὶ ὑπέστρεψαν εἰς τὴν
ἐκκλησίαν τὴν ἐν τῷ οἴκῳ τῆς Λυδίας.

ὁ δὲ Ὀνήσιμος οὐκ ἦν μετ᾽ αὐτῶν, ἀλλ᾽ ἐπορεύετο ἐν τῇ ὁδῷ
εὑρεῖν ἄρτον φαγεῖν, ἀλλ᾽ οὐχ εὗρεν. ἤμελλεν οὖν ἀποθανεῖν ὅτι
20 οὐδὲ ἱμάτιον καλὸν εἶχεν.

τότε ἤκουσεν φωνῶν ἀνθρώπων. προσῆλθεν οὖν ταῖς φωναῖς
ἐν τῷ οἴκῳ καὶ πάλιν εὗρεν Παῦλον καὶ Σιλᾶν. ὁ δὲ Ὀνήσιμος
ἐθαύμασεν ὅτι ὁ Παῦλος καὶ οἱ ἄνθρωποι οἱ σὺν αὐτῷ ἤσθιον
25 ἄρτον καὶ ἔπινον οἶνον. καὶ Παῦλος ἔλεγεν, "Νῦν πίνομεν τὸν
οἶνον τοῦτον καὶ ἐσθίομεν τὸν ἄρτον τοῦτον, ἀλλ᾽ ἐλεύσεται
ὁ κύριος καὶ τότε ἕξομεν οἶνον πιεῖν ἀπ᾽ οὐρανοῦ καὶ ἄρτον
φαγεῖν μετὰ τοῦ κυρίου καὶ τῶν ἁγίων αὐτοῦ ἐν τῇ βασιλείᾳ!"
τότε ἤρξατο Παῦλος κηρύσσειν ὅτι ἔδει Ἰησοῦν ἀποθανεῖν
30 ὑπὲρ αὐτῶν.

καὶ οἱ ἅγιοι προσέφερον δῶρα τῷ Παύλῳ ἀλλ᾽ οὐκ ἐδέξατο αὐτά.
ἐπέστρεψεν δὲ πρὸς Ὀνήσιμον καὶ εἶπεν, "Ὦ, Ὀνήσιμε! διὰ τί
μένεις ἐκεῖ; ἔχομεν τόπον σοι ἐν τῷ οἴκῳ τούτῳ. βλέπεις τὰ δῶρα
35 ταῦτα; οὐκ ἐδεξάμην τὰ δῶρα ὅτι σοῦ ἐστιν τὰ δῶρα!"

καὶ ἄλλος ἄνθρωπος εἶπεν, "Ναί, Ὀνήσιμε. Παῦλος ἔλεγεν περὶ

ἔδει, impf. act. ind. 3s of δεῖ (it is necessary, + inf.)

ἐδέξατο, aor. mid. ind. 3s of δέχομαι (I accept, receive)

εἶπαν, 2nd aor. act. ind. 3p of λέγω (I say; sometimes, the 3p in 2nd aor. can end in -αν instead of -ον)

εἶχεν, impf. act. ind. 3s of ἔχω (I have)

ἐκεῖ, there, in that place

ἐπέστρεψεν, aor. act. ind. 3s of ἐπιστρέφω (I turn)

ἔπινον, impf. act. ind. 3p of πίνω (I drink)

εὗρεν, 2nd aor. act. ind. 3s of εὑρίσκω (I find)

ἤγαγεν, 2nd aor. act. ind. 3s of ἄγω (I lead)

ἤνεγκεν, 2nd aor. act. ind. of φέρω (I bring)

ἤρξατο, aor. mid. ind. 3s of ἄρχομαι (I begin)

ἱμάτιον, ου, τό, garment, cloak, robe

Λυδία, ας, ἡ, Lydia

ναί, yes

πιεῖν, to drink (2nd aor. inf. of πίνω, I drink)

προσῆλθεν, 2nd aor. act. ind. 3s of προσέρχομαι (I approach, + dat.)

φαγεῖν, to eat (2nd aor. inf. of ἐσθίω, I eat)

Φιλίππων, of Philippi

4 ἐπίστευσαν εἰς τὸν κύριον Ἰησοῦν ὁ δεσμοφύλαξ τε καὶ ὁ οἶκος αὐτοῦ – what is the subject? ὁ δεσμοφύλαξ τε καὶ ὁ οἶκος αὐτοῦ.

9 ἤσθιον . . . ἔπινον . . . ἔλεγον – note the use of imperfect verbs here to highlight the progressive nature of these actions.

29 ἔδει Ἰησοῦν ἀποθανεῖν ὑπὲρ αὐτῶν – the subject of the infinitive ἀποθανεῖν is the accusative Ἰησοῦν, "it was necessary for Jesus to die for their sake."

35 ὅτι σοῦ ἐστιν τὰ δῶρα – the genitive σου denotes possession.

1 σου. οὐκ ἔχεις ἱμάτιον; ἰδού. καὶ τὸ ἱμάτιον τοῦτο σού ἐστιν.
   προσφέρομεν ταῦτα ὑπέρ σου."

   ὁ δὲ Ὀνήσιμος ἐθαύμασεν καὶ ἐν αὐτῇ τῇ ὥρᾳ ἤνοιξεν ὁ θεὸς τοὺς
5 ὀφθαλμοὺς τοὺς τῆς καρδίας αὐτοῦ. τότε ἐπίστευσεν ὁ Ὀνήσιμος
   καὶ ἐγένετο μαθητὴς τοῦ Χριστοῦ. ἀλλ᾽ οὐ διὰ τὰ δῶρα ἐγένετο
   μαθητής, ἀλλὰ διὰ τὴν ἀγάπην τῶν ἁγίων.

   μετὰ τοῦτο, ἐβάπτισεν αὐτὸν ὁ Παῦλος ἐν θαλάσσῃ καὶ ἐδόξασαν
10 τὸν θεὸν οἱ ἅγιοι. ὁ δὲ Παῦλος εἶπεν τῷ Ὀνησίμῳ, "Σὺ ἦς ποτε
   δοῦλος τοῦ Φιλήμονος, ἀλλὰ νῦν δοῦλος εἶ τοῦ Χριστοῦ. σὺ ἦς
   ποτε τοῦ κόσμου τούτου, ἀλλὰ νῦν τῆς ὁδοῦ εἶ."

ἐγένετο, 2nd aor. mid. ind. 3s of γίνομαι (I become)

ἤνοιξεν, aor. act. ind. 3s of ἀνοίγω (I open)

ποτέ, once, before

4   ἐν αὐτῇ τῇ ὥρᾳ – intensive use of αὐτός, "in that very hour."

11 σὺ ἦς ποτε τοῦ κόσμου τούτου, ἀλλὰ νῦν τῆς ὁδοῦ εἶ – the genitives τοῦ κόσμου τούτου and τῆς ὁδοῦ (of the Way) can denote source. "You were of this world."

1   *Λογος Α (Ὀνήσιμος κηρύσσει ἐν τῇ ἀγορᾷ)*

μετὰ ταῦτα, Ὀνήσιμος ἐπορεύετο διὰ τῆς ἀγορᾶς. τί ἐστιν ἡ
ἀγορά; ἡ δὲ ἀγορά ἐστιν τόπος ὅπου ἄνθρωποι πωλοῦσιν ἄρτον
5   τε καὶ οἶνον καὶ ἱμάτια καὶ ἄλλα. ὁ δὲ Ὀνήσιμος πολλάκις ἤρχετο
εἰς ἄλλην ἀγορὰν ἐν Κολοσσαῖς. τότε δὲ ἐλάμβανεν ἄρτον παρ᾽
ἄλλων ἀνθρώπων, ἀλλὰ νῦν ἕτερος ἄνθρωπός ἐστιν ὁ Ὀνήσιμος,
ὅτι γέγονεν μαθητὴς τοῦ Χριστοῦ. οὐ θέλει οὖν ἐλθεῖν εἰς τὴν
ἀγορὰν εὑρίσκειν ἄρτον, ἀλλὰ θέλει κηρύξαι τοῖς ὄχλοις ἐν τῇ
10   ἀγορᾷ περὶ Χριστοῦ.

ἀλλὰ Λυδία εἰρήκει τῷ Ὀνησίμῳ, "Οὐ καλόν ἐστιν εἰσελθεῖν εἰς
τὴν ἀγορὰν, ὅτι κακοὶ ἄνθρωποί εἰσιν ἐκεῖ. μένειν οὖν θέλω σε ἐν
τῷ οἴκῳ μου." ὁ δὲ Ὀνήσιμος ἀκήκοεν τῆς Λυδίας; οὐκ ἀκήκοεν!
15   κακὸς οὖν μαθητής ἐστιν Ὀνήσιμος;

ὁ οὖν Ὀνήσιμος ἐπορεύετο διὰ τῆς ἀγορᾶς καὶ εἶδεν ἄρτον καλὸν
καὶ ἱμάτια καλά, ἀλλ᾽ εἶπεν ἑαυτῷ, "Οὐ διὰ τὸν ἄρτον ἐλήλυθας,
ἀλλὰ διὰ τὰς ψυχὰς τῶν ἀνθρώπων! ναί, Λυδία εἶπεν ὅτι ἐγὼ
20   οὐκ ὀφείλω ἐλθεῖν εἰς τὴν ἀγοράν, ἀλλ᾽ αὐτὴ οὐ γινώσκει διὰ
τί ἐλήλυθα."

ὁ οὖν Ὀνήσιμος ἤρξατο κηρύσσειν, "Ἤγγικεν ἡ βασιλεία τοῦ
θεοῦ! εἰ οὐ θέλετε ἀποθανεῖν διὰ τὰς ἁμαρτίας ὑμῶν, δεῖ ὑμᾶς
25   ἐπιστρέψαι πρὸς τὸν θεόν!"

ἄνθρωπος δὲ ἐκ τοῦ ὄχλου εἶπεν, "Τίς εἶ; διὰ τί εἴρηκας ταῦτα;
κηρύσσεις ἕτερον θεόν; ἔχομεν ἤδη θεούς! οὐ δεῖ ἡμᾶς δέξασθαι
ἕτερον θεόν. ἑώρακας τὸ ἱερὸν τῶν θεῶν ἡμῶν; καλόν ἐστιν!"
30

καὶ ἄλλος ἄνθρωπος εἶπεν, "Γινώσκω σε! οὐκ εἴδομέν σε ἐν τῇ
ἐκκλησίᾳ; ναί! εἴδομεν! ἐβάλομέν σε εἰς τὴν φυλακήν, ἀλλὰ
πέφευγας ἐκ φυλακῆς;"

35   ὁ δὲ ὄχλος ἤρξατο προσελθεῖν αὐτῷ. ὁ οὖν Ὀνήσιμος οὐκ ἐδύνατο
φυγεῖν. ἄλλος δὲ ἄνρθωπος πάλιν εἶπεν, "Ὁ ἄνθρωπος οὗτος
πέφευγεν ἐκ φυλακῆς! καὶ εἴρηκεν κατὰ τῶν θεῶν ἡμῶν, ὅτι
κηρύσσει ἑτέρους θεούς. λέλυκεν οὖν τὴν εἰρήνην ἡμῶν!"

ἀγορά, ᾶς, ἡ, market

ἀκήκοεν, perf. act. ind. 3s of ἀκούω (I hear)

ἀποθανεῖν, to die (aor. inf. of ἀποθνήσκω, I die)

γέγονεν, perf. act. ind. 3s of γίνομαι (I become)

δέξασθαι, aor. mid. inf. of δέχομαι (I receive, accept)

διὰ τί, on account of what, why?

ἑαυτῷ, (dat.) to himself

ἐβάλομεν, 2nd aor. act. ind. 1p of βάλλω (I throw)

εἰρήκει, pluperf. act. ind. 3s of λέγω (I say)

εἴρηκεν, perf. act. ind. 3s of λέγω (I say)

ἐλήλυθας, perf. act. ind. 2s of ἔρχομαι (I come)

ἐπιστρέψαι, to turn (aor. inf. of ἐπιστρέφω, I turn)

ἕτερος, α, ον, other, different

ἑώρακας, perf. act. ind. 2s of ὁράω (I see)

ἤγγικεν, perf. act. ind. 3s of ἐγγίζω (I draw near)

κηρύξαι, to preach (aor. inf. of κηρύσσω, I preach, proclaim)

Κολοσσαῖς, Colossae (dat. of Κολοσσαί)

λέλυκεν, perf. act. ind. 3s of λύω (I destroy)

ναί, yes

ὅπου, where

πέφευγας, perf. act. ind. 2s of φεύγω (I flee)

πωλοῦσιν, pres. act. ind. 3p of πωλέω (I sell)

πολλάκις, often, many times

τίς, who?

φυλακή, ῆς, ἡ, prison

12 **οὐ καλόν ἐστιν εἰσελθεῖν** – "it is not good to enter."

13 **μένειν οὖν θέλω σε** = θέλω οὖν σε μένειν.

31 **ἐν τῇ ἐκκλησίᾳ** – that is, in the "city assembly," not the church.

PERFECT ACTIVE INDICATIVE OF λύω

	Singular		Plural	
1	λέλυκα	*I have loosened*	λελύκαμεν	*we have loosened*
2	λέλυκας	*you have loosened*	λελύκατε	*you have loosened*
3	λέλυκε(ν)	*he, she, it has loosened*	λελύκασι(ν), λέλυκαν	*they have loosened*

1 ὁ δὲ Ὀνήσιμος εἶπεν, "Πεπίστευκα εἰς τὸν κύριον καὶ γέγονα
μαθητής. ἔγνωκα οὖν ὅτι καὶ ἐξ ὑμῶν δύναται σῶσαί με ὁ θεός.
ὑμεῖς οὖν οὐ δύνασθε ἀποκτείνειν με."

5 ὁ ὄχλος οὖν ἔβαλεν λίθους ἐπ᾽ αὐτὸν καὶ ἔπεσεν Ὀνήσιμος ἐπὶ τὴν
γῆν. τί δὲ γενήσεται τῷ Ὀνησίμῳ; δυνήσεται Ὀνήσιμος φυγεῖν;

Λογος Β (Λυδία εὑρίσκει Ὀνήσιμον)
10
νὺξ ἐγένετο, ἀλλ᾽ Ὀνήσιμος οὔπω ἐληλύθει πρὸς οἶκον. Λυδία
οὖν ἤρξατο πιστεύειν ὅτι κακόν τι ἐγένετο τῷ Ὀνησίμῳ. καὶ Λυδία
εἶπεν ἑαυτῇ, "Τί γέγονεν; ἤδη νύξ ἐστιν ἀλλ᾽ οὔπω ἐλήλυθεν
Ὀνήσιμος." τότε ἦρεν Λυδία τὸ ἱμάτιον αὐτῆς καὶ ἐξῆλθεν, ὅτι
15 ἠθέλησεν εὑρεῖν Ὀνήσιμον.

Λυδία οὖν διήρχετο τὰς ὁδοὺς τῶν Φιλίππων, ἀλλ᾽ οὐκ ἐδύνατο
εὑρεῖν Ὀνήσιμον. εἶδεν δὲ τὸν ἀγοράν. ἀλλ᾽ ἦν Ὀνήσιμος ἐκεῖ;
εἰρήκει γὰρ ἡ Λυδία τῷ Ὀνησίμῳ, "Οὐκ ὀφείλεις ἐλθεῖν εἰς τὴν
20 ἀγοράν!" ἀλλ᾽ ἔτι ἐληλύθει ἐκεῖ;

ἡ δὲ Λυδία ἔκραξεν, "Ὀνήσιμε! Ὀνήσιμε!" τότε εἶδεν ἀνθρώπους
καὶ εἶπεν αὐτοῖς, "Ἑωράκατε Ὀνήσιμον;" καὶ ἀπεκρίθησαν, "Οὐκ
ἑωράκαμεν οὐδὲ ἀκηκόαμεν περὶ αὐτοῦ." ἡ Λυδία οὖν προσηύξατο
25 τῷ θεῷ, "Ὦ, θεέ! δεῖ σε ἄγειν με πρὸς Ὀνήσιμον, ἐγὼ γὰρ οὐ
δύναμαι εὑρεῖν αὐτόν."

καὶ Λυδία ἤνοιξεν τοὺς ὀφθαλμοὺς καὶ εἶδεν ἄλλον ἄνθρωπον
ἐν τῇ ὁδῷ. τότε προσῆλθεν τῷ ἄλλῳ ἀνθρώπῳ τούτῳ καὶ εἶπεν,
30 "Καὶ σύ, ἑώρακας αὐτόν;" ὁ δὲ ἄνθρωπος ἀπεκρίθη, "Ναί! ἐχθὲς οἱ
ὄχλοι ἔβαλον αὐτὸν ἐκ τῆς ἀγορᾶς. ἄξω σε πρὸς αὐτόν."

ὁ οὖν ἄνθρωπος οὗτος ἤγαγεν Λυδίαν ἐκ τῆς ἀγορᾶς καὶ πρὸς
ἄλλον ἄνθρωπον παρὰ τῇ ὁδῷ. καὶ Λυδία ἤγγισεν τῷ ἀνθρώπῳ
35 τούτῳ καὶ εἶδεν τὸ πρόσωπον τοῦ Ὀνησίμου. ἡ Λυδία οὖν
ἔκραξεν, "Ὀνήσιμε! διὰ τί μένεις ἐπὶ τῆς ὁδοῦ; τί ἐγένετο; διὰ
τί οὐκ ἀνοίγεις τοὺς ὀφθαλμούς; τέθνηκας;" ὁ δὲ Ὀνήσιμος
οὐκ ἀπεκρίθη οὐδὲ ἤνοιξεν τοὺς ὀφθαλμούς. ἡ Λυδία οὖν ἦρεν

ἀγορά, ᾶς, ἡ, market

ἀπεκρίθη, aor. pass. ind. 3s of
  ἀποκρίνομαι (I answer)

ἀπεκρίθησαν, aor. pass. ind. 3p of
  ἀποκρίνομαι (I answer)

διὰ τί, why?

ἐαυτῇ, to herself (dat.)

ἐγγίζω, I draw near

ἔγνωκα, I have come to know,
  perf. act. ind. 1s of γινώσκω

εἰρήκει, pluperf. act. ind. 3s of
  λέγω (I say)

ἐληλύθει, pluperf. act. ind. 3s of
  ἔρχομαι (I come)

εὑρεῖν, to find (2nd aor. inf. of
  εὑρίσκω, I find)

ἐχθές, yesterday

ἤγαγεν, 2nd aor. act. ind. 3s of ἄγω
  (I lead)

ἠθέλησεν, aor. act. ind. 3s of θέλω
  (I wish)

ἦρεν, aor. act. ind. 3s of αἴρω (I lift
  up, take up)

θεέ, God (voc.)

κακόν τι, something bad

ναί, yes

νύξ, νυκτός, ἡ, night

οὔπω, not yet

πεπίστευκα, perf. act. ind. 1s of
  πιστεύω (I believe)

προσηύξατο, aor. mid. ind. 3s of
  προσεύχομαι (I pray)

τέθνηκα, I have died, I am dead
  (perfect of θνῄσκω, I die)

Φιλίππων, Philippi (gen. of
  Φίλιπποι)

2 καὶ ἐξ ὑμῶν δύναται σῶσαί με ὁ θεός = ὁ θεὸς δύναται σῶσαί με καὶ ἐξ
   ὑμῶν.

11 ἐληλύθει – the pluperfect tense is characterized by the -ει ending. The
    narrative takes place in past time, so the pluperfect is used to indicate
    action completed *prior* to a point in the past.

17 διήρχετο τὰς ὁδούς – διέρχομαι can take an acc. object to describe what
    the subject was going through.

23 καὶ ἀπεκρίθησαν – this is the aor. pass. deponent of ἀποκρίνομαι, to be
    learned in lesson 16.

38 ἀπεκρίθη – another aorist passive indicative, from ἀποκρίνομαι. Some
    deponent verbs in the aorist take the passive form, though they are active
    in meaning. See Croy lesson 16.

1   αὐτὸν καὶ ἤνεγκεν πρὸς οἶκον. ὁ δὲ ἄνθρωπος οὐκ ἦν μετ᾽ αὐτῶν, ἀπεληλύθει γάρ.

    μετὰ ταῦτα, ὁ Ὀνήσιμος καὶ Λυδία ἦσαν ἐν τῷ οἴκῳ αὐτῆς. καὶ

5   Ὀνήσιμος οὐκ ἀπέθανεν, ἡ γὰρ Λυδία ἐθεράπευσεν αὐτόν. τότε ἤνοιξεν Ὀνήσιμος τοὺς ὀφθαλμοὺς καὶ εἶπεν, "Τίς εἶ; τέθνηκα ἐγώ; νεκρός εἰμι; ἐγήγερμαι ἐκ νεκρῶν; ἄγγελος εἶ σύ;"

ἀπέθανεν, 2nd aor. act. ind. 3s of
ἀποθνῄσκω (I die)
ἀπεληλύθει, pluperf. act. ind. 3s of
ἀπέρχομαι (I go away, depart)

ἐγήγερμαι, I have been raised,
perf. pass. ind. 1s of ἐγείρω
(I raise)
τίς, who?

PLUPERFECT ACTIVE INDICATIVE OF λύω

	Singular		Plural	
1	ἐλελύκειν	I had loosened	ἐλελύκειμεν	we had loosened
2	ἐλελύκεις	you had loosened	ἐλελύκειτε	you had loosened
3	ἐλελύκει	he, she, it had loosened	ἐλελύκεισαν	they had loosened

1   μετὰ ταῦτα, ὁ Ὀνήσιμος καὶ Λυδία ἦσαν ἐν τῷ οἴκῳ αὐτῆς. καὶ
Ὀνήσιμος οὐκ ἀπέθανεν, ἡ γὰρ Λυδία ἐθεράπευεν αὐτόν. τότε
ἤνοιξεν Ὀνήσιμος τοὺς ὀφθαλμοὺς καὶ εἶπεν, "Τίς εἶ; τέθνηκα
ἐγώ; νεκρός εἰμι; ἐγήγερμαι ἐκ νεκρῶν; ἄγγελος εἶ σύ;"

5   ἡ δὲ Λυδία ἀπεκρίθη αὐτῷ, "Οὐκ εἰμὶ ἄγγελος, ὦ τέκνον, καὶ οὐ
τέθνηκας, ὅτι οὐκ ἤγγικεν ἡ ὥρα σου. ἐγώ εἰμι Λυδία, καὶ εὗρόν σε
παρὰ τῇ ὁδῷ. ἤμελλες γὰρ ἀποθανεῖν, ἀλλ᾽ ἤγαγέν με ἄνθρωπός
τις πρός σε καὶ ἤνεγκά σε πρὸς οἶκον. ἀλλὰ τί ἐγένετο, ὦ Ὀνήσιμε;
10   οὐκ εἶπόν σοι ὅτι οὐκ ὀφείλεις ἐλθεῖν εἰς τὴν ἀγοράν;"

ὁ δὲ Ὀνήσιμος οὐκ ἀπεκρίθη. ἡ οὖν Λυδία εἶπεν, "Νῦν δεῖ
σε μένειν ἐν τῷ οἴκῳ μου καὶ φαγεῖν τὸν ἄρτον τοῦτον." ὁ δὲ
Ὀνήσιμος ἀπεκρίθη, "Ἀλλὰ τίς ἦν ὁ ἄνθρωπος ἐκεῖνος; πῶς
15   ἐδύνατό με εὑρεῖν;"

ἡ δὲ Λυδία ἀπεκρίθη, "Πιστεύω ὅτι ἄγγελος θεοῦ ἦν. ἐγὼ γὰρ
προσηυξάμην τῷ θεῷ καὶ ἠκούσθην ὑπ᾽ αὐτοῦ, ὅτι ἐπορευόμην
ἐν τῇ ὁδῷ ὅτε ὁ ἄνθρωπος ἐκεῖνος ὤφθη μοι καὶ ἤχθην ὑπ᾽ αὐτοῦ
20   πρός σε. ὁ οὖν ἄνθρωπος ἐκεῖνος ἀπεστάλη ὑπὸ θεοῦ! γινώσκω
οὖν ὅτι ὁ θεὸς τοῦ οὐρανοῦ ἀκούει ἡμῶν!"

ὁ δὲ Ὀνήσιμος ἀπεκρίθη, "Ἀλλὰ πῶς γινώσκεις ὅτι
ἄγγελος ἦν;"

25   ἡ δὲ Λυδία εἶπεν, "Ἤδη εἶπόν σοι ὅτι ὁ ἄνθρωπος ἐκεῖνος
ἀπεστάλη ὑπὸ θεοῦ. καὶ μετὰ τοῦτο, ἐπέστρεψα λέγειν αὐτῷ, ἀλλ᾽
οὐκ ἐδυνάμην ἰδεῖν αὐτόν, ἐλήμφθη γὰρ πάλιν εἰς τὸν οὐρανόν."

30   μετὰ ταῦτα, ἡ Λυδία ἀπῆλθεν καὶ ἄλλος ἄνθρωπος ἦλθεν, ὄνομα
αὐτῷ Ἐπαφρόδιτος. ὁ δὲ Ἐπαφρόδιτος εἶπεν, "Χαῖρε, τίς εἶ;"

ὁ δὲ Ὀνήσιμος ἀπεκρίθη, "Χαῖρε, Ὀνήσιμός εἰμι. καὶ σύ; τίς εἶ;"

35   ὁ δὲ Ἐπαφρόδιτος εἶπεν, "Ὄνομά μοι Ἐπαφρόδιτος, καὶ μαθητής
εἰμι τοῦ Χριστοῦ. πολλάκις ἔρχομαι πρὸς τὴν ἐκκλησίαν τὴν ἐν τῷ
οἴκῳ τῆς Λυδίας."

ἀγορά, ᾶς, ἡ, market

ἄνθρωπός τις, a certain person

ἀπεκρίθη, aor. pass. ind. 3s of ἀποκρίνομαι (I answer)

ἀπεστάλη, aor. pass. ind. 3s of ἀποστέλλω (I send)

ἐλήμφθη, aor. pass. ind. 3s of λαμβάνω (I take)

Ἐπαφρόδιτος, ου, ὁ, Epaphroditus

ἤγγικεν, perf. act. ind. 3s of ἐγγίζω (I draw near)

ἠκούσθην, aor. pass. ind. 1s of ἀκούω (I hear)

ἤχθην, aor. pass. ind. 1s of ἄγω (I lead)

ἰδεῖν, 2nd aor. act. inf. of ὁράω (I see)

ὄνομα, ὀνόματος, τό, name

ὅτε, when

ποτέ, once, before

προσηυξάμην, aor. mid. ind. 1s of προσεύχομαι (I pray)

πῶς, how?

τίς, who?

χαῖρε, hello! (lit. rejoice!)

ὤφθη, aor. pass. ind. 3s of ὁράω (I see)

AORIST PASSIVE INDICATIVE OF λύω

	Singular		Plural	
1	ἐλύθην	I was loosened	ἐλύθημεν	we were loosened
2	ἐλύθης	you (sing.) were loosened	ἐλύθητε	you (pl.) were loosened
3	ἐλύθη	he, she, it was loosened	ἐλύθησαν	they were loosened

1   ὁ δὲ Ὀνήσιμος εἶπεν, "Καὶ ἐγώ εἰμι μαθητής, ὅτι ἐδιδάχθην τε
τὴν ἀλήθειαν καὶ ἐβαπτίσθην ὑπὸ Παύλου. ἐγενήθην μὲν δοῦλος
Χριστοῦ καὶ θεοῦ, ἤμην δέ ποτε δοῦλος ἄλλου ἀνθρώπου." ὁ δὲ
Ἐπαφρόδιτος εἶπεν, "Θέλω ἀκούειν. πῶς ἐγενήθης μαθητὴς τοῦ
5   Χριστοῦ; πῶς ἦς ποτε δοῦλος ἄλλου ἀνθρώπου; καὶ πῶς ἤχθης
πρὸς Φιλίππους;"

τότε Ὀνήσιμος ἤρξατο λέγειν περὶ τῆς ζωῆς αὐτοῦ . . .

ἐβαπτίσθην, aor. pass. ind. 1s of
    βαπτίζω (I baptize)
ἐγενήθην, aor. pass. ind. 1s of
    γίνομαι (I become)

ἐδιδάχθην, aor. pass. ind. 1s of
    διδάσκω (I teach)
ποτέ, once, before
Φιλίππους, acc. of Φίλπποι
    (Philippi)

2 ἐγενήθην – verbs that are deponent in the present are often deponent in
   the aor. pass. Here, the aor. pass. form of γίνομαι has the same meaning as
   the aor. mid. form, ἐγενόμην.

1   ἐν τῇ αὐτῇ ὥρᾳ, ὁ Παῦλος ἦν ἐν τῇ συναγωγῇ τῇ ἐν Φιλίπποις,
     καὶ ἐκήρυσσεν τοῖς ἀνδράσι τε καὶ ταῖς γυναιξὶ διὰ τοῦ ἁγίου
     πνεύματος. καὶ οὕτως ἐκήρυσσεν·

5   "Ὦ, ἄνδρες Φιλιππήσιοι! ἰδού! κατὰ τὸν νόμον καὶ τὰς προφήτας
     ἔδει τὸν Χριστὸν ἀποθανεῖν καὶ ἐγερθῆναι ὑπὲρ τῶν ἁμαρτιῶν
     ὑμῶν. ὑμεῖς γὰρ νεκροί ἐστε ἐν ταῖς ἁμαρτίαις ὑμῶν, ὅτι ἄγεσθε τῷ
     ἄρχοντι τοῦ πονηροῦ αἰῶνος τούτου, καὶ ἔτι ὑπὸ τὸν νόμον τῆς
     ἁμαρτίας καὶ θανάτου ἐστέ. *εἰ δὲ πνεύματι ἄγεσθε, οὐκ ἐστὲ ὑπὸ*
10   *νόμον* (Gal 5:18), ἀλλὰ ζωὴν ἔχετε ἐν Χριστῷ. *εἰ γὰρ Χριστὸς ἐν*
     ὑμῖν, τὸ μὲν σῶμα νεκρόν [ἐστιν] διὰ ἁμαρτίαν, τὸ δὲ πνεῦμα ζωὴ
     διὰ δικαιοσύνην (Rom 8:10)."

     οἱ δὲ ἄνδρες τε καὶ αἱ γυναῖκες ἀπεκρίθησαν, "Τί λέγεις, ὦ Παῦλε;
15   οὐ δυνάμεθα δέξασθαι τὰ ῥήματα ταῦτα. πῶς γὰρ δύναται
     ἄνθρωπος ἀποθανεῖν, καὶ τότε ἐγερθῆναι;"

     ὁ δὲ Παῦλος ἀπεκρίθη, "Οὐ δέχεσθε τὰ ῥήματά μου ὅτι ἔτι ἐν
     σαρκί ἐστε. εἰ δὲ προσεύχεσθε τῷ θεῷ, δύναται αὐτὸς σῶσαι ὑμᾶς.
20   ἕως γὰρ ὁ κύριος ὑποστρέφει, θέλει ὁ θεὸς ἐπιστρέψαι τὰς καρδίας
     τῶν ἀνδρῶν τε καὶ γυναικῶν πρὸς Χριστόν."

     οἱ δὲ ἄνθρωποι ἤγγισαν αὐτῷ, ἠθέλησαν γὰρ ἐκβαλεῖν
     αὐτόν. ὁ δὲ Παῦλος ἔκραξεν, "Ἐν τῇ ἐσχάτῃ ἡμέρᾳ, οἱ νεκροὶ
25   ἐγερθήσονται!"

     οἱ ἄνθρωποι οὖν οὐκ ἔλαβον αὐτόν, ἤρξαντο γὰρ λέγειν περὶ τοῦ
     ῥήματος τούτου. Φαρισαῖοι γὰρ καὶ Σαδδουκαῖοι ἦσαν ἐκεῖ, καὶ
     οἱ μὲν Φαρισαῖοι πιστεύουσιν ὅτι ἄνθρωποι ἐγερθήσονται ἐν τῇ
30   ἐσχάτῃ ἡμέρᾳ, οἱ δὲ Σαδδουκαῖοι οὐ πιστεύουσιν τούτῳ.

     ὁ δὲ Παῦλος ἔφυγεν καὶ ἀπῆλθεν εἰς ἕτερον τόπον, ὅτι ἐπέμφθη
     ὑπὸ θεοῦ ἕως ἐσχάτου τῆς γῆς.

αἰών, αἰῶνος, ὁ, age, world

ἀνήρ, ἀνδρός, ὁ, man, husband

ἄρχων, ἄρχοντος, ὁ, ruler

γυνή, γυναικός, ἡ, woman, wife

δέξασθαι, aor. mid. inf. of δέχομαι (I receive)

ἐγερθῆναι, aor. pass. inf. of ἐγείρω (I raise)

ἐγερθήσονται, fut. pass. ind. 3p of ἐγείρω (I raise)

ἔλαβον, aor. act. ind. 3p of λαμβάνω (I take, I seize)

ἐπέμφθη, aor. pass. ind. 3s of πέμπω (I send)

ἐπιστρέψαι, aor. act. inf. of ἐπιστρέφω (I turn)

ἔφυγεν, aor. act. ind. 3s of φεύγω (I flee)

ἕως, until; (+ gen.) to, as far as

ἠθέλησαν, aor. act. ind. 3p of θέλω (I want)

πνεῦμα, πνεύματος, τό, spirit

ῥῆμα, ῥήματος, τό, word

Σαδδουκαῖοι, Sadducees

σάρξ, σαρκός, ἡ, flesh

συναγωγή, ῆς, ἡ, synagogue

σῶμα, σώματος, τό, body

ὑποστρέφω, I return

Φαρισαῖοι, Pharisees

Φιλιππήσιος, ου, ὁ, person from Philippi

Φιλίπποις, dat. of Φίλιπποι (Philippi)

7   ἄγεσθε τῷ ἄρχοντι – dative of agency or means here, to express the one who is leading.

10   εἰ γὰρ Χριστὸς ἐν ὑμῖν – ἐν can be used to mean not just "in" a place, but "among." It could be either here.

1 Φιλήμων ἦν ἔτι ἐν Κολοσσαῖς, ὅτι ἤθελεν εὑρεῖν τὸν δοῦλον
αὐτοῦ. διήρχετο οὖν τὰς ὁδοὺς τῶν Κολοσσῶν. ἀλλὰ μὴ
δυνάμενος εὑρεῖν Ὀνήσιμον, ὑπέστρεψεν πρὸς οἶκον. ἡ δὲ γυνὴ
τοῦ Φιλήμονος, ὄνομα αὐτῇ Ἀπφία, βλέπουσα τὸν ἄνδρα αὐτῆς
5 ὑποστρέφοντα πρὸς οἶκον, ἦλθεν πρὸς αὐτὸν καὶ εἶπεν, "Χαῖρε,
ἀνήρ μου! πῶς ἔχεις;"

ὁ δὲ Φιλήμων ἀπεκρίθη λέγων, "Χαῖρε, γυνή μου. κακῶς ἔχω, μὴ
δυνάμενος εὑρεῖν τὸν δοῦλον ἡμῶν. τί δὲ ἐγένετο αὐτῷ; ἔφυγεν
10 πρὸς ἕτερον οἶκον; τέθνηκεν;"

ἡ δὲ Ἀπφία ἀπεκρίθη λέγουσα, "Ἀλλὰ κακὸς δοῦλος ἦν ὁ
Ὀνήσιμος ἐκεῖνος, ὅτι ἔλαβεν τὰ ὑπάρχοντα ἡμῶν!"

15 ὁ δὲ Φιλήμων εἶπεν, "Τί ἔλαβεν;" ἡ δὲ Ἀπφία ἀπεκρίθη, "Ἄρτον
ἔλαβεν! καὶ γινώσκεις ὅτι ἡμῶν εἰσιν οἱ δοῦλοι, κύριοι αὐτῶν
ὄντες. ὅλον οὖν τὸ σῶμα τοῦ Ὀνησίμου ἡμῶν ἐστιν, καὶ ἡ κεφαλὴ
καὶ τὸ στόμα καὶ ἡ σάρξ!"

20 ὁ δὲ Φιλήμων ἀπεκρίθη λέγων, "Ἀλλὰ ἔχων κύριον ἐν οὐρανῷ, τὸν
Ἰησοῦν Χριστόν, γέγονα ἕτερος ἄνθρωπος. ἤχθην γὰρ ὑπὸ Παύλου
πρὸς τὴν ἀλήθειαν."

ἡ δὲ Ἀπφία εἶπεν, "Βούλομαι ἀκούειν περὶ τούτου. ὀφείλομεν οὖν
25 καθῆσθαι." ἡ οὖν Ἀπφία ἡτοίμασεν ἄρτον καὶ οἶνον, καὶ ἤγαγεν
Φιλήμονα εἰς τὸν οἶκον. ἐσθίοντες δὲ καὶ πίνοντες, ἡ γυνή τε καὶ ὁ
ἀνὴρ ἤρξαντο λέγειν περὶ Παύλου.

ὁ δὲ Φιλήμων εἶπεν, "Παῦλος ἐπορεύετο διὰ τῶν ὁδῶν τῶν
30 Κολοσσῶν κηρύσσων εἰρήνην καὶ ζωήν. καὶ πορευόμενος ἐν τῇ
ὁδῷ τῇ παρὰ τῷ οἴκῳ ἡμῶν, εἶδέν με λέγοντα κακὸν κατὰ τοῦ
δούλου μου. ὁ Παῦλος οὖν προσῆλθεν καὶ εὐηγγελίσατό μοι τὸν
Ἰησοῦν τοῦτον. καὶ ἤθελον ἐγὼ πιστεῦσαι εἰς Χριστόν, ἀλλ᾽ οὐκ
ἐδυνάμην, ἁμαρτωλὸς ὤν. εἶπον οὖν τῷ Παύλῳ· ὦ, Παῦλε! πῶς
35 δύναται ὁ θεός σου σῶσαί με, ἁμαρτωλὸν ὄντα; ἥμαρτον γὰρ εἰς
τοὺς δούλους μου καὶ εἰς τὴν γυναῖκα. ὁ δὲ Παῦλος ἀπεκρίθη μοι
λέγων· ὁ θεὸς δύναται σῶσαι καὶ σέ, ἔχων ἐξουσίαν ἐπὶ ζωὴν καὶ
θάνατον. καὶ ἐγὼ ἤμην ἁμαρτωλός, ὅτι ἐδίωκον τοὺς πιστεύοντας

ἁμαρτωλός, οῦ, ὁ, sinner

Ἀπφία, ας, ἡ, Apphia (Phlm 2)

βούλομαι, I want, wish

ἐδίωκον, impf. act. ind. 1s of διώκω (I persecute, pursue)

ἐν Κολοσσαῖς, in Colossae

εὐαγγελίζομαι, I bring good news, preach

ἥμαρτον, 2nd aor. act. ind. 1s of ἁμαρτάνω (I sin)

καθῆσθαι, pres. mid. inf. of κάθημαι (I sit)

κακῶς, (adv.) badly; κακῶς ἔχω, I'm not well

κεφαλή, ῆς, ἡ, head

στόμα, στόματος, τό, mouth

ὑπάρχω, I am, exist (τὰ ὑπάρχοντα, possessions)

ὤν, οὖσα, ὄν, being (present participle of εἰμί)

---

4   βλέπουσα τὸν ἄνδρα αὐτῆς ὑποστρέφοντα – there are two participles in this phrase. What nouns does each participle go with? Identify the gender and case of each participle and you'll see.

6   πῶς ἔχεις; – idiomatic way of asking, "How are you?"

8   ἀπεκρίθη λέγων – "he answered, saying," an awkward phrase, but common in the NT. It comes from the Hebrew Bible, which often has "and she spoke, saying."

8   κακῶς ἔχω – the phrase πῶς ἔχεις is answered with adv. + ἔχω. Adverbs are often formed by changing the *omicron* at the end of an adjective (e.g., κακός) to an *omega* (e.g., κακός/κακῶς, καλός/καλῶς).

26 ἐσθίοντες δὲ καὶ πίνοντες – participles often function temporally, describing when another action happened.

30 καὶ πορευόμενος . . . εἶδέν με λέγοντα – consider again the *case* of each participle to identify what noun it goes with. Sometimes, the noun is not explicitly stated in the sentence but is implied by a verb.

35 εἰς τοὺς δούλους μου καὶ εἰς τὴν γυναῖκα – εἰς + acc. can mean "against."

1 εἰς Χριστὸν ἕως ἐσχάτου τῆς γῆς. ἀλλὰ θεός, ἔχων ἀγάπην εἰς
ἁμαρτωλούς, ἔσωσεν καὶ ἐμέ. οὐ γὰρ ἐλογίσατο ὁ θεὸς τὰς
ἁμαρτίας μου.”

5 ἡ δὲ Ἀπφία ἀπεκρίθη, “Καὶ σὺ νῦν λογίζῃ τὸν Χριστὸν τὸν
κύριόν σου;”

ὁ δὲ Φιλήμων εἶπεν, “Ναί! νῦν ἔχω εἰρήνην, τέκνον θεοῦ ὑπάρχων.
καὶ σὺ θέλεις πιστεῦσαι εἰς Χριστόν;”

10

ἡ δὲ Ἀπφία ἀπεκρίθη, “Ἐγὼ οὔπω δύναμαι πιστεῦσαι τῷ Χριστῷ,
Ἑλληνικὴ γυνὴ οὖσα. σὺ δὲ οὐκ ὀφείλεις ἀκοῦσαι τῶν ῥημάτων
ἀνθρώπου πορευομένου διὰ τῶν ὁδῶν κηρύσσοντος ἑτέρους
θεούς. ἔχομεν γὰρ ἤδη ἰδίους θεούς. οὐ δεῖ οὖν δέξασθαι
15 ἑτέρους θεούς.”

ὁ δὲ Φιλήμων εἶπεν, “Οὐ δύναμαι δέξασθαι τοὺς πονηροὺς θεοὺς
ἡμῶν, μὴ ὄντας θεοὺς ἀλλὰ δαιμόνια! εἰ δὲ πιστεύεις εἰς Χριστόν,
καὶ σὺ ἕξεις εἰρήνην εἰς τὸν αἰῶνα. ὁ θεὸς γὰρ ἐργάζεται ἡμέρας
20 καὶ νυκτὸς συνάγειν τοὺς πιστεύοντας αὐτῷ εἰς τὴν βασιλείαν.”

εἰς τὸν αἰῶνα, forever
Ἑλληνικός, ή, όν, (adj.) Greek
ἐλογίσατο, aor. mid. ind. 3s of
  λογίζομαι (I reckon, count,
  consider)

ἕξεις, fut. act. ind. 2s of ἔχω
  (I have)
ἐργάζομαι, I work
ναί, yes
νύξ, νυκτός, ἡ, night

1 ἔχων ἀγάπην εἰς ἁμαρτωλούς – εἰς + acc. can also mean "for."
13 ἀνθρώπου πορευομένου – participle in attributive position functions like an adjective describing the noun
19 ἡμέρας καὶ νυκτός – the time when something is done is often given in the genitive ("day and night").
20 τοὺς πιστεύοντας αὐτῷ – participles can also take objects, like here.

1 θεραπεύσασα τὸν Ὀνήσιμον, ἀπῆλθεν ἡ Λυδία πρὸς τὸν οἶκον
τὸν τῆς Εὐοδίας. ἠθέλησεν γὰρ λέγειν αὐτῇ περὶ τούτων τῶν
γενομένων τῷ Ὀνησίμῳ. τίς ἐστιν Εὐοδία; ἀδελφή ἐστιν τῆς
Λυδίας ἐν Χριστῷ.

5

παραγενομένη δὲ πρὸς τὸν οἶκον, εὗρεν Εὐοδίαν λέγουσαν
σὺν Συντύχῃ. τίς δέ ἐστιν Συντύχη; ἀδελφή ἐστιν καὶ Συντύχη.
ἀσπασαμένη οὖν αὐτάς, εἰσῆλθεν ἡ Λυδία καὶ ἐκάθισεν παρ᾽
αὐταῖς. τί δὲ ἔλεγον αἱ ἀδελφαί; ἔλεγεν Εὐοδία λόγον περὶ Ἰησοῦ
10 καὶ ἤκουεν Συντύχη. καὶ οὕτως ἔλεγεν,

"Ἰησοῦς παραγενόμενος πρὸς οἶκον γυναικός, ὄνομα αὐτῇ Μάρθα,
ἠσπάσατο καὶ αὐτὴν καὶ τὴν μητέρα αὐτῆς καὶ τὸν πατέρα καὶ ὅλον
τὸν οἶκον. ἀσπασάμενοι δὲ Ἰησοῦν, ἐδέξαντο αὐτὸν εἰς τὸν οἶκον. καὶ
15 εἶχεν Μάρθα ἀδελφήν, ὄνομα αὐτῇ Μαριάμ, καὶ καθίσασα Μαριὰμ
παρὰ τοὺς πόδας τοῦ Ἰησοῦ, ἤκουεν τὸν λόγον αὐτοῦ. ἡ δὲ Μάρθα
ἡτοίμαζεν ἄρτον καὶ οἶνον καὶ ἄλλα τοῖς οὖσιν ἐν τῷ οἴκῳ.

ἡ Μάρθα οὖν ἐλθοῦσα πρὸς Ἰησοῦν, εἶπεν αὐτῷ· κύριε! ἡ ἀδελφή
20 μου οὐκ ἐργάζεται! καὶ ἡ μὴ ἐργάζουσα οὐ φάγεται ἄρτον οὐδὲ
πίεται οἶνον! ἡ δὲ Μαριὰμ ἀπεκρίθη· ἀλλὰ βούλομαι φαγεῖν τε καὶ
πιεῖν! ὁ δὲ Ἰησοῦς ἐπιστρέψας πρὸς Μάρθα καὶ λαβὼν τὰς χεῖρας
αὐτῆς εἶπεν· Μάρθα Μάρθα, ἡ ἀδελφή σου ἐδέξατο ἀγαθόν τι,
ἀκούουσα τοῦ λόγου μου. καὶ οὐκ ἀρθήσεται τοῦτο ἀπ᾽ αὐτῆς."

25
ἡ δὲ Συντύχη εἶπεν, "Ἔγνωκα τί ἔλεγεν ὁ κύριος. σὺ εἶ Μάρθα καὶ
ἐγώ εἰμι Μαριάμ! σὺ μὲν ἐργάζῃ πολλάκις ἑτοίμασαι ἄρτον καὶ
οἶνον καὶ ἄλλα τοῖς παραγενομένοις πρὸς οἶκον τοῦτον, ἐγὼ δὲ
πολλάκις καθίζουσα ἀκούω τῶν ῥημάτων τοῦ Παύλου. ἐγὼ οὖν
30 ἐδεξάμην ἀγαθόν τι."

ἡ δὲ Εὐοδία ἀπεκρίθη λέγουσα, "Οὐκ εἰμὶ Μάρθα! ἀλλὰ λέγεις τὴν
ἀλήθειαν, ὅτι πολλάκις ἐλθοῦσα πρὸς οἶκόν μου, οὐκ ἐργάζῃ οὐδὲ
ἀσπάζῃ τοὺς παραγενομένους. κακὴ οὖν ἀδελφὴ εἶ σύ!"

35
ἡ δὲ Λυδία ἀκούσασα ταῦτα εἶπεν αὐταῖς, "Οὐκ ὀφείλετε οὕτως
λέγειν, ἀδελφαὶ ὑπάρχουσαι ἐν Χριστῷ." αἱ δὲ ἀδελφαὶ οὐκ
ἤκουσαν τῆς Λυδίας, ἀλλὰ ἄρασα τὸ ἱμάτιον αὐτῆς, ἀπῆλθεν ἡ
Συντύχη εἰς τὰ ἴδια.

ἀγαθόν τι, something good

ἄρασα, aor. act. ptcpl. nom. fem. sing. of αἴρω (I take up, take away)

ἀρθήσεται, fut. pass. ind. 3s of αἴρω (I take up, take away)

ἀσπάζομαι, I greet, salute

εἰς τὰ ἴδια, to her own (i.e., to her home or family)

ἐκάθισεν, aor. act. ind. 3s of καθίζω (I sit)

Εὐοδία, ας, ἡ, Euodia (Phil 4:2)

ἠθέλησεν, aor. act. ind. 3s of θέλω (I wish, desire)

Μάρθα, ας, ἡ, Martha

Μαριάμ, ἡ, Mary, Miriam (indeclinable)

μή, not (usual negative for nonindicative moods)

μήτηρ, μητρός, ἡ, mother

παραγίνομαι, I come, arrive

πατήρ, πατρός, ὁ, father

πίεται, fut. act. ind. 3s of πίνω (I drink)

πούς, ποδός, ὁ, foot

Συντύχη, ης, ἡ, Syntyche

τί, what?

τίς, who?

φάγεται, fut. act. ind. 3s of ἐσθίω (I eat)

χείρ, χειρός, ἡ, hand

1   θεραπεύσασα . . . ἀπῆλθεν – aorist participles often denote action prior to the main verb (ἀπῆλθεν).

2   τούτων τῶν γενομένων – the gender of this participle is neuter, "the *things* that happened."

17 τοῖς οὖσιν – example of a substantive use of the participle from εἰμί.

20 ἡ μὴ ἐργάζουσα – another substantive participle, "the one who does not work."

23 ἐδέξατο ἀγαθόν τι, ἀκούουσα τοῦ λόγου μου – participles can have the sense of the *means* by which something is done. In this case, "*by* listening . . ."

29 καθίζουσα – compare the use of this present participle with the aorist participle in line 15 (καθίσασα). Present participles often denote action simultaneous with the main verb (ἀκούω).

LESSON 20 ΤΑ ΤΩ ΟΝΗΣΙΜΩ ΓΕΝΟΜΕΝΑ*

1   *Λογος Α (ἡ πρώτη τοῦ Ὀνησίμου ζωή)*

     Λεγούσης δὲ Λυδίας τῇ Εὐοδίᾳ, Ὀνήσιμος ἦν λέγων
     σὺν Ἐπαφροδίτῳ περὶ τῆς ζωῆς αὐτοῦ ἐν ἄλλῃ γῇ. καὶ
5   οὕτως ἔλεγεν·

     "Σὺ γινώσκεις ὅτι οὐκ ἔχω τέκνα οὔτε γυναῖκα οὔτε οἶκον, ἀλλὰ
     ἔσχον ταῦτα ἐν ἄλλῃ γῇ. ἔσχον γὰρ γυναῖκα, ὄνομα αὐτῇ Ῥόδη,
     καὶ οἶκον καλὸν ἔσχομεν παρὰ τῇ θαλάσσῃ καὶ υἱὸν ἔσχομεν
10   ἀγαθόν, ὄνομα αὐτῷ Τίτος.

     ἐν δὲ ταῖς ἡμέραις ἐκείναις πολλάκις ἐπορευόμεθα ἐν τῷ μικρῷ
     πλοίῳ ἡμῶν ἐπὶ τῆς θαλάσσης. εἰρήνην οὖν ἔχοντες ἐν ταῖς
     καρδίαις ἡμῶν, οὐκ ἔγνωμεν τί ἤμελλεν γενέσθαι.

15
     μετὰ δὲ ταῦτα, κακὸν ἐγένετο ἡμῖν. ὁ γὰρ ἄρχων τῆς ἄλλης γῆς,
     θέλων ἆραι καὶ τὴν γῆν ἡμῶν, ἔπεμψεν πονηροὺς ἀνθρώπους
     ἐφ᾽ ἡμᾶς. ἐργαζομένου δέ μου ἐν πλοίῳ ἐπὶ τῆς θαλάσσης—ἤμην
     γὰρ ἐγὼ ὁ κτίσας πλοῖα ὑπὲρ τοῦ λαοῦ ἡμῶν—ἦλθαν οἱ πονηροὶ
20   ἄνθρωποι ἐκεῖνοι καὶ ἔλυσαν τὴν βασιλείαν ἡμῶν. ἐγὼ δὲ ἐπὶ
     τῆς θαλάσσης ὤν, οὐκ ἔγνων τί ἐγίνετο. ἀλλ᾽ ἀκούσας [ἐγὼ] τῆς
     γυναικός μου κραζούσης ἀπὸ τοῦ οἴκου, ἔβαλον τὸ σῶμά μου εἰς
     τὴν θάλασσαν καὶ ἐπορεύθην πρὸς τὸν οἶκον. παραγενόμενος δὲ
     ἐπὶ τὸν οἶκον, ἤνοιξα τὴν θύραν καὶ εἰσῆλθον. εὑρὼν δὲ τὸν υἱόν
25   μου καὶ τὴν γυναῖκα ἤδη τεθνηκότας, ἔπεσα ἐπὶ πρόσωπόν μου καὶ
     ἔκραξα· διὰ τί γέγονεν τὸ κακὸν τοῦτο; ὦ, θεοί μου! οὐκ ἐδύνασθε
     σῶσαι αὐτούς; οὐκ οὖν πιστεύσω ὑμῖν, τοῖς μὴ δυναμένοις σῶσαι
     τὴν γυναῖκα καὶ τὸν υἱόν!

30   καὶ λαβὼν τὰς χεῖρας τῆς γυναικός μου, ἔκραξα πάλιν· ὦ, γύναι
     μου! ἤδη ἀπελήλυθεν ἡ ψυχή σου; καὶ ἡ ψυχή μου ἀπελεύσεται
     πρός σε.

---

* If your first semester of Greek ends with lesson 20 of Croy, the second
story of lesson 20 (τὰ ἕως τοῦ νῦν γεγονότα) is a good refresher to use
at the beginning of the second semester.

ἀπελήλυθεν, perf. act. ind. 3s of
  ἀπέρχομαι (I depart, go away)
ἆραι, aor. act. inf. from ἦρα, the
  aor. act. ind. 1s of αἴρω (I take up,
  seize)
ἄρχων, ἄρχοντος, ὁ, ruler
γύναι, voc. of γυνή
ἔγνων, aor. act. ind. 1s of γινώσκω
  (I know)
ἐνεχθείς, aor. pass. ptcpl. nom.
  masc. sing. of φέρω (I bring,
  bear, carry)
Ἐπαφρόδιτος, ου, ὁ, Epaphroditus
ἔπεσα, aor. act. ind. 1s of πίπτω
  (I fall)

ἔσχον, aor. act. ind. 1s of ἔχω
  (I have)
Εὐοδία, ας, ἡ, Euodia
ἤνοιξα, aor. act. ind. 1s of ἀνοίγω
  (I open)
θύρα, ας, ἡ, door
κτίζω, I create
παραγενόμενος, aor. mid. ptcpl.
  nom. masc. sing. of παραγίνομαι
  (I come, arrive)
Ῥόδη, ης, ἡ, Rhoda
τεθνηκότας, perf. act. ptcpl. acc.
  masc. pl. of ἀποθνῄσκω (I die)
Τίτος, ου, ὁ, Titus

3 λεγούσης δὲ Λυδίας – genitive absolute.

3 Ὀνήσιμος ἦν λέγων – periphrastic participle, "was speaking."

18 ἐφ᾽ ἡμᾶς – ἐπὶ ἡμᾶς, the rough breathing on ἡμᾶς causes the π to change
   to a φ.

18 ἐργαζομένου δέ μου – genitive absolute, "while I was working."

25 ἤδη τεθνηκότας – the perfect participle τεθνηκότας denotes the state they
   were in.

28 τοῖς μὴ δυναμένοις – participle is masculine plural dative. Why? It must
   modify a noun that matches its case, gender, number.

1 οἱ δὲ πονηροὶ ἄνθρωποι ἔτι ἐν τῷ οἴκῳ ὄντες, ἤκουσάν μου
λέγοντος καὶ ἐδίωξάν με. ἐγὼ οὖν ἀπῆλθον ἐκ τοῦ οἴκου, ἀλλ᾽
οὐκ ἐδυνάμην φυγεῖν. εὑρόντων γάρ με τῶν πονηρῶν ἀνθρώπων,
ἐλήμφθην καὶ ἠνέχθην πρὸς ἑτέραν γῆν. ἐνεχθεὶς οὖν ἀπὸ τῆς γῆς
5 μου, δοῦλος ἐγενήθην κακοῦ κυρίου λεγομένου Φιλήμονος."

Λογος Β (τὰ ἕως τοῦ νῦν γεγονότα)

10 Ἐν τῷ λόγῳ ἡμῶν τῷ περὶ τοῦ Φιλήμονος καὶ Ὀνησίμου
γέγονεν κακὰ καὶ ἀγαθά. θέλετε ἀκούειν πάλιν περὶ τούτων τῶν
ἀνθρώπων; δεῖ σε ἀκούειν ὅλον τὸν λόγον.

πρῶτον δὲ Φιλήμων ἦν κύριος πονηρὸς τῶν δούλων αὐτοῦ. ἀλλ᾽
15 ἀκούσας περὶ τῆς χάριτος τοῦ θεοῦ, ἐγενήθη ἕτερος ἄνθρωπος,
ἐπίστευσεν γὰρ τῷ Χριστῷ. καὶ μετὰ τοῦτο, ἠθέλησεν ὁ Φιλήμων
εὐαγγελίζεσθαι τοῖς ἐν τῷ οἴκῳ αὐτοῦ οὖσιν, ἀλλὰ καὶ ὁ ἀδελφὸς
αὐτοῦ καὶ ἡ ἀδελφὴ οὐκ ἔλαβον τὰ ῥήματα αὐτοῦ τὰ περὶ τοῦ
εὐαγγελίου. κηρύσσοντος δὲ τοῦ Φιλήμονος, ὁ δοῦλος αὐτοῦ,
20 ὄνομα αὐτῷ Ὀνήσιμος, ἔφυγεν ἐκ τοῦ οἴκου καὶ πρὸς ἑτέραν
γῆν. καὶ ὁ Φιλήμων, ὑποστρέψας πρὸς οἶκον, οὐκ ἐδύνατο εὑρεῖν
Ὀνήσιμον, ἤδη ἀπεληλύθει γάρ.

ὁ οὖν Ὀνήσιμος ἐσώθη ἀπὸ κακοῦ; εἰρήνην εὗρεν ἐν ἄλλῳ τόπῳ;
25 οὐχ εὗρεν εἰρήνην οὐδὲ ἐσώθη ἀπὸ κακοῦ, ἀλλ᾽ εὑρέθη ὑπὸ ὄχλου
κακοῦ. ἐγγίζοντες δὲ οἱ ἄνθρωποι οὗτοι, εἶδον ὅτι δοῦλος ἦν ὁ
Ὀνήσιμος καὶ ἔβαλον αὐτὸν εἰς φυλακήν.

μετὰ ταῦτα, καθίζων ἐν τῇ φυλακῇ, ἤκουσεν ὁ Ὀνήσιμος τοῦ
30 Παύλου λέγοντος περὶ δικαιοσύνης τε καὶ χάριτος καὶ τῆς
βασιλείας τοῦ οὐρανοῦ. τοῦ δὲ θεοῦ θέλοντος σῶσαι αὐτούς,
σημεῖον ἐγένετο ἐν τῇ ὥρᾳ ἐκείνῃ· αἱ θύραι ἠνεῴχθησαν καὶ ὁδὸν
εὗρεν Ὀνήσιμος ἐκ τῆς φυλακῆς. ὁ μὲν οὖν Ὀνήσιμος ἐξῆλθεν ἐκ
τῆς φυλακῆς, ὁ δὲ Παῦλος ἔμεινεν ἐκεῖ σὺν Σιλᾷ.

35 μετὰ ταῦτα, διερχόμενος διὰ τῶν ὁδῶν τῶν Φιλίππων εἶδεν πάλιν
ὁ Ὀνήσιμος τὸν Παῦλον ἐν τῇ ἐκκλησίᾳ τῇ ἐν τῷ οἴκῳ τῆς Λυδίας.

ἀπεληλύθει, pluperf. act. ind. 3s of ἀπέρχομαι (I depart, go away)

ἐλήμφθην, aor. pass. ind. 1s of λαμβάνω (I take, receive)

ἔμεινεν, aor. act. ind. 3s of μένω (I remain)

ἐνεχθείς, aor. pass. ptcpl. nom. masc. sing. of φέρω (I bring, bear, carry)

ἐσώθη, aor. pass. ind. 3s of σῴζω (I save)

εὐαγγέλιον, ου, τό, good news, gospel

ἕως, until (+ gen.)

ἠθέλησεν, aor. act. ind. 3s of θέλω (I wish, desire)

ἠνέχθην, aor. pass. ind. 1s of φέρω (I bring, bear, carry)

ἠνεῴχθησαν, aor. pass. ind. 3p of ἀνοίγω (I open)

ἤχθη, aor. pass. ind. 3s of ἄγω (I lead)

θύρα, ας, ἡ, door

οὖσιν, pres. act. ptcpl. dat. masc. pl. of εἰμί

παρεγένοντο, from παραγίνομαι (I come, arrive)

πρῶτον, (adv.) first

ὑπάρχουσα, pres. act. ptcpl. nom. fem. sing. of ὑπάρχω (I am, exist)

φυλακή, ῆς, ἡ, prison, watch, guard

χάρις, χάριτος, ἡ, grace, favor

3 εὑρόντων γάρ με τῶν πονηρῶν ἀνθρώπων, ἐλήμφθην – the participle εὑρόντων is part of a genitive absolute, because the subject of this participle (τῶν πονηρῶν ἀνθρώπων) is different from the subject of the main verb ἐλήμφθην.

5 κακοῦ κυρίου λεγομένου Φιλήμονος – λεγομένου is a passive participle that comes from λέγω, and here can mean "called."

8 τὰ ἕως τοῦ νῦν γεγονότα – "The things that have happened up to now." Greek often splits nouns from their definite articles with various modifiers, such as ἕως τοῦ νῦν.

11 γέγονεν κακὰ καὶ ἀγαθά – neuter plural subjects (κακὰ καὶ ἀγαθά) often take singular verbs (γέγονεν).

19 κηρύσσοντος δὲ τοῦ Φιλήμονος – genitive absolute.

22 ἀπεληλύθει – pluperfect of ἀπέρχομαι. Note the 4th principal part with the pluperfect ending ει.

31 τοῦ δὲ θεοῦ θέλοντος – another genitive absolute, because the subject of the main verb is σημεῖον, not θεός.

33 ὁ μὲν οὖν Ὀνήσιμος ἐξῆλθεν . . . ὁ δὲ Παῦλος ἔμεινεν – the μέν . . . δέ construction emphasizes the contrast, but is often untranslated.

1 τί δὲ εἶδεν Ὀνήσιμος; εἶδεν αὐτοὺς πίνοντας οἶνον καὶ ἐσθίοντας
ἄρτον. καὶ οἱ ἅγιοι τῆς ἐκκλησίας ταύτης ἐδέξαντο αὐτὸν καὶ
ἔπεισαν πιστεύειν εἰς τὸν Χριστόν.

5 ἀλλὰ κακὰ πάλιν ἐγένετο τῷ Ὀνησίμῳ, πορευομένου γὰρ αὐτοῦ
διὰ τῆς ἀγορᾶς, πονηροὶ ἄνθρωποι παρεγένοντο καὶ λίθους
ἔβαλον ἐπ᾽ αὐτόν. Ὀνήσιμος οὖν ἔπεσεν ἐπὶ τὴν γῆν καὶ ἤγγισεν
ἕως θανάτου. ἡ δὲ Λυδία, πιστὴ γυνὴ τοῦ κυρίου ὑπάρχουσα,
προσευξαμένη τῷ θεῷ, ἤχθη ὑπὸ θεοῦ πρὸς Ὀνήσιμον καὶ ἤνεγκεν
10 αὐτὸν πρὸς οἶκον. ὁ δὲ Ὀνήσιμος, ἀνοίξας τοὺς ὀφθαλμοὺς εἶδεν
τὴν Λυδίαν θεραπεύουσαν αὐτόν.

τί δὲ γενήσεται τῷ Ὀνησίμῳ μετὰ ταῦτα; γνωρίσω ὑμῖν!

ἀγορά, ᾶς, ἡ, market

γνωρίζω, I make known, reveal

ἔπεισεν, aor. act. ind. 3s of πείθω
 (I persuade)

ἔπεσεν, aor. act. ind. 3s of πίπτω
 (I fall)

ἤχθη, aor. pass. ind. 3s of ἄγω
 (I lead)

παρεγένοντο, from παραγίνομαι
 (I come, arrive)

ὑπάρχουσα, pres. act. ptcpl. nom.
 fem. sing. of ὑπάρχω (I am, exist)

8 ἡ δὲ Λυδία . . . ἤχθη – the main subject (Λυδία) and verb (ἤχθη) are
 separated by two participles (ὑπάρχουσα and προσευξαμένη) that provide
 additional information.

9 προσευξαμένη . . . ἤχθη – aorist participles such as προσευξαμένη often
 denote action prior to the main verb (ἤχθη).

1 ὁ Φιλήμων καὶ ἡ γυνὴ αὐτοῦ Ἀπφία περιπατοῦντες ἦσαν ἐν τῇ
ὁδῷ τῇ πρὸς τὸν οἶκον τοῦ Ἀρχίππου. καὶ ἤρχοντο πρὸς τὸν οἶκον
τοῦτον, ὅτι ἡ ἐκκλησία πολλάκις συνήχθη ἐκεῖ. ὁ μὲν Φιλήμων ἤδη
ἠκολούθει τῷ Χριστῷ, πιστεύσας γὰρ τῷ εὐαγγελίῳ ἐβαπτίσθη
5 ὑπὸ Παύλου τοῦ ἀποστόλου, ἡ δὲ Ἀπφία οὔπω ἐπίστευσεν,
φοβουμένη γὰρ τοὺς θεοὺς αὐτῆς οὐκ ἐδύνατο δέξασθαι
ἕτερον θεόν.

ὁ δὲ Φιλήμων θέλων πεῖσαι αὐτὴν εἶπεν, "Γύναι μου! ἰδού! ὁ θεὸς
10 τοῦ οὐρανοῦ ὁ ποιήσας πάντα ζητεῖ σε! γινώσκεις γὰρ ὅτι ἐκλήθην
ὑπ᾽ αὐτοῦ εἰς τὴν σωτηρίαν ταύτην καὶ νῦν περιπατῶ ἐν τῇ
ἀληθείᾳ. ὁρᾷς γὰρ ὅτι νῦν οὐ λαλῶ κακὰ κατὰ τῶν δούλων ἡμῶν
οὐδὲ ζῶ ἐμαυτῷ ἀλλὰ παντὶ τῷ οἴκῳ μου. καὶ σὲ καλεῖ ὁ θεός!"

ἡ δὲ Ἀπφία ἀπεκρίθη λέγων, "Ναί! καὶ ταῦτα πάντα ἀγαθά! ἀλλὰ
15 καὶ ὁρῶ ὅτι νῦν οὐκ ἀναβαίνεις μετ᾽ ἐμοῦ πρὸς τὸ ἱερὸν τῶν θεῶν
ἡμῶν οὐδὲ προσεύχῃ αὐτοῖς. καὶ τοὺς θεοὺς ἡμῶν τοὺς κτισθέντας
ἐκ λίθου ἐξέβαλες ἐκ τοῦ οἴκου. οὐ φοβῇ τοὺς θεοὺς ἡμῶν τοὺς
ὁρῶντας πάντα;"

20 Φιλήμων δὲ ἀπεκρίνατο, "Πᾶς θεὸς κτισθεὶς ταῖς χερσὶν τῶν
ἀνθρώπων οὐκ ἔστιν θεὸς ἀλλὰ ἔργον πονηρόν. ὁ θεός μου ὁ
ἐξουσίαν ἔχων ἐπὶ πᾶσαν τὴν γῆν καλεῖ νῦν πάντας ἀνθρώπους,
ὅτι ἀγαπᾷ καὶ τοὺς πονηροὺς καὶ τοὺς πιστούς."

25 ἀπεκρίθη δὲ ἡ Ἀπφία καὶ εἶπεν, "Ἀλλὰ πῶς δύναται ὁ θεός σου
ποιεῖν ταῦτα; σὺ εἶπας ὅτι ὁ θεὸς γεννηθεὶς ἐκ γυναικὸς ἔζησεν ἐπὶ
τῆς γῆς ἕως τοῦ θανάτου. σταυρωθεὶς δὲ ἠγέρθη ἐκ νεκρῶν; πῶς
δύναμαι πιστεῦσαι ταῦτα πάντα;"

30 ὁ δὲ Φιλήμων παρεκάλει αὐτὴν λέγων, "Ἐληλύθαμεν πρὸς
ἐκκλησίαν. ἐκεῖ ἀκούσῃ πάντων ἀπὸ τῶν ἁγίων περὶ τούτων."

ἀγαπάω, I love

ἀκολουθέω, I follow (+ dat.)

ἀκούσῃ, fut. mid. ind. 2s of ἀκούω
(I hear)

Ἄρχιππος, ου, ὁ, Archippus
(Phlm 2)

γεννάω, I beget, bear (ἐγεννήθην,
I was begotten)

γύναι, voc. of γυνή

ἐκλήθην, aor. pass. ind. 1s of
καλέω (I call)

ἐληλύθαμεν, perf. act. ind. 1p of
ἔρχομαι (I come, go)

ἐμαυτοῦ, of myself

ἔζησε, aor. act. ind. 3s of ζάω
(I live)

ζάω, I live

ζητέω, I seek

καλέω, I call, name, invite

λαλέω, I speak

ναί, yes

ὁράω, I see

οὔπω, not yet

παρακαλέω, I exhort, encourage,
comfort

παντί, masc. dat. sing. of πᾶς
(every, all)

πεῖσαι, aor. act. inf. of πείθω
(I persuade)

περιπατέω, I walk

ποιέω, I make, I do

σταυρόω, I crucify

συνήχθη, aor. pass. ind. 3s of
συνάγω (I gather)

σωτηρία, ας, ἡ, salvation, safety

φοβέομαι, I fear

χερσίν, pl. dat. of χείρ (hand)

1 περιπατοῦντες ἦσαν – periphrastic participle construction (εἰμί + ptcpl. = "is/was . . .").

4 ἠκολούθει – impf. act. ind. 3s. ἀκολουθέω, contracted from ἠκολούθεε.

4 ἐβαπτίσθη – aor. pass. ind. 3s βαπτίζω (remember the θη is the usual marker of the aorist passive).

10 ποιήσας – (aorist) aside from the first principal part, other principal parts of contract verbs often lengthen the contract vowel before adding the tense suffix.

10 πάντα – substantive use of πᾶς.

13 ἐμαυτῷ – "dative of advantage" here, meaning the dative denotes for whose sake something is done.

13 παντὶ τῷ οἴκῳ μου – predicate position of πᾶς, "all my house." οἶκος can mean household or family.

32 ἀκούσῃ – some verbs become deponent in the future such as ἀκούω.

1 *Λογος Α (τέκνον κακὸν καὶ πατὴρ ἀγαθός)*

ἄνθρωπός τις ἔσχεν τέκνον κακόν. διὰ τί ἦν κακὸν τὸ τέκνον;
κακὸν ἦν τὸ τέκνον ὅτι πολλάκις οὐκ ἤκουεν τοῦ πατρός.

5

ἐγένετο δὲ ὅτι περιεπάτουν αὐτοὶ παρὰ θαλάσσῃ οὐ μικρᾷ. ὁ μὲν
τέκνον ἔβαλλεν λίθους εἰς τὸ ὕδωρ, ὁ δὲ πατὴρ ἡτοίμαζεν ἄρτον
φαγεῖν. ἀγαθὸς οὖν ἦν ὁ πατήρ, ὅτι ἠγάπησεν τὸ τέκνον. διὰ τοῦτο,
ἐλάλησεν τῷ τέκνῳ λέγων, "Οὐκ ὀφείλεις καταβαίνειν παρὰ τῷ
10 ὕδατι! εἰ οὐκ ἀκούεις τοῦ λόγου τοῦ ἐμοῦ, πεσῇ εἰς τὸ ὕδωρ!"

ἤκουσεν δὲ τὸ τέκνον; τὸ τέκνον ἀκούει ἑαυτοῦ, ἀλλ᾽ οὐκ ἀκούει
τῆς φωνῆς τοῦ πατρός. ἐλθὸν οὖν πρὸς τὸ ὕδωρ ἔπεσεν εἰς αὐτὸ
καὶ οὐκ ἐδύνατο ἀναβαίνειν ἐκ τοῦ ὕδατος. ὁ δὲ πατὴρ ὁρῶν τὸ
15 τέκνον καταβαῖνον εἰς τὴν θάλασσαν ἔβαλεν ἑαυτὸν εἰς τὸ ὕδωρ.
ἀλλὰ ἐδύνατο ὁ πατὴρ σῶσαι αὐτό; τί δοκεῖτε;

ὁ δὲ τέκνον ἔκραξεν, "Πάτερ! φοβοῦμαι! καταβαίνω εἰς τὴν
θάλασσαν!" ὁ δὲ πατὴρ ἐλθὼν πρὸς τὸ τέκνον ἠθέλησεν ἆραι
20 αὐτό, ἀλλ᾽ οὐκ ἐδύνατο, οὐ μικροῦ ὄντος τοῦ τέκνου. διὰ τοῦτο,
καὶ τὸ κακὸν τέκνον καὶ ὁ ἀγαθὸς πατὴρ ἀπέθανον ἐν τῷ ὕδατι.
πᾶν τέκνον οὖν ὀφείλει ἀκούειν τοῦ πατρὸς αὐτοῦ!

ἄνθρωπός τις, a certain person

ἀπαγγέλλω, I report, announce, declare

ἆραι, aor. act. inf. of αἴρω (I lift up)

δοκέω, I think, seem, seem good

ἐμός, ἐμή, ἐμόν, my, mine

ἔσχεν, aor. act. ind. 3s of ἔχω (I have)

πεσοῦμαι, I will fall (fut. mid. ind. of πίπτω)

ὕδωρ, ὕδατος, τό, water

Χανάαν, ἡ, Canaan (indeclinable)

ὡς, as

6   ἐγένετο – a common biblical idiom from the Hebrew Bible ("it came to pass . . ." or "it happened . . .").

12   ἑαυτοῦ – this reflexive pronoun is in the genitive because it is the object of ἀκούει.

13   ἐλθὸν – this is a neuter participle. These are rare, but do sometimes occur with neuter subjects. There are also other neuter participles in the story.

20   οὐ μικροῦ ὄντος τοῦ τέκνου – genitive absolute providing the cause for the previous phrase.

1 *Λογος Β (Μωϋσῆς ἀπαγγέλλει τὰς ἐντολάς)*

ὁ λαὸς τοῦ Ἰσραὴλ εἶδεν Μωϋσῆν τὸν ἄρχοντα αὐτῶν πορευθέντα ἐκ ὄρους πυρός.

5

ὁ δὲ Μωϋσῆς ἔφερεν ἐν ταῖς χερσὶν αὐτοῦ λίθους δύο ἔχοντας τὰς ἐντολὰς τοῦ θεοῦ. καὶ προσελθὼν τῷ λαῷ εἶπεν, "Ἀπαγγέλλω ὑμῖν πάσας τὰς ἐντολὰς τοῦ θεοῦ τοῦ ἡμετέρου! ἕκαστος ὑμῶν ὀφείλει τηρεῖν πᾶσαν ἐντολήν."

10

ὁ δὲ λαὸς ἀπεκρίνατο, "Τί ἐστιν ἡ ἐντολὴ τοῦ θεοῦ;"

ὁ δὲ Μωϋσῆς εἶπεν, "*Ἀγαπήσεις κύριον τὸν θεόν σου ἐξ ὅλης τῆς καρδίας σου καὶ ἐξ ὅλης τῆς ψυχῆς σου . . . καὶ ἀγαπήσεις*
15 *τὸν πλησίον σου ὡς σεαυτόν* (Mark 12:30; Deut 6:5; Lev 19:18). εἰ ἀγαπᾶτε ἀλλήλους καὶ προσκυνεῖτε τῷ θεῷ, ἄρτον ἀποστελεῖ ὁ κύριος ἀπ᾽ οὐρανοῦ ἑκάστῳ ὑμῶν. ἀλλὰ εἰ οὐ περιπατεῖτε ἐν τῷ φωτὶ καὶ οὐ τηρεῖτε τὰς ἐντολὰς πάσας καὶ προσκυνεῖτε θεοῖς ἑτέροις, πεσεῖται πῦρ ἀπ᾽ οὐρανοῦ ἐπὶ πάντα οἶκον ὑμέτερον. τότε
20 ἀποθανεῖσθε ὑμεῖς πάντες ἐν τῇ γῇ ταύτῃ καὶ οὐκ ἐλεύσεσθε εἰς γῆν Χανάαν."

ἀλλήλων, of each other, of one another

ἀπαγγέλλω, I report, announce, declare

δύο, two (acc.)

ἕκαστος, η, ον, each, every

ἐντολή, ῆς, ἡ, commandment

ἡμέτερος, α, ον, our

ὄρους, mountain (gen. of τὸ ὄρος)

πλησίον, ὁ, neighbor

προσκυνέω, I worship, bow down to (usu. + dat.)

πῦρ, πυρός, τό, fire

σεαυτοῦ, of yourself

τί, what?

τηρέω, I keep, observe, obey

ὑμέτερος, α, ον, your (pl.)

φῶς, φωτός, τό, light

ὡς, as

3   πορευθέντα – aor. pass. ptcpl. πορεύομαι.

4   ἐκ ὄρους πυρός – out of a mountain *of fire*. The genitive πυρός can also be adjectival (i.e., a fiery mountain).

16 ἀποστελεῖ – future form of the liquid verb ἀποστέλλω. See the partial list in Croy p. 133.

1 ὁ Ὀνήσιμος καὶ ὁ Ἐπαφρόδιτος ἔλεγον μετ᾽ ἀλλήλων ἐν τῷ τῆς
Λυδίας οἴκῳ περὶ πάντων τῶν γενομένων. ἀκούσας δὲ περὶ τοῦ
κακοῦ κυρίου Φιλήμονος, ἐθαύμασεν ὁ Ἐπαφρόδιτος ἐπὶ τῇ χάριτι
τοῦ θεοῦ. καὶ εἶπεν, "Τί ποιήσεις; δεῖ σε ὑποστρέψαι ἐπὶ τὸν κύριόν
5 σου ἐν Κολοσσαῖς."

ὁ δὲ Ὀνήσιμος ἀπεκρίνατο, "Οὐ μὴ ὑποστρέψω πρὸς ἐκεῖνον!
σωθεὶς ἐκ θανάτου ὑποστρέψω πάλιν εἰς τὴν κώμην τοῦ
Φιλήμονος ἵνα σταυρωθῶ; οὐκέτι δοῦλός εἰμι ἐκείνου."

10 ὁ δὲ Ἐπαφρόδιτος εἶπεν, "Ἀλλ᾽ ἔφυγες ἀπ᾽ αὐτοῦ καὶ ὁ νόμος
λέγει ὅτι ἐὰν φύγῃ δοῦλος ἀπὸ τοῦ κυρίου αὐτοῦ, δύναται ὁ
κύριος ζητεῖν τε καὶ ἀποκτεῖναι τὸν ἴδιον δοῦλον. ἐὰν οὖν ὁ
Φιλήμων ζητῇ σε καὶ εὕρῃ, τί γενήσεταί σοι;"

15 ὁ δὲ Ὀνήσιμος εἶπεν, "Τί σοι δοκεῖ; φοβοῦμαι τὸν κύριόν μου
Φιλήμονα. μὴ λέγωμεν οὖν περὶ αὐτοῦ. λέγωμεν δὲ περὶ τῶν
τέκνων σου. πῶς ἔχουσιν;"

20 λέγοντος δὲ τοῦ Ὀνησίμου εἰσῆλθεν ἡ Λυδία εἰς τὸν οἶκον καὶ
ἠσπάσατο τοὺς ἀδελφούς. καὶ εἶπεν, "Ἤδη νὺξ ἐγένετο. ὥρα
ἐστὶν ἐσθίειν! φάγωμεν καὶ πίωμεν!" καθίσαντες οὖν ἤρξαντο
ἐσθίειν. ἀλλὰ ἄρτον μὴ ἔχουσα, ᾐτήσατο ἡ Λυδία τὸν Ὀνήσιμον
πορεύεσθαι εἰς τὴν ἀγορὰν ἵνα ἀγοράσῃ ἄρτον.

25 ὁ οὖν Ὀνήσιμος ἀπῆλθεν πρὸς τὴν ἀγορὰν ὅπως ἔχωσιν αὐτοὶ
ἄρτον ἐσθίειν.

πολλοὶ δὲ ἄνθρωποι ἦσαν ἐν τῇ ἀγορᾷ. ὅτε οὖν παρεγένετο ὁ
30 Ὀνήσιμος, οὐκ ἐδύνατο ἄρτον εὑρεῖν, ἄλλοι γὰρ ἤδη ἠγόρασαν
πάντα τὸν ἄρτον. εἶπεν οὖν Ὀνήσιμος, "Παρεγενόμην ἵνα
ἀγοράσω ἄρτον, ἀλλὰ ὅταν ἔλθω οὐ δύναμαι ἄρτον εὑρεῖν,
ὄχλου ὄντος."

35 λέγοντος δὲ τοῦ Ὀνησίμου, ὄχλος ἕτερος ἐγίνετο. ὁ δὲ ὄχλος
οὗτος συνήχθη ἵνα ἀκούῃ τῶν λόγων τοῦ Παύλου! καὶ Παῦλος
καὶ Ὀνήσιμος ἦσαν ἐν τῇ αὐτῇ ἀγορᾷ! ὁ οὖν Ὀνήσιμος ἐκάθητο
ὅπως ἀκούῃ.

ἀγορά, ᾶς, ἡ, market
ἀγοράζω, I buy, redeem
ἐάν, if (+ subj.; = εἰ + ἄν)
ᾐτήσατο, aor. mid. ind. 3s of αἰτέω (I ask)
ἵνα, in order that, so that (+ subj.)
Κολοσσαῖς, Colossae (dat. of Κολοσσαί)
κώμη, ης, ἡ, village

νόμος, ου, ὁ, law
ὅπως, in order that, that (+ subj.)
ὅταν, whenever (usu. + subj.)
ὅτε, when (+ ind.)
οὐκέτι, no longer (+ ind.)
πολλοί, many
σταυρωθῶ, aor. pass. subj. 1s of σταυρόω (I crucify)

3   ἐπὶ τῇ χάριτι – ἐπί + dat. is used after verbs expressing feelings (e.g., θαυμάζω) to mean *at* or *because of*.

4   ὑποστρέψαι ἐπὶ τὸν κύριον – ὑποστρέφω can take ἐπί + acc. to indicate returning to a person. These two examples indicate the flexibility of Greek prepositions such as ἐπί.

7   Οὐ μὴ ὑποστρέψω – subjunctive used for emphatic negation.

8   ὑποστρέψω πάλιν . . . ; – deliberative subjunctive, "shall I return again . . . ?" Note that ὑποστρέψω could be either the aorist subjunctive or future indicative of ὑποστρέφω.

9   ἵνα σταυρωθῶ – subjunctive to express purpose. These examples show how the translation of a subjunctive depends on its particular use.

12 ἐὰν φύγῃ δοῦλος – subjunctive for future or present general conditional clauses.

16 Τί σοι δοκεῖ; – lit. "What does it seem like to you?" Idiomatically, "what do you think?" δοκέω is often used in an impersonal way (i.e., "it seems . . .").

18 πῶς ἔχουσιν; – idiomatic way to ask "How are they?" One would respond with an adverb (e.g., καλῶς ἔχουσιν).

22 φάγωμεν καὶ πίωμεν! – hortatory subjunctive.

23 ᾐτήσατο – "she asked," the aorist middle and aorist active forms of αἰτέω have the same meaning.

1   μετὰ ταῦτα ὑπέστρεψεν ὁ Ὀνήσιμος πρὸς Λυδίαν καὶ
     Ἐπαφρόδιτον. ἄρτον δὲ μὴ ἔχοντος τοῦ Ὀνησίμου, οἱ ὀφθαλμοὶ
     τῆς Λυδίας ἐγένοντο ὡς πῦρ. ὁ δὲ Ὀνήσιμος ἀπεκρίνατο λέγων,
     "Οὐ γινώσκεις; αἱ γραφαὶ λέγουσιν ὅτι *Οὐκ ἐπ᾽ ἄρτῳ μόνῳ*
5   *ζήσεται ὁ ἄνθρωπος, ἀλλ᾽ ἐπὶ παντὶ ῥήματι ἐκπορευομένῳ διὰ*
     στόματος θεοῦ."

     ἐκβαλοῦσα οὖν ἡ Λυδία τὸν Ὀνήσιμον εἶπεν τῷ Ἐπαφροδίτῳ,
     "Μηκέτι πέμψωμεν αὐτὸν εἰς τὴν ἀγοράν." ὁ δὲ Ὀνήσιμος ἀπῆλθεν
10   ἵνα εὕρῃ Παῦλον ὡς τέκνον ζητοῦν τὸν πατέρα αὐτοῦ.

γραφή, ῆς, ἡ, writing, Scripture
μηκέτι, no longer (+ subj.)

μόνος, η, ον, only, alone
ὡς, as, how, that, about

4   ἐπ᾽ ἄρτῳ μόνῳ – ἐπί + dat. here denotes the basis for an action or state
    of being.

1 ἐγένετο ἐν ταῖς ἡμέραις ἐκείναις ὅτε Καῖσαρ Αὔγουστος ὁ κύριος
ἦν ἐπὶ πᾶσαν τὴν γῆν ἐπορεύοντο παιδίον τι καὶ ἡ μήτηρ καὶ
ὁ πατὴρ αὐτοῦ εἰς Ἰερουσαλὴμ ἵνα προσκυνήσωσι τὸν θεόν.
προσκυνήσαντες δὲ οὗτοι ὑπέστρεψαν εἰς οἶκον.

5

ἐν δὲ τῷ ὑποστρέφειν αὐτοὺς ἔμεινεν τὸ παιδίον ἐν Ἰερουσαλὴμ
καὶ οὐκ ἔγνωσαν οἱ γονεῖς αὐτοῦ, ὅτε γὰρ ἡ μήτηρ καὶ ὁ πατὴρ
ἤρχοντο ἐν τῇ ὁδῷ τῇ πρὸς Ναζαρὲθ τὸ παιδίον οὐκ ἦν μετ᾽
αὐτῶν. ὄντων δὲ ὄχλων ἐν τῇ αὐτῇ ὁδῷ, οὐκ ἔγνωσαν οἱ γονεῖς
10 τὸν υἱὸν μὴ εἶναι μετ᾽ αὐτῶν.

πρὸ δὲ τοῦ παραγενέσθαι τὸν πατέρα καὶ τὴν μητέρα εἰς οἶκον,
ἐθεώρει ἡ μήτηρ τὸ παιδίον μηκέτι εἶναι μετ᾽ αὐτῶν, καὶ εἶπεν,
"Ὁ ἐμὸς υἱὸς ὁ ἀγαπητός! Ἰωσήφ! δεῖ ἡμᾶς ἐπιστρέφειν εἰς τὸ
15 ζητεῖν αὐτόν!"

οἱ γονεῖς οὖν ἐπέστρεψαν τοῦ εὑρεῖν τὸ παιδίον. ἐν δὲ τῷ ζητεῖν
τὸν πατέρα καὶ τὴν μητέρα, τὸ παιδίον διδάσκων ἦν ἐν τῷ ἱερῷ,
ὥστε τοὺς ἀνθρώπους θαυμάζειν. ἐδίδασκεν γὰρ οὐχ ὡς παιδίον
20 ἀλλὰ ὡς ἄνθρωπος σοφίαν ἔχων. ἐμαρτύρει γὰρ περὶ θεοῦ ἐν
παραβολαῖς. τί ἔλεγεν; οὕτως ἔλεγεν,

"Ἰδοὺ ἐξῆλθεν ὁ σπείρων σπεῖραι. καὶ ἐγένετο ἐν τῷ σπείρειν ὃ μὲν
ἔπεσεν παρὰ τὴν ὁδόν, καὶ ἦλθεν τὰ πετεινὰ καὶ ἔφαγεν αὐτό."
25 (Mark 4:3–4)

ἐν δὲ τῷ λέγειν τὸ παιδίον τὴν παραβολὴν ταύτην, ἡ μήτηρ
παρεγένετο καὶ ἔκραξεν, "Τέκνον! τί ἐποίησας ἡμῖν οὕτως; ἰδού,
ὁ πατήρ σου κἀγὼ . . . ἐζητοῦμέν σε." (Luke 2:48)

30

τὸ δὲ παιδίον ἀποκριθεὶς εἶπεν, "Ἔμεινα ἐν τῷ ἱερῷ τούτῳ
διὰ τὸ μὴ ἔχειν σοφίαν τοὺς ἀνθρώπους τούτους. ἔδει οὖν
διδάσκειν αὐτούς."

ἀγαπητός, ή, όν, beloved

ἀρχή, ῆς, ἡ, beginning, ruler

γονεῖς, γονέων, οἱ, parents

ἔγνωσαν, aor. act. ind. 3p of
γινώσκω (I know)

εἶναι, inf. of εἰμί, to be

ἔμεινεν, aor. act. ind. 3s of μένω
(I remain)

ἔπεσεν, aor. act. ind. 3s of πίπτω
(I fall)

ᾖ, pres. act. subj. 3s of εἰμί (I am)

θεωρέω, I notice, observe, behold

καγώ, καί + ἐγώ

Καῖσαρ Αὔγουστος, Caesar
Augustus

μαρτυρέω, I testify, witness, bear
witness

Ναζαρέθ, ἡ, Nazareth
(indeclinable)

ὅ, one or some (neut. sing. rel.
pron.)

παιδίον, ου, τό, child, infant

παραβολή, ῆς, ἡ, parable, proverb

πετεινόν, οῦ, τό, bird

πρό, (+ gen.) before

σοφία, ας, ἡ, wisdom

σπεῖραι, aor. act. inf. of σπείρω
(I sow)

σπείρω, I sow

τί, why?

τι, a certain (indef. pron.)

ὥστε, so that (often + inf.)

6 ἐν δὲ τῷ ὑποστρέφειν αὐτούς – ἐν is used with the infinitive to express simultaneous time, "while . . ."

9 ὄντων δὲ πολλῶν ὄχλων – genitive absolute.

10 τὸν υἱὸν μὴ εἶναι μετ᾽ αὐτῶν – this infinitival construction acts as the object of the verb ἔγνωσαν.

14 εἰς τὸ ζητεῖν – infinitive with εἰς to express purpose.

17 τοῦ εὑρεῖν – infinitive with genitive article τοῦ expresses purpose, "in order to find . . ."

18 διδάσκων ἦν – periphrastic participle, "was teaching."

19 ὥστε τοὺς ἀνθρώπους θαυμάζειν – ὥστε introduces the actual result here, though it can sometimes introduce intended results like ἵνα.

23 ὅ μὲν ἔπεσεν – ὅ is a neut. sing. relative pronoun that corresponds to what the sower was sowing. The μέν introduces a contrast with the other seeds that show up later in the parable.

28 τί ἐποίησας ἡμῖν οὕτως; – ποιέω is used here to indicate behavior or actions done to someone, "Why have you acted thus to us?"

32 διὰ τὸ μὴ ἔχειν σοφίαν – διά + acc. indicates the cause or reason.

1   ἡ δὲ μήτηρ καὶ ὁ πατὴρ ἐθαύμασαν. τὸ δὲ παιδίον ἀκολουθῆσαν τῇ μητρὶ ἐπέστρεψεν πρὸς οἶκον, ἵνα ἀγαθὸν παιδίον ᾖ.

οἱ δὲ ἄνθρωποι οἱ ἐν τῷ ἱερῷ εἶπον, "Ἡκούσαμεν τῆς ἀρχῆς τῆς
5   παραβολῆς μόνον. οὐκ ἔξεστιν ἄρξασθαι παραβολὴν λέγειν καὶ μὴ τελέσαι!"

ἐκέλευον οὖν τὸ παιδίον ἐπιστρέψαι καὶ τελέσαι τὴν παραβολήν, ἀλλὰ οὐκ ἤκουσεν τὸ παιδίον διὰ τὸ ἤδη ἀπελθεῖν.

ἀρχή, ῆς, ἡ, beginning, ruler
ἔξεστι(ν), it is permitted, lawful
κελεύω, I command, order, urge
μόνον, (adv.) only

παιδίον, ου, τό, child, infant
τελέσαι, aor. act. inf. of τελέω
  (I complete)

1 τὸ δὲ παιδίον ἀκολουθῆσαν – note the lack of an augment on
   ἀκολουθῆσαν. Though it looks like the aor. act. ind. 3p form of ἀκολουθέω
   (ἠκολούθησαν), it is a neut. ptcpl. See Croy p. 211 for the forms.

9 διὰ τὸ ἤδη ἀπελθεῖν – the aorist tense of the infinitive ἀπελθεῖν tells you
   the *kind* of action (undefined), not the time. The time of the infinitive is
   determined by the context and its use in the sentence.

1 "Παῦλε! Παῦλε! ἰδού, Ὀνήσιμός εἰμι!"

ἀπεληλύθει ὁ Ὀνήσιμος μετὰ τὸ λαλεῖν σὺν τῇ Λυδίᾳ, ἵνα
εὕρη τε καὶ ἀκολουθῇ τῷ Παύλῳ. διελθὼν οὖν τὴν πόλιν τὴν
5 Θεσσαλονίκην καὶ τὴν πόλιν τὴν Βέροιαν, εὗρεν Παῦλον ἐν πλοίῳ
μέλλοντι ἀπελθεῖν.

ἐγγίζων δὲ τῇ θαλάσσῃ, εἶδεν Σιλᾶν καὶ εἶπεν αὐτῷ, "Σιλᾶ, ποῦ
πορεύεται ὁ Παῦλος; θέλω ἀκολουθεῖν." ὁ δὲ Σιλᾶς ἀπεκρίθη
10 λέγων, "Ὦ Ὀνήσιμε, οὐ δύνη ἀκολουθεῖν, μέλλει γὰρ ἀπελθεῖν
τὸ πλοῖον. πορεύονται γὰρ ἕως Ἀθηνῶν καὶ Παῦλος καὶ Λουκᾶς
ὁ ἀδελφός."

πάλιν οὖν ἔκραξεν ὁ Ὀνήσιμος, "Παῦλε! θέλω καὶ ἐγὼ πορεύεσθαι
15 μεθ᾽ ὑμῶν!"

μὴ ἀποκρινομένων δὲ τῶν ἀνδρῶν, ἐφοβεῖτο ὁ Ὀνήσιμος μὴ
ἀπέλθῃ τὸ πλοῖον. ἔβαλεν οὖν τὸ σῶμα αὐτοῦ εἰς τὸ ὕδωρ! διὰ τί
ἔβαλεν ἑαυτὸν εἰς τὸ ὕδωρ; ἔβαλεν ἑαυτὸν ἵνα ἀναβαίνῃ εἰς τὸ
20 πλοῖον. ἐβούλετο μὲν γὰρ ἀναβαίνειν εἰς τὸ πλοῖον, οὐκ ἐδύνατο
δέ, ἀσθενὴς ὤν. τὸ ὕδωρ γὰρ ἐπλήρου τὸ στόμα αὐτοῦ ὥστε
καταβαίνειν αὐτὸν εἰς τὴν καρδίαν τῆς θαλάσσης.

καταβαίνοντος δὲ τοῦ Ὀνησίμου, πλήρης ὕδατος ἐγίνετο τὸ
25 σῶμα αὐτοῦ. ἤγγισεν οὖν ἕως θανάτου ἡ ψυχὴ αὐτοῦ. οὐκέτι οὖν
εἶδεν τὸν Παῦλον οὐδὲ τὸ πλοῖον ὅτι τὸ ὕδωρ τὸ περὶ αὐτὸν ὡς
νὺξ ἐγένετο.

ἔλεγεν οὖν ἑαυτῳ, "Ἔδοξέν μοι τὸ βαλεῖν ἐμαυτὸν εἰς τὴν
30 θάλασσαν, ἀλλὰ νῦν τί ποιήσω; ἤγγικεν τὸ τέλος τῆς ζωῆς μου.
ἀλλ᾽ ἐὰν ἀποθάνω, ἔτι ἐρῶ τῷ θεῷ μου τῷ κυρίῳ, ὁ θεός μου εἶ,
καὶ νῦν καὶ ἐν τῷ μέλλοντι. ἀπαγγελῶ οὖν τὸ ὄνομά σου καὶ ἐν τῷ
ζῆν με καὶ ἐν τῷ ἀποθανεῖν."

35 μετὰ τοῦτο, μηκέτι βλέπων τὸ πλοῖον, ἐκάμμυσεν τοὺς ὀφθαλμοὺς
καὶ ἐδέχετο τὸ μέλλον.

βεβληκότος Ὀνησίμου ἑαυτὸν εἰς τὴν θάλασσαν, Παῦλός τε

Ἀθῆναι, ῶν, αἱ, Athens

ἀπαγγελῶ, fut. act. ind. 1s of
  ἀπαγγέλλω (I declare)

ἀπεληλύθει, pluperf. act. ind. 3s of
  ἀπέρχομαι (I go away, depart)

ἀσθενής, ές, weak, sick

βεβληκότος, perf. act. ptcpl. of
  βάλλω (I throw)

Βέροια, ας, ἡ, Berea

ἐκάμμυσεν, aor. act. ind. 3s of
  καμμύω (I close)

ἐρῶ, fut. act. ind. 1s of λέγω
  (I say, speak)

ζῆν, pres. act. inf. of ζάω (I live)

ἤγγικεν, perf. act. ind. 3s of ἐγγίζει
  (he/she/it draws near)

Θεσσαλονίκη, ης, ἡ, Thessalonica

Λουκᾶς, ᾶ, ὁ, Luke

πλήρης, ες, full

πληρόω, I fill, make full of, fulfill

ποιήσω, fut. act. ind. 1s of ποιέω
  (I do, make)

πόλις, πόλεως, ἡ, city

ποῦ, where?

τέλος, τέλους, τό, end

17 ἐφοβεῖτο . . . μὴ ἀπέλθῃ – φοβοῦμαι is followed by μή and the aor. subj. to
    indicate what one fears.

21 ἐπλήρου – impf. act. ind. 3s of πληρόω, note the contraction of ο and ε.

24 πλήρης ὕδατος – the adj. πλήρης takes a genitive object.

29 Ἔδοξέν μοι τὸ βαλεῖν – δοκέω in an impersonal sense can mean not only
    "it seems," but also "it seems good" as it does here.

32 ἐν τῷ μέλλοντι – "in the future," from the verb μέλλω.

32 ἐν τῷ ζῆν με – temporal infinitive construction with accusative subject με.

36 ἐδέχετο τὸ μέλλον – "he welcomed/accepted what was coming."

38 βεβληκότος Ὀνησίμου – a genitive absolute with a perfect participle. The
    perfect here has the sense of completed action prior to the main verb.

1   καὶ Λουκᾶς εἶδον αὐτὸν καταβαίνοντα εἰς τὸ ὕδωρ. ἠτήσαντο
    οὖν τοὺς ἄνδρας τοὺς ἐν τῷ πλοίῳ ἆραι τὸν Ὀνήσιμον ἐκ
    τοῦ ὕδατος.

5   "Ἄνθρωποι! ἄρωμεν τὸν ἄνδρα τοῦτον ἐκ τῆς θαλάσσης! εἰ
    αἴρομεν αὐτὸν νῦν, ἔτι ζήσεται."

    πείσαντος οὖν τοῦ Παύλου τοὺς ἄλλους, ἤρθη ὁ Ὀνήσιμος, ἔτι
    μὲν ζῶν ἀσθενὴς δὲ γενόμενος.

10 "Ὦ Ὀνήσιμε! Ὀνήσιμε! Παῦλός εἰμι. ἀκούεις τῆς φωνῆς μου;"

    ὁ δὲ Ὀνήσιμος οὐκ ἐδύνατο τοὺς ὀφθαλμοὺς ἀνοῖξαι οὐδὲ τὸ
    στόμα, πλήρους ὕδατος ὄντος τοῦ σώματος αὐτοῦ. Παῦλος οὖν
15 προσηύξατο ἵνα θεραπευθῇ ὁ Ὀνήσιμος. οἱ δὲ ἄνθρωποι οἱ ἐν τῷ
    πλοίῳ ἐθεώρουν αὐτὸν εἰ ἀκούεται ἡ προσευχή.

    τοῦ δὲ Ὀνησίμου ἔτι μὴ ἀνοίξαντος τοὺς ὀφθαλμούς, προσελθὼν
    ἀνήρ τις τῷ Παύλῳ εἶπεν, "Ἐγώ εἰμι ἱερεὺς τοῦ Διὸς καὶ μαρτυρῶ
20 ὅτι ὑπὸ κρίσιν πέπτωκεν οὗτος, νεκρὸς μένων."

    καὶ ἄλλος ἱερεὺς εἶπεν, "Καὶ ἐγὼ ἱερεύς εἰμι τοῦ θεοῦ τῶν
    Ἰουδαίων τοῦ ἔχοντος δύναμιν ἐγείρειν τοὺς νεκρούς. δοκεῖ μοι
    ὅτι τὸ θέλημα θεοῦ ἐστιν τὸ ἐκβαλεῖν τὸν νεκρὸν ἐκ τοῦ πλοίου.
25 οὐκ ἔξεστιν γὰρ τηρεῖν σῶμα νεκρὸν ἐν ἡμῖν."

    ὁ δὲ Παῦλος ἀποκριθεὶς εἶπεν τοῖς ἱερεῦσιν, "Πῶς ἐκβάλωμεν
    τοῦτον, τὸν ἀδελφόν μου ὄντα; οὐ γάρ! ἀλλὰ τηρῶμεν αὐτὸν ἐν
    τῷ πλοίῳ ἕως τοῦ παραγενέσθαι ἡμᾶς εἰς τὴν πόλιν."

30 οἱ δὲ ἱερεῖς ἔπειθον τοὺς ἄλλους ἐν τῷ πλοίῳ λέγοντες, "Ἄνδρες!
    μηκέτι ἀκούσωμεν τοῦ ἀνδρὸς τούτου. ἐὰν μὴ ἐκβάλωμεν τὸν
    νεκρόν, ποιήσει ὁ θεὸς καὶ κατ᾽ ἡμῶν τὴν κρίσιν αὐτοῦ, ὡς
    ἐποίησεν κατὰ τοῦ νεκροῦ τούτου. τότε πῶς φευξόμεθα ἀπὸ τῆς
35 κρίσεως αὐτοῦ;"

    οἱ δὲ ἄνθρωποι οἱ ἐν τῷ πλοίῳ ἀπὸ πάντων τῶν ἐθνῶν ἦσαν.
    πεισθέντες δὲ τοῖς ἱερεῦσιν, προσῆλθαν τῷ Παύλῳ πονηρὸν
    ἔχοντες ἐν ταῖς καρδίαις αὐτῶν.

ἀνήρ τις, a certain man

ἆραι, aor. act. inf. of αἴρω (I lift up)

Διός, gen. of Ζεύς (Zeus)

ἔθνος, ἔθνους, τό, nation; pl. the nations, gentiles

ἤρθη, aor. pass. ind. 3s of αἴρω (I lift up)

ᾐτήσαντο, aor. mid. ind. 3p of αἰτέω (I ask, request)

θέλημα, θελήματος, τό, will

ἱερεύς, ἱερέως, ὁ, priest

Ἰουδαίων, gen. pl. of Ἰουδαῖος (Jew, Judean)

κρίσις, κρίσεως, ἡ, judgment

πεισθέντες, aor. pass. ptcpl. of πείθω (I persuade)

πέπτωκεν, perf. act. ind. 3s of πίπτω (I fall)

προσευχή, ῆς, ἡ, prayer

φεύξομαι, fut. act. ind. 1s of φεύγω (I flee)

8   ἔτι μὲν ζῶν ἀσθενὴς δὲ γενόμενος – a μέν . . . δέ construction contrasting the different states of Onesimus when he was pulled out of the water.

16   ἐθεώρουν . . . εἰ ἀκούεται ἡ προσευχή – εἰ with the indicative can mean "whether" (cf. Lk 6:7), so "they were observing . . . whether his prayer would be heard . . ."

23   τοῦ ἔχοντος δύναμιν – note carefully the case and number of the participle to identify the noun it modifies.

25   ἐν ἡμῖν – "among us" or "in our midst."

28   οὐ γάρ – a strong denial, "no way!"

31   ἔπειθον – the imperfect tense can have the sense of attempted or desired action, "were trying to persuade . . ."

33   ποιήσει . . . τὴν κρίσιν – κρίσιν ποιεῖν means to execute judgment.

38   τοῖς ἱερεῦσιν – dative of agency, "by the priests."

1   Εἰς ἑαυτὸν ἐλθών, ἤνοιξεν Ὀνήσιμος τοὺς ὀφθαλμούς. ἀκούων
     δὲ φωνῶν ἀνθρώπων κραζόντων, εἶπεν ἑαυτῷ, "Ἔτι ζῶ ἐγώ;
     εἰσῆλθεν εἰς τὰ ὦτα κυρίου τὰ ῥήματά μου; τί δὲ αἱ φωναὶ αὗται;"
     ὅτε δὲ ἤνοιξεν τοὺς ὀφθαλμούς, ἐθαύμασεν ὁ Ὀνήσιμος ὅτι οἱ
5   ἄνθωρποι οἱ ἐν τῷ πλοίῳ ἀπὸ πάντων τῶν ἐθνῶν ἦσαν. ἐλάλουν
     γὰρ ἀλλήλοις ἐν γλώσσαις ἰδίαις, ὥστε μὴ γνῶναι τὸν Ὀνήσιμον
     τί ἔλεγον.

     οἱ δὲ ἄνθρωποι οἱ περὶ Παῦλον καὶ Λουκᾶν, πεισθέντες τοῖς
10   ἱερεῦσιν, προσῆλθαν ἵνα πείσωσιν καὶ αὐτούς. "Ἀκούετε! δεῖ ἡμᾶς
     ἐκβαλεῖν τὸ σῶμα, ἵνα σωθῇ τὸ πλοῖον ἡμῶν. ἐὰν δὲ μὴ ἀκούσητε,
     καὶ ὑμᾶς ἐκβαλοῦμεν."

     ὁ δὲ Παῦλος καὶ Λουκᾶς ἀπεκρίθησαν, "Μενέτω τὸ σῶμα ἐν τῷ
15   πλοίῳ! μὴ ἐκβάλητε τὸ σῶμα! μὴ γίνεσθε οὕτως πονηροί! ἀλλὰ
     ἐλεήσατε! ἀδελφὸς γάρ ἐστιν ἡμέτερος."

     οἱ δὲ ἄνθρωποι ἐπηρώτησαν λέγοντες, "Πῶς ἐστιν ὁ νεκρὸς οὗτος
     ὁ αδελφὸς ὁ ὑμέτερος; πῶς ἐστιν αὐτὸς ὧδε ἐν τῷ πλοίῳ;"
20

     ὁ δὲ Παῦλος ἀπεκρίθη, "Ὁ ἀδελφός ἐστιν ὁ ἐμὸς ὅτι ἔχομεν τὸν
     αὐτὸν πατέρα, τὸν θεὸν τῶν Ἰουδαίων καὶ τὸν θεὸν τοῦ κυρίου
     ἡμῶν Ἰησοῦ Χριστοῦ."

25   ὁ δὲ ἱερεὺς τῶν Ἰουδαίων ὁ ἐν τῷ πλοίῳ εἶπεν, "Οὐ λέγεις
     ἀληθῆ, λέγεις γὰρ περὶ ἀνθρώπου σταυρωθέντος ἐν Ἰερουσαλήμ.
     ἤκουσα γὰρ περὶ Ἰησοῦ τούτου ἐν Ἰερουσαλήμ." ὁ δὲ Λουκᾶς
     ἀπεκρίνατο, "Ναί! ἀλλὰ μετὰ τὸ σταυρωθῆναι ἠγέρθη ἐν
     δυνάμει." ὁ δὲ ἱερεὺς τοῦ Διὸς εἶπεν, "Ἐὰν δύνηται ὁ θεός σου
30   ἐγεῖραι τὸν Ἰησοῦν τοῦτον, δυνήσεται καὶ ἐγεῖραι ὑμᾶς ἐκ τῆς
     θαλάσσης! ἄνδρες! ἐκβάλωμεν πρῶτον τούτους, τότε ἐκβάλωμεν
     τὸν νεκρόν! ἔστωσαν τὰ δῶρα ἡμῶν τῷ Ποσειδῶνι τῷ θεῷ τῆς
     θαλάσσης!" ὁ δὲ ἄλλος ἱερεὺς εἶπεν, "Γενηθήτω τὸ θέλημα θεοῦ.
     προσευξάσθωσαν τῷ θεῷ ἵνα σωθῶσιν."
35

     ὁ δὲ Ὀνήσιμος ἀκούων τε καὶ βλέπων τὰ πάντα ταῦτα, ἐβούλετο
     μὲν λαλεῖν, οὐκ ἐδύνατο δέ, ἀσθενὴς ὢν ἔτι. οἱ δὲ ἄνθρωποι

ἀληθής, ές, true

γενηθήτω, aor. pass. impv. 3s of
  γίνομαι (I become)

γλῶσσα, ης, ἡ, tongue, language

γνῶναι, aor. act. inf. of γινώσκω
  (I know)

Διός, gen. of Ζεύς (Zeus)

δύναμις, δυνάμεως, ἡ, power,
  strength

ἐλεέω, I have mercy on, pity

ἐπερωτάω, I ask, question

ἔστωσαν, pres. impv. 3p of εἰμί
  (I am)

ἠγέρθη, aor. pass. ind. 3s of ἐγείρω
  (I raise)

Ἰουδαίων, gen. pl. of Ἰουδαῖος
  (Jew, Judean)

ναί, yes

οὖς, ὠτός, τό, ear

Ποσειδῶνι, dat. of Ποσειδῶν
  (Poseidon)

προσευξάσθωσαν, aor. mid. impv.
  3p of προσεύχομαι (I pray)

πρῶτον, (adv.) first

ὧδε, here, hither

1   Εἰς ἑαυτὸν ἐλθών – "having come to himself" or "woken up"
  (cf. Luke 15:17).

6   μὴ γνῶναι τὸν Ὀνήσιμον – infinitive construction with accusative subject
  Ὀνήσιμον.

10   Ἀκούετε – note the present imperative second-person plural looks the
  same as the indicative.

12   ἐκβαλοῦμεν – liquid future from ἐκβάλλω.

25   Οὐ λέγεις ἀληθῆ – the adj. ἀληθής is declined according to the third
  declension. Here, ἀληθῆ is neut. pl. acc.

33   Γενηθήτω τὸ θέλημα θεοῦ – the verb γίνομαι has the sense here that the
  will of God should come to pass or "be done" as in Matt. 6:10.

PRESENT ACTIVE IMPERATIVE OF λύω

	Singular		Plural	
2	λῦε	loosen!	λύετε	loosen!
3	λυέτω	let him/her/it loosen!	λυέτωσαν	let them loosen!

PRESENT IMPERATIVE OF εἰμί

	Singular		Plural	
2	ἴσθι	be!	ἔστε	be!
3	ἔστω	let him/her/it be!	ἔστωσαν	let them be!

1 ἐκράτησαν τὸν Παῦλον τῆς χειρὸς καὶ ἤνεγκαν αὐτὸν καὶ Λουκᾶν
πρὸς τὴν θάλασσαν. ὁ δὲ Παῦλος φερόμενος πρὸς τὴν θάλασσαν
εἶπεν, "Μετανοήσατε ἀπὸ τῆς ἁμαρτίας ὑμῶν καὶ ζήσετε!"

5 ἐκβαλλόντων δὲ τῶν ἀνθρώπων τοὺς ἄνδρας, ὁ Ὀνήσιμος πάλιν
ἔκραξεν, "Ἐγὼ ζῶ! ἴδετε ὧδε! οὐ νεκρός εἰμι! μὴ τοῦτο ποιεῖτε!
ἐλεήσατε! μὴ βάλητε τοὺς ἄνδρας τούτους εἰς τὴν θάλασσαν!"

ἐκβεβληκότες δὲ ἤδη τοὺς ἄνδρας, ἤκουσαν τῆς φωνῆς τοῦ
10 Ὀνησίμου καὶ εἶπαν, "Σὺ ζῇς; διὰ τί οὐκ ἐλάλησας ἕως τοῦ νῦν;
ἤδη ἐξεβάλομεν τοὺς ἄνδρας καὶ οὐ δυνάμεθα ἀνάγειν αὐτούς."
ὁ δὲ Ὀνήσιμος εἶπεν ἑαυτῷ, "Ἐλήλυθα ὧδε ἵνα ἀκολουθῶ τῷ
Παύλῳ, ἀλλὰ σωθεὶς ἐκ θαλάσσης πάλιν ἔλθω εἰς αὐτήν; τί δεῖ
με ποιῆσαι;"

ἀνάγω, I bring up, lead up

κρατέω, I seize, grasp, hold

μετανοέω, I repent

1   **ἐκράτησαν τὸν Παῦλον τῆς χειρός** – κρατέω + object + τῆς χειρός means "seize [someone] by the hand."

9   **ἐκβεβληκότες δὲ ἤδη τοὺς ἄνδρας** – the perf. ptcpl. ἐκβεβληκότες denotes action prior to the main verb ἤκουσαν.

13   **πάλιν ἔλθω εἰς αὐτήν;** – deliberative subjunctive ἔλθω.

13   **τί δεῖ με ποιῆσαι;** – lit., "what is necessary for me to do?" Note that the accusative με is the subject of the infinitive ποιῆσαι. Idiomatically, this question means something like "what should I do?"

1 *Λογος A (Ὀνήσιμος ζῇ)*

Προσελθὼν ἠρώτησέν τις τῶν ἀνθρώπων, "Πῶς ἔχεις; ἤραμέν
σε ἐκ τῆς θαλάσσης νεκρὸν ὄντα, νῦν δὲ ζῇς πάλιν! πῶς ἐγένετο
5 ταῦτα πάντα;" ἄλλος δέ τις εἶπεν, "Καθὼς ὁ ἀνὴρ ἐκεῖνος εἶπεν,
ὃν ἐξεβάλομεν εἰς θάλασσαν, ὁ θεὸς αὐτοῦ ἤγειρεν τοῦτον ἐκ
νεκρῶν!" ἄλλοι δέ τινες εἶπαν, "Ἐγείρωμεν ἐκ θαλάσσης τοὺς
ἄνδρας οὓς ἐξεβάλομεν; ἐὰν ὁ θεὸς οὕτως ἀκούσῃ αὐτῶν, τίνα
κρίσιν ποιήσει κατ᾽ ἡμῶν;" ἄλλος δὲ εἶπεν, "Οὐ δυνάμεθα ἐγεῖραι
10 οὓς ἐξεβάλομεν, τεθνήκασιν γὰρ ἤδη."

λεγόντων δὲ ἀλλήλοις τῶν ἀνθρώπων, ὁ Ὀνήσιμος εἶπεν ἑαυτῷ,
"Ὁ θεὸς ἐκάλεσέν με ἀκολουθεῖν τῷ Παύλῳ. νῦν δὲ τί ποιήσω;
τίνι ἀκολουθήσω; μένω ὧδε σὺν τοῖς ἀνθρώποις οἳ ἐξέβαλον τοὺς
15 ἀδελφούς μου; οὐ μὴ μένω ὧδε! οὐ γὰρ λογίζομαι τὴν ζωὴν ἐμὴν
εἶναι, ἀλλὰ τοῦ θεοῦ. ἐλπίδα γὰρ ἔχω ἐπὶ τὸν θεόν, ὃς ἔσωσέν
με καὶ σώσει με εἰς τὸν αἰῶνα. διὰ τοῦτο, τοῖς ἀδελφοῖς μου
ἀκολουθήσω ἕως θανάτου." λέγοντες δὲ οἱ ἄνθρωποι οἱ παρὰ
Ὀνησίμῳ, ἐθεώρουν αὐτὸν μέλλοντα βαλεῖν ἑαυτὸν εἰς τὸ ὕδωρ.
20 ὁ οὖν ἱερεὺς εἶπεν, "Τί ποιεῖς; ποῦ πορεύῃ;" ἀλλὰ οὐκ ἤκουσεν ὁ
Ὀνήσιμος, ἔβαλον γὰρ ἑαυτὸν ἔξω τοῦ πλοίου. οἱ δὲ ἄνθρωποι οὐκ
ᾔδεισαν τί τοῦτο ἐποίησεν. προσῆλθαν οὖν τῷ ὕδατι ἵνα ἴδωσιν τί
γένηται τῷ Ὀνησίμῳ.

25

Λογος B (Φιλήμων χαίρει τε καὶ φοβεῖται)

"Ὀνήσιμε! Ὀνήσιμε!" ἠγέρθη ὁ Φιλήμων ἐξ ὕπνου. νὺξ ἦν ἔτι,
ἡμέρα γὰρ οὐκ ἐγένετο. εἶπεν δὲ Φιλήμων ἑαυτῷ, "Τί ἔλεγον;
30 εἶδον τὸν δοῦλόν μου τὸν ἀγαπητὸν ἐν κινδύνῳ. ποῦ ἐστιν
αὐτός; ὦ θεέ μου, ὅπου ἐὰν ᾖ, τήρει αὐτόν! παρακαλῶ σε, σῶσον
αὐτὸν ἀπὸ πάντων κακῶν ἃ ἐὰν γένηται αὐτῷ!" μὴ δυνάμενος
καθεύδειν, περιεπάτει διὰ τοῦ οἴκου εὑρεῖν τινα μεθ᾽ οὗ λαλεῖν
δύναται. εἰσελθὼν δὲ εἰς τὸ τῆς θυγατρὸς ταμεῖον, εὗρεν αὐτὴν ἔτι
35 καθεύδουσαν. καὶ μὴ θέλων ἐγεῖραι αὐτήν, ἐξῆλθεν εἰς τὸν ἀγρὸν
εἰς τὸ ἐργάζεσθαι.

ἀγρός, οῦ, ὁ, field, country
ἐλπίς, ἐλπίδος, ἡ, hope
ἔξω, outside (sometimes + gen.)
ἐρωτάω, I ask, request, entreat
ᾔδεισαν, they knew (from οἶδα, I know, understand)
Θέκλα, ης, ἡ, Thecla
θυγάτηρ, θυγατρός, ἡ, daughter
καθεύδω, I sleep
καθώς, as, even as, just as
καρπός, οῦ, ὁ, fruit
κίνδυνος, ου, ὁ, danger
λογίζομαι, I reckon, consider
οἶδα, I know, understand
ὅς, ἥ, ὅ, who, which (rel. pron.)

ὅσος, η, ον, as many as, as great as
ὅστις, ἥτις, ὅτι, whoever, whichever, whatever (indef. rel. pron.)
περιεπάτει, impf. act. ind. 3s of περιπατέω (I walk)
ποῦ, where?
σπέρμα, σπέρματος, τό, seed
ταμεῖον, ου, τό, room
τεθνήκασιν, perf. act. ind. 3p of θνήσκω (I die)
τίς, τί, who? which? what? why?
τις, τι, someone, something, a certain (indef. pron.)
ὕπνος, ου, ὁ, sleep

8   τίνα κρίσιν – the interrogative pronoun τίνα matches κρίσιν in case, gender, number.

10 οὓς ἐξεβάλομεν – the antecedent of the relative pronoun οὕς is omitted, so it must be supplied in English ("the ones whom we threw out").

14 τίνι ἀκολουθήσω – τίνι is dat. as the object of ἀκολουθήσω. Note that ἀκολουθήσω could be either fut. ind. or aor. subj.

14 μένω . . . ; – deliberative subj.

16 ἀλλὰ τοῦ θεοῦ – the genitive construction here denotes possession, in contrast with ἐμήν.

22 τί τοῦτο ἐποίησεν – so far τί has mostly been used for "what?" However, it can also mean "why?" as it does here.

22 τί γένηται τῷ Ὀνησίμῳ – deliberative subj. used in an indirect question.

28 ἠγέρθη – ἐγείρω in the passive can mean "raised" or the intransitive "wake up, rise up."

31 ὅπου ἐάν – a conditional relative clause, "wherever."

32 ἃ ἐὰν γένηται – a conditional relative clause, "whatever happens."

33 μεθ᾽ οὗ λαλεῖν δύνηται – "with whom he could speak." οὗ refers to τινά, but is gen. as the obj. of μετά.

1 ἐλθὼν δὲ εἰς ἀγρὸν εἶδεν σπέρματά τινα ἐπὶ τῆς γῆς. συναγαγὼν οὖν τὰ σπέρματα, ὅσα ἐδύνατο κρατεῖν ἐν ταῖς χερσίν, ἔσπειρεν παρὰ τὰς ὁδοὺς τὰς διερχομένας δι᾽ ἀγροῦ.

5 ἔτι δὲ ἐργαζόμενος ἤκουσέν τινος ἐγγίζοντος. ἡ θυγάτηρ ἦν, ἣ ἠγέρθη ἐξ ὕπνου τῇ φωνῇ τοῦ πατρὸς αὐτῆς ἐργαζομένου, ὄνομα αὐτῇ Θέκλα. καὶ εἶπεν αὐτῇ, "Πάτερ, τί ποιεῖς; ἔτι νύξ ἐστιν." ὁ δὲ Φιλήμων, μὴ ἀποκρινόμενος τῇ θυγατρί, ᾖρεν καρποὺς τινας ἀπὸ τῆς γῆς καὶ εἶπεν, "Ἴδε τοὺς καρποὺς τούτους. ὁ μὲν ἀγαθός,
10 ἕτερος δὲ κακός. ἐγὼ ἤμην ὡς ὁ κακὸς καρπὸς οὗτος, κακὸν ποιῶν κατὰ τῶν δούλων μου. ἀλλὰ ἄνθρωπός τις ἐδίδαξέν με ὅτι ὅστις ἂν μετανοήσῃ καὶ πιστεύσῃ εἰς Χριστὸν σωθήσεται. πιστεύσας οὖν Χριστῷ, ἐγενήθην ἕτερος ἄνθρωπος ὡς ὁ ἀγαθὸς καρπὸς οὗτος. οἶδας ὃ λέγω, ὦ θύγατερ;"

15

ἡ δὲ Θέκλα, μὴ εἰδυῖα τὴν παραβολὴν τῶν καρπῶν εἶπεν, "Οὐκ οἶδα τί λέγεις, ἀλλὰ νῦν θέλω καρποὺς τινας φαγεῖν! πάτερ, ἐπιστρέψωμεν εἰς οἶκον ἵνα φάγωμέν τι!" ὁ οὖν Φιλήμων, κρατήσας τῆς χειρὸς αὐτῆς ὑπέστρεψεν, χαίρων μὲν ἐπὶ τῇ
20 θυγατρί, ᾗ καρδίαν εἶχεν καλήν, φοβούμενος δὲ ἔτι ἐπὶ τῷ Ὀνησίμῳ ὃν εἶδεν καθεύδων.

ἔσπειρεν, aor. act. ind. 3s of
  σπείρω (I sow)

ἴδε, aor. act. impv. 2s of ὁράω
  (I see)
καρπός, οῦ, ὁ, fruit

14 ὃ λέγω – another example where the antecedent of the relative pronoun is omitted.

16 εἰδυῖα – perf. act. ptcpl. nom. fem. sing. of οἶδα.

19 χαίρων . . . ἐπὶ τῇ θυγατρί – ἐπί + dat. is used after verbs expressing feelings (e.g., χαίρω and φοβοῦμαι) to mean *at* or *because of*.

20 χαίρων μὲν . . . φοβούμενος δέ – the μέν . . . δέ construction contrasts Philemon's conflicting emotions.

1   Ἐπέστρεψαν Φιλήμων καὶ Θέκλα εἰς οἶκον. ἀνοίξαντες δὲ τὴν
     θύραν, εἶδον Ἀπφίαν ἤδη ἐγηγερμένην. ἡ δὲ Θέκλα εἶπεν, "Μήτηρ!
     ἀγαπῶ σέ!" καὶ ἡ μήτηρ, "Κἀγὼ ἀγαπῶ σε, τί θέλεις;" ἡ δὲ Θέκλα,
     "Φάγωμεν!" ἡ οὖν Ἀπφία καὶ ὁ Φιλήμων ἡτοίμασαν ἄρτον καὶ
5   καρπὸν φαγεῖν καὶ ὕδωρ πίνειν. καθίσαντες δὲ πάντες ἤμελλον
     ἐσθίειν. ὁ δὲ Φιλήμων εἶπεν τῇ θυγατρί, "Δός μοι τὴν χεῖρα."
     δοῦσα οὖν αὐτῷ τὴν χεῖρα, ἐθεώρει τὸν πατέρα καὶ τὴν μητέρα
     προσευχομένους. καὶ ὁ πατὴρ εἶπεν,

10   Σὺ κύριε, δίδως ἡμῖν πάντα ὅσα ἔχομεν ἐσθίειν.

     καὶ ὃ ἐὰν ἔχωμεν σὺ ἔδωκας ἡμῖν.

     παρακαλῶ σε, ὦ κύριε, δίδου ἡμῖν ἡμέρας ἀγαθὰς καὶ ἔτη
15 . πλήρη χαρᾶς, ὅπως διδῶμεν ἐκ τῶν ὑπαρχόντων ἡμῶν τοῖς
     μὴ ἔχουσιν.

     ὡς σὺ ἔδωκας ἡμῖν ζωὴν καὶ πνεῦμα καὶ πάντα, καὶ ἡμεῖς δώσομεν
     ἄλλοις. ἀμήν.
20
     ἡ δὲ θυγάτηρ ἐθαύμασεν τὴν πίστιν τῶν γονέων. ἐπερώτησεν οὖν
     τῷ πατρί, "Πάτερ, τί προσεύχομεν πρὸ τοῦ ἐσθίειν;" ἀπεκρίθη δὲ
     ὁ πατὴρ λέγων, "Προσεύχομεν τῷ θεῷ, ὃς δίδωσιν ἡμῖν ταῦτα
     πάντα, ὅτι χαίρει ὅτε αἰτοῦμεν ἀπ᾽ αὐτοῦ ὃ ἐὰν θέλωμεν. καὶ σύ,
25   τέκνον, αἴτησον αὐτὸν ὃ ἐὰν θέλῃς καὶ δώσει σοι!"

     ἡ οὖν Θέκλα ἦρεν τοὺς ὀφθαλμοὺς καὶ εἶπεν, "Κύριε, παρακαλῶ
     σε, ἔγειρε τὸν ἀδελφόν μου, ὃς ἔτι καθεύδει!"

30   ἡ δὲ Ἀπφία γνοῦσα τὸν υἱὸν μὴ εἶναι μετ᾽ αὐτῶν, ἠγέρθη ἐλθεῖν
     αὐτῷ. ἡ δὲ Θέκλα εἶπεν, "Κάθισον, μήτηρ! ἐγὼ ἐλεύσομαι καὶ
     ἐγερῶ αὐτόν." ὁ δὲ πατὴρ εἶπεν, "Ὕπαγε, θύγατερ, καὶ ἔγειρε
     αὐτόν. κακὸν δὲ μὴ ποίησον!"

35   ἡ οὖν Θέκλα εὐθὺς ἐξῆλθεν τοῦ ἐγεῖραι τὸν ἀδελφόν, ὄνομα
     αὐτῷ Δημᾶς. εὑροῦσα οὖν τὸν Δημᾶν ὡς λίθον καθεύδοντα
     ἔκραξεν φωνῇ μεγάλῃ, "Ἔγειρε! ἔγειρε! ὥρα ἐστὶν ἐσθίειν!"

αἷμα, αἵματος, τό, blood

αἴτησον, aor. act. impv. 2s of αἰτέω (I ask)

γονέων, gen. of γονεῖς (parents)

Δημᾶς, ᾶ, ὁ, Demas

δίδωμι, I give, grant

δός, aor. act. impv. 2s of δίδωμι

δώσομεν, fut. act. ind. 1p of δίδωμι (I give)

ἐγερῶ, fut. act. ind. 1s of ἐγείρω (I raise)

ἔτος, ἔτους, τό, year

εὐθύς, immediately, at once

ἐχάρησεν, aor. act. ind. 3s of χαίρω (I rejoice)

καγώ, καί + ἐγώ

καθεύδω, I sleep

μέγας, μεγάλη, μέγα, large, great

τί, what? why?

ὑπάγω, I go, go away

χαρά, ᾶς, ἡ, joy

2 ἤδη ἐγηγερμένην – perf. mid. ptcpl. acc. fem. sg. of ἐγείρω, the perf. ptcpl. denotes the state Apphia is in.

10 πάντα ὅσα ἔχομεν – πᾶς + ὅσος is difficult to render in English. Woodenly, "everything, as much as we have" or simply "all that we have."

14 δίδου – pres. act. impv. of δίδωμι. The difference between the present δίδου and the aorist δός (line 6) is one of *aspect*. The former expresses a progressive giving, "give us good days." Note the different uses in the Lord's Prayer in Matt 6:11 and Luke 11:3.

15 τοῖς μὴ ἔχουσιν – ptcpl. acting as the indirect obj. of διδῶμεν, "to those who don't have."

21 ἐθαύμασεν τὴν πίστιν – the verb θαυμάζω can take an acc. object as the object of marveling or wonder.

30 ἡ δὲ Ἀπφία γνοῦσα – the verb γινώσκω can have the sense of "noticing" or "realizing" something.

35 τοῦ ἐγεῖραι – τοῦ + infinitive expresses purpose.

1 τοῦ δὲ ἀδελφοῦ ἔτι μὴ ἐγερθέντος ἔκραξεν πάλιν, "Ἔγειρε!
ἜΓΕΙΡΕ! ἜΓΕΙΡΕ!"

ὁ οὖν Δημᾶς ἀνοίξας τοὺς ὀφθαλμοὺς καὶ βλέπων τὴν αὑτοῦ
5 ἀδελφὴν ἀπεκρίθη, "Οὐ θέλω ἐγερθῆναι! ὕπαγε καὶ μὴ οὕτως
κράζε!" ἡ δὲ Θέκλα οὐκ ἐχάρησεν ἐπὶ τῷ ἀδελφῷ ὃς πολλάκις οὐκ
ἤκουσεν αὐτῆς. ἡ γὰρ ἀδελφὴ πρεσβυτέρα ἦν, ἡ μὲν γὰρ ἔτη πέντε
εἶχεν, ὁ δὲ ἀδελφὸς ἔτη τέσσαρα.

10 τότε ἰδοῦσα λίθους τινοὺς ἐπὶ τῆς γῆς οἶδεν τί δεῖ αὐτὴν ποιεῖν.
ἄρασα οὖν λίθον μικρὸν ἔβαλεν πρὸς αὐτόν! τοῦ δὲ λίθου
πεσόντος ἐπὶ τὸ πρόσωπον τοῦ Δημᾶ, ἠγέρθη καὶ ἔκραξεν, "Ἄ, ἄ!
τί ἐγένετο; τί ἐστιν τοῦτο ἐπὶ τοῦ προσώπου μου; αἷμά ἐστιν;" ἡ
δὲ Θέκλα, φοβουμένη καὶ τὸν πατέρα καὶ τὸν ἀδελφόν, εὐθὺς
15 ἔφυγεν ἐξ οἴκου. ὁ δὲ Δημᾶς ἐγερθεὶς ἠκολούθησεν ἵνα κρατήσῃ
αὐτήν. καὶ ἔκραξεν, "Ἀποδώσω σοι ὡς σὺ ἀπέδωκάς μοι, κακὸν
ἀντὶ κακοῦ!

αἷμα, αἵματος, τό, blood
ἀντί, (+ gen.) for, in place of, as
ἀποδίδωμι, I render, recompense,
  give back

ἐχάρησεν, aor. act. ind. 3s of χαίρω
  (I rejoice)
πέντε, five
πρεσβύτερος, α, ον, older
τέσσαρα, four

5 μὴ οὕτως κράζε! – prohibitions are expressed using μή + aor. subj. or +
  pres. impv. (as here).
7 ἡ μὲν γάρ . . . – the article before μέν or δέ with no noun following it acts
  like a pronoun to continue the narrative.
7 ἔτη πέντε εἶχεν – age is expressed with ἔχω + number of ἔτη.
12 πεσόντος – aor. ptcpl. from πίπτω.
12 Ἄ, ἄ – an interjection like the English "ah!" Cf. Judg 6:22 (LXX).
16 κακὸν ἀντὶ κακοῦ – "evil for evil."

PRESENT ACTIVE INDICATIVE OF *δίδωμι*

	Singular		Plural	
1	δίδωμι	I give	δίδομεν	we give
2	δίδως	you (sing.) give	δίδοτε	you (pl.) give
3	δίδωσι(ν)	he, she, it gives	διδόασι(ν)	they give

1   Ἐφέρετο Ὀνήσιμος ὑπὸ τῆς θαλάσσης, ἐλπίδα μὴ ἔχων σωτηρίας.
οἱ δὲ ἄνθρωποι οἱ ἐν τῷ πλοίῳ ἰδόντες αὐτὸν οὐκ οἴδασι τί
ποιήσωσιν. εἷς δὲ αὐτῶν εἶπεν, "Ἐὰν ἀφῶμεν αὐτὸν οὕτως,
ἀποθανεῖται, τότε τὸ αἷμα αὐτοῦ ἐπὶ τὴν κεφαλὴν ἡμῶν ἔσται!"
5   ἄλλος δέ τις εἶπεν, "Ἄφες αὐτόν! ὃ ἐὰν γένηται αὐτῷ, ταῖς ἰδίαις
χερσὶν ἐποίησεν. ἀλλὰ βάλωμεν αὐτῷ σανίδα ἵνα κρατήσῃ αὐτὴν
καὶ μὴ εὐθὺς ἀποθάνῃ."

     ἔβαλον οὖν σανίδα, ἣν Ὀνήσιμος ἐκράτησεν τῇ χειρί. καὶ οἱ
10 ἄνθρωποι ἀφέντες αὐτὸν ἐν τῇ θαλάσσῃ ἀπῆλθον. ἔκραξεν δὲ
Ὀνήσιμος φωνῇ μεγάλῃ, "Παῦλε! Λουκᾶ! ποῦ ἐστε;" οὐδενὸς δὲ
ἀκούων, προσηύξατο, "Ὦ θεέ μου, ἔσωσάς μέ ποτε ἐκ φυλακῆς καὶ
ὄχλων κακῶν. δύνασαι οὖν σῶσαι ἡμᾶς νῦν ἐκ θαλάσσης. τί γάρ
ἐστιν ἡ θάλασσα; οὐδέν σοί ἐστιν! παρακαλῶ οὖν, μὴ ἀφῇς με ὧδε,
15 ἀλλὰ δεῖξόν μοι ποῦ εἰσιν οἱ ἀδελφοί."

     καὶ ἐν αὐτῇ τῇ ὥρᾳ εἶδέν τι ἀναβαῖνόν τε καὶ καταβαῖνον ἐν τῷ
ὕδατι. χεὶρ ἦν τοῦ Παύλου! παρεκάλει οὖν ὁ Ὀνήσιμος, "Δός
μοι τὴν χεῖρα!" τοῦ δὲ Παύλου μὴ ἀποκρινομένου, προσελθὼν
20 Ὀνήσιμος ἐκράτησεν αὐτὸν τῆς χειρὸς καὶ ἦρεν τὸ σῶμα αὐτοῦ ἐκ
τῆς θαλάσσης. τότε ἐπέθηκεν αὐτὸν ἐπὶ τὴν σανίδα.

     οὐκ ἐλάλει ὁ Παῦλος οὐδὲ ἤνοιξεν τοὺς ὀφθαλμούς, ἀλλὰ ἔμενεν
ἐπὶ τῆς σανίδος ὡς νεκρός. εἶπεν οὖν Ὀνήσιμος, "Ὦ Παῦλε.
25 μὴ ἀποθάνῃς. προστίθης γὰρ καὶ τοῦτο ἐπὶ πᾶσιν τοῖς κακοῖς
μου. φοβοῦμαι γὰρ μὴ ἀπολώμεθα." εἶπεν δὲ ὁ Παῦλος ἐν φωνῇ
ἀσθενεῖ, "Μὴ φοβοῦ, Ὀνήσιμε. οὐδεὶς ἡμῶν ἀπολεῖται, ὅτι ἡ ψυχὴ
ἡμῶν ἐν ταῖς χερσὶν θεοῦ."

30 ἐφέροντο δὲ ὑπὸ τῆς θαλάσσης νύκτα καὶ ἡμέραν. τὸν πάντα
χρόνον οὐκ ἔφαγον οὐδὲν οὐδὲ ἔπιον. ἤγγισαν οὖν ἕως
τοῦ θανάτου. γενομένης δὲ ἡμέρας, ἠγέρθησαν ὑπὸ φωνῶν
ἀνθρώπων. ἀνοίξαντες οὖν τοὺς ὀφθαλμοὺς εἶδον πλοῖον μικρὸν
ἐγγίζον αὐτοῖς!

35
     φωνῆς δὲ ἤκουσαν ἐκ τοῦ πλοίου κραζούσης, "Ἴδετε ὧδε! Λουκᾶς
εἰμι! ἐληλύθαμεν σῶσαι ὑμᾶς! ἐκεῖ μένετε!"

ἀποθανεῖται, fut. mid. ind. 3s of
  ἀποθνήσκω (I die)

ἀπολεῖται, fut. mid. ind. 3s of
  ἀπόλλυμι (I destroy, lose)

ἀπόλλυμι or ἀπολλύω, I destroy,
  lose; (mid.) perish

ἀσθενεῖ, dat. fem. sing. of ἀσθενής
  (weak, sick)

ἄφες, aor. act. impv. 2s of ἀφίημι
  (I let go, leave, forgive, permit)

ἀφῆς, aor. act. subj. 2s of ἀφίημι
  (I let go, leave, forgive, permit)

ἀφίημι, I let go, leave, forgive,
  permit

ἀφῶμεν, aor. act. subj. 1p of ἀφίημι
  (I let go, leave, forgive, permit)

δείκνυμι/δεικνύω, I show, point
  out

δεῖξον, aor. act. impv. 2s of
  δείκνυμι (I show, point out)

εἷς, μία, ἕν, one, a, an, single

ἐπιτίθημι, I place upon, lay upon

οὐδείς, οὐδεμία, οὐδέν, no one,
  nothing, no

ποτέ, once, formerly, before

προστίθημι, I add (to), increase

σανίς, σανίδος, ἡ, board, plank
  (cf. Acts 27:44)

σωτηρία, ας, ἡ, salvation, safety

τίθημι, I place, put, appoint

χρόνος, ου, ὁ, time

17 ἐν αὐτῇ τῇ ὥρᾳ – intensive use of αὐτός, "in that very hour."

26 φοβοῦμαι . . . μὴ ἀπολώμεθα – φοβοῦμαι is followed by μή and the aor.
    subj. to indicate what one fears.

30 νύκτα καὶ ἡμέραν – the time *within* which something is done is often
    given in the gen. (see lesson 18, p. 82, line 19). The dat. is used for the
    moment an action is done, while the acc. is used for the entire duration of
    an action (as here).

31 οὐκ ἔφαγον οὐδέν – double negatives add emphasis and do not cancel
    each other in Greek, "they ate nothing."

PRESENT ACTIVE INDICATIVE OF τίθημι

	Singular		Plural	
1	τίθημι	I place	τίθεμεν	we place
2	τίθης	you (sing.) place	τίθετε	you (pl.) place
3	τίθησι(ν)	he, she, it places	τιθέασι(ν)	they place

1 ἔμειναν οὖν ἐπὶ τῆς σανίδος ἕως τοῦ παραγενέσθαι τὸ πλοῖον.
εἰσελθόντες δὲ εἰς τὸ πλοῖον ἔχαιρον ἐπὶ τῷ Λουκᾷ τῷ εὑρηκότι
αὐτούς. ὁ δὲ Ὀνήσιμος εἶπεν, "Λουκᾶ! πῶς ζῇς ἔτι;" εἶπεν δὲ
Λουκᾶς, "Οἱ ἀγαθοὶ ἄνθρωποι οὗτοι εὑρόντες με φερόμενον
5 ὑπὸ τῆς θαλάσσης ἐδέξαντο εἰς τὸ πλοῖον." εἷς δὲ τῶν ἀνθρώπων
εἶπεν, "Μὴ λαλεῖτε περὶ τούτου. ἀλλὰ ἐλθόντες φάγετε καὶ πίετε!"
ἔδωκαν οὖν οἱ ἄνθρωποι τοῖς ἀδελφοῖς ἄρτον φαγεῖν καὶ οἶνον
πιεῖν. ἔδοξαν οὖν αὐτοῖς ὡς ἄγγελοι θεοῦ.

10 εὐθὺς οὖν ἤρξαντο Παῦλος καὶ Ὀνήσιμος φαγεῖν πάντα ὅσα
ἂν δύνωνται βάλλειν εἰς τὸ στόμα, ὥστε οὐδὲν λοιπὸν εἶναι
τοῖς ἄλλοις.

εὑρηκότι, perf. act. ptcpl. of
εὑρίσκω (I find)

λοιπός, ή, όν, remaining, rest

6   ἐλθόντες φάγετε καὶ πίετε – the participle ἐλθόντες denotes action prior
to the imperatives and is translated like an imperative ("come, eat and
drink"). Cf. Matt 28:19.

11 ὥστε οὐδὲν λοιπὸν εἶναι – infinitive clauses are difficult to render word
for word into English, so it's best to understand the sense of the entire
clause first, instead of translating εἶναι as "to be."

AORIST ACTIVE INDICATIVE OF τίθημι

	Singular		Plural	
1	ἔθηκα	I placed	ἐθήκαμεν	we placed
2	ἔθηκας	you (sing.) placed	ἐθήκατε	you (pl.) placed
3	ἔθηκε(ν)	he, she, it placed	ἔθηκαν	they placed

1   Ἀναστὰς ὁ Δημᾶς ἐξῆλθεν τοῦ εὑρεῖν τε καὶ κρατῆσαι τὴν
     ἀδελφὴν τὴν φυγοῦσαν ἀπὸ προσώπου αὐτοῦ. ἤθελεν γὰρ
     ἀποδοῦναι αὐτῇ ὡς καὶ αὐτὴ ἀπέδωκεν αὐτῷ.

5   ὁ δὲ Δημᾶς μὴ ἐν τῷ οἴκῳ εὑρὼν τὴν Θέκλαν ἐξῆλθεν εἰς τὸν
     ἀγρὸν ζητεῖν αὐτὴν ἔξω τοῦ οἴκου. ἡ δὲ Θέκλα, μὴ θέλουσα
     εὑρεθῆναι, ἔστη παρὰ λίθῳ μεγάλῳ. σταθεὶς δὲ ὁ ἀδελφὸς ἐπὶ
     ἄλλου λίθου μεγάλου, ἔφη, "Ἔξελθε! οἶδα γὰρ ὅτι εἶ ὧδε! μὴ
     φεῦγε! θέλω λαλεῖν μόνον περὶ τοῦ γενομένου." ἡ δὲ Θέκλα μὴ
10   πιστεύσασα τῷ ἀδελφῷ οὐκ ἀπεκρίνατο.

     ὁ οὖν Δημᾶς πάλιν ἔφη, "Ἐὰν μὴ ἐξέλθῃς, ὄψῃ πῦρ καταβαῖνον
     ἐπὶ σε ἐξ οὐρανοῦ. τότε οὐ μὴ φύγῃς ἐκ χειρός μου." καὶ τούτῳ μὴ
     πιστεύσασα ἡ Θέκλα, οὐκ ἀνέστη ἀλλὰ ἔμεινεν ὅπου ἦν.

15

     εὐθὺς οὖν ἐλθὼν ὁ ἀδελφὸς εἰς τὸν οἶκον ὑπέστρεψεν πῦρ ἔχων
     ἐν τῇ χειρί. ἤρξατο δὲ βάλλειν τὸ πῦρ εἰς τὸν ἀγρὸν ὅπως ἐκβάλῃ
     τὴν Θέκλαν.

20   ἡ δὲ Θέκλα ἰδοῦσα τὸ πῦρ ἀνέστη καὶ ἔφη, "Παρακαλῶ σε,
     ἐλέησον! μὴ τοῦτο ποιήσῃς!" χαίρων δὲ ὁ Δημᾶς ὅτι εὗρεν αὐτήν,
     ἤγγισεν ἵνα κρατήσῃ καὶ κακὸν ποιήσῃ, ἀλλ᾽ οὐκ ἐδύνατο.
     μέγα γὰρ ἐγένετο τὸ πῦρ ὥστε ἤμελλεν καὶ τὸν οἶκον ἐσθίειν.
     τότε ὁ Δημᾶς ἔγνω ὅτι κακὸν μέγα ἐποίησεν, πλήρης γὰρ πυρὸς
25   ἐγίνετο ὁ ἀγρός, ὥστε οὐκ ἐδύνατο τὰ τέκνα φυγεῖν. οἱ δύο
     οὖν ἔκραξαν φωναῖς μεγάλαις, "ΠΑΤΕΡ! ΜΗΤΕΡ! σώσατε
     ἡμᾶς! ἀπολλύμεθα!"

     ὁ δὲ Φιλήμων καὶ ἡ Ἀπφία ἀκούσαντες τῶν τέκνων εὐθὺς
30   ἐλθόντες ἐκράτησαν τὰ τέκνα καὶ ἦραν αὐτοὺς ἐκ τοῦ πυρός. ὁ
     δὲ Φιλήμων ἐκέλευσεν τοὺς δούλους βάλλειν ὕδωρ εἰς τὸ πῦρ
     ἵνα σώσῃ καὶ τὸν οἶκον καὶ τὸν ἀγρὸν καὶ πάντα ἄλλα ὑπάρχοντα
     αὐτοῦ. οἱ οὖν δοῦλοι ἔβαλλον πολὺ ὕδωρ εἰς τὸ πῦρ, ἀλλὰ οὐδὲν
     ἐγένετο, μέγα γενόμενον ἤδη. ἐλπίδα δὲ ἔτι ἔχων, Φιλήμων αὐτὸς
35   ἤνεγκεν ὕδωρ καὶ ἔβαλλεν εἰς τὸ πῦρ. ἡ δὲ Ἀπφία ἔκραξεν, "Ἄφες
     τὸν οἶκον! οὐ δύνῃ σῶσαι αὐτόν, ἤδη μεγάλου γενομένου τοῦ
     πυρός. ἀλλὰ φύγωμεν καὶ σώσωμεν ἑαυτούς!"

ἀναστάς, aor. act. ptcpl. of
  ἀνίστημι (I arise, cause to rise)
ἀνέστη, 2nd aor. act. ind. 3s of
  ἀνίστημι (I arise, cause to rise)
ἀνίστημι, I arise, cause to rise
δύο, two
ἔγνω, aor. act. ind. 3s of γινώσκω
  (I know)

ἔστη, 2nd aor. act. ind. 3s of ἵστημι
  (I stand, cause to stand)
ἔφη, aor. act. ind. 3s of φήμι (I say)
ἵστημι, I stand; cause to stand
μόνον, (adv.) only
πολύς, πολλή, πολύ, much, many
σταθείς, aor. pass. ptcpl. of ἵστημι
  (I stand, cause to stand)
φημί, I say

1 τοῦ εὑρεῖν – τοῦ + infinitive expresses purpose.
2 ἀπὸ προσώπου αὐτοῦ – "from his presence," a common idiom in the LXX
  and NT.
7 ἔστη παρὰ λίθῳ μεγάλῳ – the second aor. of ἵστημι has an intransitive
  meaning, "she stood . . ."
7 σταθεὶς δὲ ὁ ἀδελφός – the aor. pass. of ἵστημι has an active meaning.
23 τὸν οἶκον ἐσθίειν – "consume the house."

PRINCIPAL PARTS OF ἵστημι

1. ἵστημι	2. στήσω	3. ἔστησα	4. ἔστηκα	5. ἔσταμαι	6. ἐστάθην
		or ἔστην			

1   οἱ τέσσαρες οὖν ἔφυγον ἀπὸ τοῦ οἴκου οὗ ἠγάπησαν. καὶ
    ἀπώλλυτο ὁ οἶκος τοῦ Φιλήμονος, ὥστε οὐδὲν ἔμεινεν τῶν
    ὑπαρχόντων αὐτοῦ. βλέπων δὲ ὁ Φιλήμων τὸ πῦρ ἐσθίον τὸν
    οἶκον, ἠσπάσατο αὐτὸν καὶ ἀφῆκεν πάντα ὅσα εἶχεν.

ἀπώλλυτο, impf. mid. ind. 3s of
  ἀπολλύω (I destroy, mid. perish)

ἀφῆκεν, aor. act. ind. 3s of ἀφίημι
  (I leave)
τέσσαρες, τέσσαρα, four

1 ἀπὸ τοῦ οἴκου οὗ ἠγάπησαν – the relative pronoun οὗ is gen. by attraction to its antecedent. We would expect the acc. ὅν as the object of ἠγάπησαν.

4 ἠσπάσατο – ἀσπάζομαι more commonly means "I greet," but can also mean "I bid farewell."

1 Παραγενόμενοι ὁ Παῦλος καὶ ὁ Ὀνήσιμος εἰς τὴν πόλιν τὴν
τῶν Ἀθηνῶν, ἤρξαντο κηρύσσειν ἐν τῇ ἀγορᾷ περὶ τοῦ Χριστοῦ,
ἤνοιξεν γὰρ ὁ θεὸς θύραν εὐαγγελίσασθαι τοῖς ἑστῶσιν ἐκεῖ. τινὲς
μὲν τῶν ἐκεῖ ἑστηκότων οὐκ ἐδέξαντο τὸν λόγον, ἄλλοι δὲ εἶπαν,
5 "Ἀκουσόμεθά σου περὶ τούτου πάλιν," ἐν οἷς καὶ Διονύσιος ὁ
Ἀρεοπαγίτης καὶ γυνὴ αὐτοῦ ὀνόματι Δάμαρις.

οὗτοι οὖν ἐκάλεσαν τοὺς ἀδελφοὺς εἰς τὸν ἴδιον οἶκον ἵνα
ἀκούσωσιν πάλιν περὶ τῆς πίστεως. εἰσελθὼν δὲ εἰς τὸν οἶκον,
10 εἶδεν ὁ Παῦλος ὄχλον μέγαν συναχθέντα. ὁ δὲ ἔφη, "Τί τοῦτο;"

ὁ οὖν Διονύσιος ἀπεκρίνατο, "Θέλομεν ἡμεῖς πάντες ἀκούειν περὶ
τοῦ Χριστοῦ τούτου οὗ κηρύσσεις!"

15 ὁ δὲ Παῦλος ἐθαύμασεν θεωρῶν τοὺς ἀνθρώπους τοὺς οὕτως
βουλομένους ἀκούειν. ἡ δὲ Δάμαρις ἡ τοῦ Διονυσίου γυνὴ
κρατήσασα αὐτοῦ τῆς χειρὸς ἔστησεν αὐτὸν ἐνώπιον πάντων.

σταθεὶς οὖν Παῦλος ἔμπροσθεν αὐτῶν ἔφη, "Ἐπιγινώσκω νῦν ὅτι
20 ὁ θεός μου ἀληθῶς ἀγαπᾷ ἀνθρώπους ἀπὸ παντὸς ἔθνους ὑπὸ
τὸν οὐρανόν, ὑμεῖς γὰρ ἐλθόντες ὧδε βούλεσθε ἀκούειν περὶ θεοῦ
τούτου οὗ οὐκ οἴδατε. ὁ γὰρ θεὸς οὗτος ὁ θεὸς τῶν Ἰουδαίων
ἐστίν, ὃς ἔκτισεν τὸν οὐρανὸν καὶ τὴν γῆν καὶ τὴν θάλασσαν καὶ
πάντα ἐν αὐτοῖς, καὶ . . ."
25
λέγοντος δὲ τοῦ Παύλου, ἔφη ἄνθρωπός τις λέγων,
"Ἀλλὰ ἰσχυρότερός ἐστιν ὁ θεός σου ἢ Ποσειδῶν ὁ θεὸς
τῆς θαλάσσης;"

30 καὶ ἀπεκρίθη ὁ Παῦλος, "Ναί, ἰσχυρότερός ἐστιν ὁ θεός μου τοῦ
Ποσειδῶνος."

ἄλλος δὲ εἶπεν, "Ἀλλὰ κρείσσων ἐστὶν αὐτὸς ἢ Ἀθηνᾶ ἡ θεὰ τῆς
πόλεως ἡμῶν;"
35
ὁ δὲ Παῦλος ἔφη, "Οὐ μόνον κρείσσων ἐστὶν ἢ Ἀθηνᾶ, ἀλλὰ καὶ
κρείσσων καὶ μείζων καὶ ἰσχυρότερος τῶν πάντων θεῶν ὧν ὑμεῖς
προσκυνεῖτε!"

ἀγορά, ᾶς, ἡ, market
Ἀθηνᾶ, ᾶς, ἡ, Athena
Ἀθηνῶν, gen. of Ἀθῆναι (Athens)
ἀληθῶς, (adv.) truly
Ἀρεοπαγίτης, ου, ὁ, Areopagite
Δάμαρις, Δαμάριδος, ἡ, Damaris
Διονύσιος, ου, ὁ, Dionysius
ἔμπροσθεν, before, in front of
   (+ gen.)
ἐνώπιον, before, in the sight of, in
   the presence of (+ gen.)
ἐπιγινώσκω, I recognize, know,
   understand
ἑστηκότων, 1st perf. act. ptcpl.
   masc. gen. pl. of ἵστημι (I stand,
   intransitive)
ἔστησεν, 1st aor. act. ind. 3s
   of ἵστημι (I cause to stand,
   transitive)

ἑστῶσιν, 2nd perf. act. ptcpl.
   masc. dat. pl. of ἵστημι (I stand,
   intransitive)
ἤ, or, than
θεά, ᾶς, ἡ, goddess
ἰσχυρός, ά, όν, strong, mighty
κρείσσων, ον, better (compar. of
   ἀγαθός, good)
μείζων, ον, greater (compar. of
   μέγας, great)
μόνον, (adv.) only
ναί, yes
Ποσειδῶν, Ποσειδῶνος, ὁ,
   Poseidon
συναχθέντα, aor. pass. ptcpl. of
   συνάγω (I gather together)
μόνον, (adv.) only

5   ἐν οἷς – "among whom," relative pronouns such as οἷς sometimes lack an
    explicit antecedent.
6   ὀνόματι Δάμαρις – names are sometimes given with ὄνομα in the dat.
13 οὗ κηρύσσεις – gen. by attraction to its antecedent Χριστοῦ.
17 ἔστησεν αὐτόν – the first aor. of ἵστημι has a transitive meaning, "she set
    him . . ."
22 οὗ οὐκ οἴδατε – another relative pronoun which is gen. by attraction.
27 ἰσχυρότερός ἐστιν ὁ θεός σου ἤ Ποσειδῶν – when comparisons are made
    with ἤ the nouns are in the same case.
30 ἰσχυρότερός ἐστιν . . . τοῦ Ποσειδῶνος – without ἤ, comparisons are
    made with the second noun in the gen.
37 ὧν ὑμεῖς προσκυνεῖτε – gen. ὧν by attraction to θεῶν.

1   οἱ δὲ ἀκούοντες ἐθαύμασαν ἐπὶ τῷ λόγῳ τούτῳ. ὁ δὲ Παῦλος ἔφη,
"Ὁ θεός μου ἔκτισεν οὐ μόνον τὴν γῆν, ἀλλὰ καὶ ὑμᾶς πάντας.
καὶ κτίσαντος τοῦ θεοῦ ταῦτα πάντα, ἡ ἁμαρτία εἰς τὸν κόσμον
εἰσῆλθεν δι᾽ ἑνὸς ἀνθρώπου καὶ διὰ τῆς ἁμαρτίας ὁ θάνατος.

5   διὸ ἔπεμψεν ὁ θεὸς τὸν ἴδιον υἱὸν τὸν Ἰησοῦν, ὃν ἐσταύρωσαν
οἱ ἄνθρωποι ἐν Ἰερουσαλήμ. ἀλλὰ μετὰ τρεῖς ἡμέρας ἠγέρθη
ἐκ νεκρῶν."

Διονύσιος δὲ εἶπεν, "Ἀλλὰ νῦν ποῦ ἐστιν αὐτός; μή ἐστιν ἔτι ἐν

10   Ἰερουσαλήμ;"

Παῦλος δὲ ἀπεκρίθη, "Οὐχί! ἀλλὰ κάθηται ἐπὶ θρόνου
δόξης ἐν οὐρανῷ, καὶ ἐλεύσεται ἐν τῇ ἐσχάτῃ ἡμέρᾳ κρίνειν
ζῶντας καὶ νεκρούς. ὅστις δ᾽ ἂν μετανοήσῃ καὶ πιστεύσῃ εἰς

15   αὐτὸν σωθήσεται."

οὕτως οὖν ἐδίδασκεν αὐτοὺς πολλὰς ἡμέρας καὶ πολλοὶ ἐδέξαντο
τὸ εὐαγγέλιον, βαπτισθέντες εἰς τὸ ὄνομα τοῦ Ἰησοῦ. καὶ μετὰ
δώδεκα ἡμέρας ἡτοίμασαν Παῦλος καὶ Ὀνήσιμος τοῦ ἀπελθεῖν.

20

πρὸ δὲ τοῦ ἀπελθεῖν αὐτούς, ὁ Διονύσιος προσελθὼν εἶπεν
αὐτοῖς, "Εἰ μὴ ἤλθατε ὧδε, οὐκ ἂν ἐδεξάμεθα τὸ εὐαγγέλιον.
χάριν οὖν ἔχω σοί!"

25   ὁ δὲ Ὀνήσιμος ἔφη, "Εἰ μὴ ἐκαλέσατε ἡμᾶς εἰς τὸν οἶκον ὑμῶν,
οὐκ ἂν ἐκηρύξαμεν ὑμῖν! χάριν ἔχομεν ὑμῖν!"

καὶ ὁ Παῦλος ἔφη, "Μᾶλλον δὲ Ὀνήσιμε, εἰ μὴ ἔσωσάς με ἐκ τῆς
θαλάσσης, οὐκ ἂν ἔζων ἔτι. χάριν σοι ἔχω!"

30

ὁ δὲ Ὀνήσιμος ἔφη, "Μᾶλλον δέ, ὦ Παῦλε, εἰ μὴ ἐδίδαξάς με τὸ
εὐαγγέλιον ἐν Φιλίπποις, οὐκ ἂν ἤμην μαθητὴς τοῦ Χριστοῦ."

ἡ δὲ Δάμαρις προσελθοῦσα ἔφη, "Μᾶλλον δέ, ὦ ἄνδρες, ἐὰν μὴ

35   ἀπέλθητε νῦν, ἐγὼ αὐτὴ ἐκβαλῶ ὑμᾶς πάντας!"

εὐθὺς οὖν ἐξῆλθον οἱ ἀδελφοί.

Δάμαρις, Δαμάριδος, ἡ, Damaris
διό, therefore, for this reason
Διονύσιος, ου, ὁ, Dionysius
δώδεκα, twelve
ἑνός, gen. of εἷς (one)
μᾶλλον, more, rather
οὐχί, not (stronger form of οὐ)

πολλάς, acc. fem. pl. of πολλή
   (many)
πολλοί, nom. masc. pl. of πολύς
   (many)
τρεῖς, three
Φιλίπποις, dat. of Φίλιπποι
   (Philippi)

9   μή ἐστιν – questions beginning with μή expect a "no" answer.

14 ὅστις δ᾽ ἂν μετανοήσῃ – conditional relative clause, "whoever . . ."

22 Εἰ μή ἤλθατε ὧδε, οὐκ ἂν ἐδεξάμεθα . . . – note the various contrary to
    fact conditions in this story. The aor. tense verb in the apodosis denotes
    past tense, while the impf. tense (e.g., ἔζων) denotes present tense.

23 χάριν οὖν ἔχω σοί – ἔχω χάριν + dat. of person is a common way to ex-
    press thanks.

1 διδάσκοντες οὖν καὶ εὐαγγελιζόμενοι ἦσαν οἱ δύο ἀδελφοὶ κατὰ
πᾶσαν πόλιν εἰς ἣν ὁ θεὸς ἀπέστειλεν αὐτούς. ὅτε γὰρ εἰσῆρχοντο
εἰς πόλιν τινά, πρῶτον ἐν ταῖς συναγωγαῖς καὶ τότε ἐν μέσῳ τῆς
πόλεως ἐκήρυσσον τὸ εὐαγγέλιον, τοῖς τε Ἰουδαίοις καὶ τοῖς
5 ἔθνεσιν. οὕτως οὖν ἐπορεύοντο Παῦλος καὶ Ὀνήσιμος καὶ ἄλλοι
ὅσοι ἤθελον κηρύσσειν τὴν ἐπαγγελίαν τῆς σωτηρίας διὰ τῆς
γῆς. ἀλλὰ οὐ μόνον ἀγαθὰ ἐγίνετο αὐτοῖς, ἀλλὰ καὶ κακὰ πολλά,
παρεδόθησαν γὰρ πολλάκις εἰς χεῖρας ἀνθρώπων πονηρῶν.
διὸ παραδοθεὶς ὁ Παῦλος εἰς τὰς χεῖρας τῶν Ῥωμαίων ἐπέμφθη
10 εἰς Ῥώμην.

καὶ νῦν ἐν Ῥώμῃ ἐστὶν Παῦλος σὺν Ὀνησίμῳ καὶ Τιμοθέῳ. οὐ
δύναται μὲν ἐξελθεῖν ἔξω τοῦ οἴκου, δέξασθαι δὲ δύναται εἰς τὸν
οἶκον πάντας ὅσους θέλοντας ἀκούειν αὐτοῦ. ἐν δὲ ἡμέρᾳ τινὶ
15 πορευομένου τοῦ Παύλου περὶ τὸν οἶκον, ἐλθὼν ὁ Τιμόθεος φησιν,
"Παῦλε, ἄγγελοι ἐληλύθασιν ἀπὸ τῆς ἐκκλησίας τῆς ἐν Κολοσσαῖς,
καὶ θέλουσιν λαλεῖν σοι."

Παῦλος οὖν δεξάμενος αὐτοὺς ἑτοιμάζει τι φαγεῖν. οἱ δέ φασιν,
20 "Παῦλε, μὴ ἑτοιμάσῃς οὐδέν! ἠνέγκαμεν γὰρ τὰ δῶρα ταῦτα
ἀπὸ Κολοσσῶν."

καὶ θέντες τὰ δῶρα ἐν μέσῳ αὐτῶν δεικνύουσιν αὐτῷ καρπόν τε
καὶ ἄρτον, βιβλία τε καὶ ἱμάτια καὶ ἄλλα δῶρα τοιαῦτα.
25

ὁ δὲ Παῦλός φησιν, "Ἐληλύθατε ἕως τοῦ Ῥώμης ἵνα ἱμάτια δῶτέ
μοι; οὐκ οἴδατε ὅτι ταῦτα πάντα δύναμαι ἀγοράσαι καὶ ὧδε
ἐν Ῥώμῃ;"

30 οἱ δὲ ἀποκρίνονται, "Ὦ Παῦλε, πατὴρ εἶ ἡμῶν πάντων οἳ
πεπιστεύκασιν ἐν Κολοσσαῖς. ἀλλὰ ἡμεῖς αὐτοὶ οὐδέποτε εἴδομέν
σε, ἀλλὰ μόνον ἠκούομεν περὶ σοῦ ἀπὸ Φιλήμονος. διὸ οὐ
μόνον ἤλθαμεν διὰ τὰ δῶρα, ἀλλὰ καὶ ἵνα ἴδωμέν σε πρόσωπον
πρὸς πρόσωπον."

35 ὁ δὲ Παῦλος, μὴ εἰδὼς τί λέγῃ, χαίρει ἐπὶ τῇ πίστει αὐτῶν καὶ
λέγει, "Καλῶς. ἀλλὰ πῶς ἔχει ὁ Φιλήμων;"

δῶτε, aor. act. subj. 2p of δίδωμι (I give)

ἐπαγγελία, ας, ἡ, promise

ἐπέμφθη, aor. pass. ind. 3s of πέμπω (I send)

θέντες, aor. act. ptcpl. of τίθημι (I put, place)

καιρός, οῦ, ὁ, season, time

κατά, (+ acc.) in

Κολοσσαῖς, dat. of Κολοσσαί (Colossae)

μέσος, η, ον, middle, in the midst

ὅσος, η, ον, as many as, as great as

οὐδέποτε, never

παρεδόθησαν, aor. pass. ind. 3p of παραδίδωμι (I hand over, betray)

πρῶτον, (adv.) first

Ῥωμαῖος, ου, ὁ, Roman

Ῥώμη, ης, ἡ, Rome

σωτηρία, ας, ἡ, salvation

Τιμόθεος, ου, ὁ, Timothy

τοιοῦτος, αὕτη, οὗτον/οὗτο, such

φασίν, pres. act. ind. 3p of φημί (I say)

φησίν, pres. act. ind. 3s of φημί (I say)

---

1 διδάσκοντες καὶ εὐαγγελιζόμενοι ἦσαν – periphrastic ptcpl.

1 κατὰ πᾶσαν πόλιν – κατά + acc. can denote location in or throughout a space.

2 εἰσήρχοντο . . . ἐκήρυσσον . . . ἐπορεύοντο – the use of imperfect verbs in the first paragraph highlights the progressive or habitual nature of these activities of Paul and Onesimus during their travels.

5 ἄλλοι ὅσοι ἤθελον – even without πάντες, ὅσοι can mean "all who . . ."

12 καὶ νῦν ἐν Ῥώμῃ ἐστίν – this story is told in the present tense, like much of the gospels. This is called the "historical present" and can add vividness to a narrative.

30 οἱ δὲ ἀποκρίνονται – the article οἱ before δέ with no noun has the force of a pronoun.

36 μὴ εἰδώς – the ptcpl. form of οἶδα (I know), which is easily confused with ἰδών, the aor. ptcpl. of ὁράω (I see). Note the lack of the epsilon in ἰδών.

37 καλῶς – adv. from καλός, "very well."

1 οἱ δέ φασιν, "Κακῶς ἔχει, ἀπώλεσεν γὰρ πάντα τὰ ἴδια ἐν πυρὶ
μεγάλῳ."

μετὰ ταῦτα, ὑποστρέψας ὁ Ὀνήσιμος ἀπὸ τῆς ἀγορᾶς ἔρχεται
5 πρὸς Παῦλον. ὁ δὲ Παῦλος λέγει, "Ποῦ ἦς;"

"Κατέβην εἰς ἀγοράν," λέγει Ὀνήσιμος, "ἵνα πλείονα ἄρτον
ἀγοράσω, ἀλλὰ τί ταῦτα; εἰ ἔγνων ὅτι ἤδη ἔχεις τοσαῦτα, οὐκ
ἂν ἦλθον."

10 ὁ δὲ Παῦλος λέγει, "Ἄγγελοι ἐληλύθασιν ἀπὸ Κολοσσῶν
ἀπαγγέλλοντές μοι περὶ Φιλήμονος τοῦ ἀδελφοῦ ἡμῶν."

ὁ δὲ λέγει, "Ἡμῶν ὁ ἀδελφός; μᾶλλον δὲ ὁ ἀδελφὸς ὁ σὸς
15 μόνον!"

Παῦλος δέ φησιν, "Ἄκουσον Ὀνήσιμε! κακὸν μέγα γέγονεν αὐτῷ
ὥστε χρείαν ἔχει σου! ἀπώλεσεν γὰρ πάντα τὰ ὑπάρχοντα αὐτοῦ
ἐν πυρί.

20 ὁ δὲ Ὀνήσιμός φησιν, "Ἀλλὰ πέμψον ἄλλον μᾶλλον ἢ ἐμέ.
Τιμόθεον πέμψον! ἐὰν γὰρ πάλιν γένωμαι δοῦλος αὐτοῦ,
τί οὖν;"

25 Παῦλος δὲ λέγει, "μὴ γένοιτο! οὐ μὴ γένῃ δοῦλος πάλιν, γράφω
γὰρ ἐπιστολὴν τῇ ἐκκλησίᾳ ἐν Κολοσσαῖς ἵνα μὴ δέξωνταί σε
ὡς δοῦλον, μᾶλλον δὲ ὡς ἀδελφόν. καὶ οὕτως φανερώσει ὁ θεὸς
τὴν χάριν αὐτοῦ ἣν δίδωσιν τοῖς πᾶσιν, ἡμεῖς γὰρ πάντες εἷς
ἐσμὲν ἐν Χριστῷ. λαβὼν οὖν τὴν ἐπιστολὴν ταύτην φέρε αὐτὴν
30 πρὸς Φιλήμονα."

(τί δὲ ἔγραψεν ὁ Παῦλος ἐν τῇ ἐπιστολῇ; εὑρήσεις ὃ ἔγραψεν ἐν τῇ
ἐπιστολῇ τῇ καλουμένῃ ΠΡΟΣ ΦΙΛΗΜΟΝΑ.)

35 μετὰ δέ τινας χρόνους ἑτοιμάσαντες Ὀνήσιμος καὶ ἄλλοι τινὲς
μετ᾽ αὐτου, πορεύονται εἰς Κολοσσάς. πρὸ δὲ τοῦ ἀπελθεῖν, ὁ
Παῦλος ἐπιθεὶς ἐπ᾽ Ὀνήσιμον τὰς χεῖρας προσεύχεται,

ἀγορά, ᾶς, ἡ, market

ἀπαγγέλλω, I report, announce, declare

γένῃ, aor. mid. subj. 2s of γίνομαι (I become)

γένοιτο, aor. mid. opt. 3s of γίνομαι (I become)

ἐπιστολή, ῆς, ἡ, letter

εὑρήσεις, fut. act. ind. 2s of εὑρίσκω (I find)

κακῶς, (adv.) badly

καλουμένῃ, dat. fem. ptcpl. of καλέω (I call)

κατέβην, aor. act. ind. 1s of καταβαίνω (I go down)

πλείων, ον, more, larger (compar. of πολύς, many)

σός, σή, σόν, your (sing.)

τοσοῦτος, αύτη, οῦτον, so much

φανερόω, I make known, reveal

χρεία, ας, ἡ, need, necessity, lack

1   τὰ ἴδια – one's own things (incl. possessions and/or family).

8   εἰ ἔγνων . . . , οὐκ ἄν ἦλθον – contrary to fact condition.

18 χρείαν ἔχει σου – ἔχω χρείαν + gen. noun expresses need.

23 τί οὖν; – "what then?"

25 μὴ γένοιτο! – a common saying in Paul's letters.

29 λαβών . . . φέρε – the participle λαβών denotes action prior to the imperative φέρε and is translated like an imperative ("take . . . [and] bring").

35 μετὰ δέ τινας χρόνους – "after some time."

1 "Ἐλεήσαι σε ὁ θεὸς ἐν τῇ ὁδῷ,

 ἀγάγοι σε ὁ κύριος μετ᾽ εἰρήνης πρὸς Φιλήμονα,

5 εἴη ἐν παντὶ καιρῷ τὸ πνεῦμα τὸ ἅγιον μετὰ σου,

 χάρις καὶ εἰρήνη εἴη μεθ᾽ ὑμῶν πάντων νῦν καὶ εἰς τὸν αἰῶνα. ἀμήν."

ἀγάγοι, aor. act. opt. 3s of ἄγω
  (I lead)

εἴη, pres. opt. 3s of εἰμί (I am)

ἐλεήσαι, aor. act. opt. 3s of ἐλεέω
  (I have mercy)

καιρός, οῦ, ὁ, season, time

1 Ἐλεήσαι σε – aor. act. opt. used to express a wish, "may God show you mercy . . ." The other optatives in Paul's prayer have the same function.

PRESENT ACTIVE OPTATIVE OF λύω

	Singular		Plural	
1	λύοιμι	may I loosen	λύοιμεν	may we loosen
2	λύοις	may you (sing.) loosen	λύοιτε	may you (pl.) loosen
3	λύοι	may he, she, it loosen	λύοιεν	may they loosen

AORIST ACTIVE OPTATIVE OF λύω

	Singular		Plural	
1	λύσαιμι	may I loosen	λύσαιμεν	may we loosen
2	λύσαις	may you (sing.) loosen	λύσαιτε	may you (pl.) loosen
3	λύσαι	may he, she, it loosen	λύσαιεν	may they loosen

ENGLISH TRANSLATIONS

CONTENTS

LESSON 1

WHO ARE YOU?

Jacob, "Hello! I am Jacob."

David, "Hello! I am David."

(Again)

Jacob, "Hello! Who are you?"

David, "I am David. Who are you?"

Jacob, "I am Jacob."

(Mary, who knows David, joins the group)

Mary, "Hello! Who is he?"

David, "He is Jacob."

Jacob (to David), "Who is she?"

David, "She is Mary"

(the teacher says hello to everyone)

Mark, "Hello!"

David, "Hello!"

Mary, "Hello! Who are you?"

Mark, "I am the teacher."

David, "What?"

Mark, "I am the teacher."

Jacob, "What is your name?"

Mark, "I am Mark! What is your name?"

Jacob, "I am Jacob."

Mark, "What is her name?"

Jacob, "Her name is Mary."

LESSON 2

DESTROYING A BOOK

Jacob, "Hello! I am Jacob. Who are you?"

David, "Hello! I am David. What are you writing?"

Jacob, "I am writing a book."

(Mary joins them)

Mary, "Hello!"

David, "Hello! Do you see that Jacob is writing?"

Mary, "I see that Jacob is writing. What is Jacob writing?"

David, "Jacob is writing a book."

Mary, "I also want to write a book."

Mary and Jacob are writing.

David is not writing. David does not want to write. David wants to destroy the book.

Mark sees that Mary and Jacob are writing.

Mark, "What are you writing? I want to see and hear."

Jacob and Mary, "We are writing a book. Do you want to write?"

Mark, "I don't want to write. I want to teach."

David, "I also want to teach . . ."

David is destroying the book! Jacob and Mary are not writing.

Mary says, "What are you doing?"

David says, "I am teaching!"

Jacob says, "You're not teaching! You're destroying the book!"

Mary and Jacob say, "We don't believe that you're destroying the book. Why are you destroying the book? We want to know!"

David says, "I am destroying the book because I don't want to write!"

Mary cries. Jacob cries. Mary and Jacob are crying.

Mark hears that Mary and Jacob are crying.

Mark says, "Why are you crying?"

Mary and Jacob, "We are crying because David is destroying the book!"

Mark says, "Oh, David! Why are you destroying the book?"

David says, "I am destroying the book because I want to teach them that I don't want to write."

Mark says, "What? Don't you know that I am the teacher?"

David says, "What is a teacher?"

Mark says, "A teacher teaches."

LESSON 3

IT IS TIME TO BELIEVE

Story A

Prisca, "My sister says that Jesus has a kingdom."

Saul, "What is the kingdom? I don't see and I don't believe. Your sister does not speak the truth."

Prisca, "The church also says that Jesus has a kingdom. Don't you believe?"

Barnabas, "I hear that Jesus wants to have the kingdom of the earth."

Prisca, "You're not speaking the truth. Don't you know that Jesus sees the heart?"

Saul and Barnabas don't believe that Jesus has a kingdom.

(Jesus appears before them)

Jesus, "What are you saying?"

Prisca, "Saul and Barnabas don't believe that you have a kingdom."

Saul and Barnabas, "We don't believe because we don't see!"

Jesus, "I speak the truth and you don't believe. I see that you don't know the truth."

Prisca and Saul and Barnabas, "What is truth? We want to know."

Jesus, "I am the truth and the life. I have a kingdom. You don't believe because you don't see? It is not time to see. It is time to believe!"

Story B

(Poseidon, the god of the sea, and Gaia, the goddess of the earth, are having a friendly chat)

Poseidon, "I have a kingdom."

Gaia, "What is your kingdom?"

Poseidon, "My kingdom is the sea."

Gaia, "I don't believe [it]! You don't have a kingdom! I want to see!"

Poseidon, "You want to see? It is not time to see. It is time to listen and believe."

Gaia, "You're not speaking the truth. I speak the truth and I have a kingdom. Do you want to see?"

Poseidon, "What is your kingdom?"

Gaia, "Do you see the earth? The earth is my kingdom. Do you see the glory of the earth?"

Poseidon, "I see the earth, but the earth does not have glory."

Gaia, "The sea also does not have glory . . ."

Story C

(John receives a vision from an angel and begins to write a letter to the church)

John is writing. The angel says that the church does not have life because she does not believe and does not listen.

The church wants to have glory and does not want to have life. John writes that the church does not know the truth and the time/hour. What time is it? It is time to believe!

Story D

(Satan meets Jesus in the desert)

Satan, "Oh, Jesus, what do you want to have?"

Jesus, ". . ."

Satan, "Don't you want to have the kingdom of the earth?"

Jesus, "I do not want to have the kingdom of the earth."

Satan, "Don't you see the kingdom of the earth? Don't you see the glory of the kingdom?"

Jesus, "I don't see the glory of the kingdom of the earth. The kingdoms of the earth don't have glory."

Satan, "Who has glory?"

Jesus, "The churches have glory because the churches hear my voice."

Satan, "The churches have glory? I don't see the glory of the churches."

Story E

(Paul is writing to the churches)

Paul writes to the church of Galatia and the church of Corinth. What does he write? Paul writes that the churches do not hear the voice of truth and do not believe the truth. Paul knows that the churches want to have glory, but do not want to have life.

Paul wants to say to the churches that the glories of the earth are destroying the hearts of the churches. Paul writes that the churches do not know the truth.

What are the churches doing? Are the churches listening to the voice of truth? Do they believe the truth? They do not listen and do not believe!

Story F

(Adapted from Acts 1 before Jesus is about to depart)

Peter and Jacob/James and John, "Is it time to see the kingdom? We know that you have a kingdom. We want to see the kingdom."

Jesus, "You want to see my kingdom? You want to see the glories of the kingdom?"

Peter and Jacob/James and John, "Yes! We want to see!"

Jesus, "It is not the day of glory. It is time to believe my voice and the truth. Do you believe?"

Peter and Jacob/James and John, "We believe!"

LESSON 4

PHILEMON HEARS THE WORD

Story A

A certain person has a slave. And the slave has a child and the child is the son of the slave. And the person is a master of the slave. What is the name of the slave? The name of the slave is Eutychus. What is the name of the son of the slave? His name is Tertius.

What does the son say? He says that he wants to have a house.

Tertius, "Father, Why don't we have a house?"

Eutychus, "Because you are a slave."

Master of the slave, "Yes, a slave does not have a house, but the master has houses. Don't you [pl.] know that I am the master?"

Tertius and Eutychus, "We know . . ."

Tertius has a brother. And the brother of Tertius is Onesimus. Onesimus has work, but he does not want to do the work(s).

Onesimus, "The work of the slave is death!"

Tertius, "Shh! Don't you know that the master is listening?"

The master is not listening, but he has a son. The name of the son is Philemon. Does Philemon hear the voices of the slaves? He does not hear, but Philemon hears the voice of a person. Who is the person? He is Paul.

Story B

Philemon hears the voice of a person. Who is the person? It is Paul. Philemon hears the words of Paul.

Philemon sees the person and speaks to the person.

Philemon, "What are you saying?"

Paul, "I am speaking the word of God. Do you want to know the word of truth?"

Philemon, "What is truth? What do you have to say? I and the master of the slaves, we have houses and slaves and children. Do you see the glory of our house?"

Paul, "Oh, man! Your house does not have glory, but the God of life and of truth has glory."

Philemon, "What? Who is god? We have gods of the earth and of the sea and of death, but we do not know the god of life and of truth."

Paul, "Your gods are not gods, but works of humans. The word of God says that God wants to have the hearts of people."

Philemon, "I do not believe your words! I want to see your god."

Paul, "It is not time to see, but to believe."

LESSON 5

PHILEMON DOES NOT RECEIVE THE MESSAGE

Story A

Philemon hears the beautiful voice of a person. Who is the person? It is Paul. Philemon sees the holy person and hears the good words and speaks to the person, for he wants to know what he is saying.

Philemon, "What are you saying?"

Paul, "I am speaking the word of the good God. Do you want to know the word of truth?"

Philemon, "What is truth? What do you have to say? I and the master of the slaves, we have houses and slaves and children. Do you see our beautiful house?"

Paul, "Oh, man! Your house is not beautiful, but the God of life and of truth is beautiful/good."

Philemon, "What? Who is the good/beautiful god? We have gods of the earth and the sea and death, but we do not know the god of life and of truth."

Paul, "Your gods are not gods, but works of evil people. Your gods are wicked, but my God is just/righteous, for my God wants to have the hearts of the people."

Philemon, "I do not receive/accept your message! You are speaking bad words! I want to see your god."

Paul, "It is not time to see, but to believe in the beautiful/good truth."

Story B

A certain person has a slave. And the slave has a child and the child is the son of the slave. And the person is the master of the slave. What is the name of the slave? The name of the slave is Eutychus. What is the name of the son of the slave? His name is Tertius. Tertius is a good slave and has a brother. And the brother of Tertius is Onesimus. Is Onesimus good [i.e., a good slave]? Onesimus has work, but he does not want to do the works. He is a bad slave.

Onesimus, "The work of the slave is death. The work is evil, for the master is wicked."

Tertius, "Shh! Don't you know that the master is listening?"

Story C

(Poseidon, the god of the sea and Gaia, the goddess of the earth, are talking)

Poseidon, "I have a beautiful and good kingdom."

Gaia, "What is your kingdom?"

Poseidon, "My kingdom is the sea."

Gaia, "I don't believe! The sea is not your kingdom! I know that the sea is beautiful and good, but your kingdom is ugly/bad and small. I have a kingdom. Do you want to see?"

Poseidon, "What is your kingdom?"

Gaia, "Do you see the beautiful/good earth? The earth is my kingdom."

Poseidon, "I see the earth, but the

earth is not beautiful/good, for it has evil people. The evil people are destroying the beautiful/good earth."

Gaia, "You speak the truth . . . the people are bad and evil!"

LESSON 6

PHILEMON BELIEVES AND ONESIMUS HEARS

Story A

Jonah is a prophet of God. The people of Nineveh are evil, but God wants to teach the people of Nineveh the word of truth. But Jonah does not want to, for he knows that the people are bad and wicked.

God sends Jonah to Nineveh because he wants to receive the evil people of Nineveh.

But does Jonah listen to the voice of God? He does not listen.

And God throws the sea toward Jonah, for God wants to teach Jonah that he wants to receive also/even the bad people. Now Jonah listens and the people of Nineveh believe in God.

Story B

Paul teaches Philemon the word from God. But Philemon believes that Paul is an angel/messenger from heaven.

Philemon says, "You are an angel/ messenger of God!"

Paul, "I am not an angel but a prophet of God, for I speak the word from God. God is sending me to the kingdoms of the world, because he wants to receive the hearts of the people. Do you believe God? Do you believe that a person does not have life from works of the law?"

Philemon, "Now I believe in your God!"

Now Philemon believes in God. Now he knows the way of truth. Now he is in Christ. Now he is a disciple.

Onesimus also hears the words of Paul and of Philemon, but he does not know what they are saying. He wants to know, but he does not have a teacher.

Story C

Jesus says, "It is good to believe in God and in Christ. For my God has houses in heaven and you are receiving the good/ beautiful houses from God. You see a bad way in the world, but you know the good way."

Thomas says, "Lord, we don't know what you're saying. We don't know the good way and we don't see the houses from God. What is the good way?"

Jesus says, "I am the way and the truth and the life. You [pl.] know God because you know me. You [pl.] see God because you see me."

Philip says, "Lord, we want to see God."

Jesus says, "I am with you [pl.] and you [sing.] don't know me, Philip? You [sing.] see God because you see me. But you say that you want to see God? Don't you [sing.] believe that I am in God and God is in me? My words are from God, and God abides in me and does his works. Do you [pl.] believe that I am in God and God is in me? You believe on account of the works."

Story D

Paul, an apostle not from people and not through a person, but through Jesus Christ and [through] God, and the brothers and sisters who are with us to the churches of Galatia. You [pl.] have grace and peace from God and [from] the Lord Jesus Christ, for God wants to receive the people from the evil world. Glory to God!

I hear about you that now you [pl.] don't believe the first word/message from Christ, but you believe in the evil word. For the evil people wish to teach the evil word and you are listening to the evil voices.

But I and an angel from heaven, we do not teach the evil word, but the good [word]. Why/on account of what do you [pl.] not believe the word of truth?

You [pl.] know the word concerning the truth. I do not receive the word from evil people, but through the Lord Jesus Christ. You know about my life in Judaism, but now I do not remain in the first life, but [I remain] in Christ. Do

you [pl.] see my life in Christ? Do you want to have the life that is in Christ? You don't have [it] because you don't believe in Christ!

Story E

John the Baptist has a small house in the desert, but he wants to see the beautiful houses in Jerusalem.

John runs toward the beautiful houses, but the people in the houses don't want to see John.

They throw stones toward John, because they don't want to listen to his words. John runs out of Jerusalem and through the desert and into his house. John doesn't have a beautiful house in Jerusalem, but he has a good kingdom in heaven.

LESSON 7

BREAD FROM HEAVEN

Story A

Paul and Philemon are talking about the truth and the kingdom and the son of God. For Philemon is now a disciple, for he believes in Christ, but his sister and brother do not believe. But Philemon wants to teach them about Christ. But do they listen?

Philemon, "Now I'm a disciple of Christ! Now I have life with God in heaven!"

His brother, "What are you saying? We are Greek people. We are not disciples of the god of Paul."

His sister, "Yes, Philemon. Your brother speaks the truth."

Philemon, "But according to the word of God, we are evil people, for our gods are not gods, but works of man/humanity. And the holy God in heaven wants to save us from sin and from death through his love."

His brother, "Oh, evil person! What are you saying to us? Do you not hear us? You are a Greek person! Who is Paul? He is a barbarian! Isn't Paul the man from Jerusalem? Paul is saying evil words to you against our gods. I want to throw him out of our house [and] into the desert!"

Now there are crowds around Philemon. His brother and sister say to them that Philemon does not believe in their gods and speaks against Caesar. The crowds throw stones toward Philemon.

What does Philemon do? The disciple of Christ looks into heaven and says, "Our Father, who is in heaven/the heavens. . . . yours is the kingdom and the power and the glory! Amen!"

Story B

(Adapted from John 6:22–42)

Jesus who is in the boat teaches the crowds around the sea concerning the bread from heaven.

Jesus says to them, ". . . for the bread of God is from heaven and is a gift to the world from God."

The crowds say to him, "Give us the bread of God!"

Jesus says to them, "I am the bread of life. The saints/holy ones eat the bread of life because they believe in me."

The crowds speak about him, "Isn't he the son of Joseph? We know his father and mother! Why does he say to us that he is bread from God?"

The crowds do not see God because they do not believe in Jesus the bread from God.

LESSON 8

PAUL BAPTIZES PHILEMON

Story A

John speaks concerning houses.

John, "I see beautiful houses in Jerusalem, but this house of mine is not beautiful, but ugly/bad and small! Therefore, I want to have those houses in Jerusalem! For there is good bread in those houses. But I don't have good bread in this house of mine."

Then, John runs toward those houses in Jerusalem. But the people in those houses see John and speak about this person John.

The people, "Who is that person? Isn't he the person from that desert? We hear that that man wants to have these houses of ours! That man wants to eat this good bread of ours!"

John sees those people in those houses, but those people do not want to see John. Therefore, the people talk to him.

The people, "What do you want? You see that we have these houses. Do you therefore want to have them?"

John, "Yes! I see that you have beautiful houses, but I don't have [them]. So I want to have those beautiful houses and that good bread."

The people, "We don't want to hear these words of yours and this voice of yours! We want to throw you into that desert! Don't you have a house in that desert? These houses are ours! Because of this, we want to send you away from these houses."

The people throw stones toward John and send him away from their houses. And after these things, John runs into his house and hears a voice from heaven.

The voice, "Oh, John! Why do you want to have those houses? Don't you know that this house of yours is good? You don't have that good bread, but you have this bread from heaven and this kingdom in heaven."

Story B

Philemon is a disciple of Christ, because he believes in God. Therefore, Paul is baptizing him in the sea in Colossae.

And the saints/holy ones in Colossae are around Philemon and they are listening to his words.

Philemon, "I myself am a Greek man. Therefore, I have in that house of mine gods of stone, but now I know that those [gods] are not gods but works of man/humanity. Therefore, I want to stay with you [pl.] in this church in Colossae. Through the love of this Paul I have this life. Therefore, Paul himself is baptizing me, for I myself am his son, and you yourselves are my brothers [and sisters]!"

LESSON 9

GOD SENDS HIS SERVANTS

Story A

(Based on the story of Philip and the eunuch in Acts 8:26–40)

Philip is walking on the road to Jerusalem. And an angel of the Lord sees him and says, "The Lord wants you to go on the road that is from Jerusalem and toward Gaza, this road is a desert."

So Philip rises and walks and sees a person. The person is going from Jerusalem to the land of the Ethiopians. And God says to Philip, "I want you to go to this man and speak with him."

And Philip hears this man. What is this man saying? He is saying the words of the prophet Isaiah. Philip says to this man, "Do you know what you are saying?" The man answers and says, "I'm not able to know because I don't have a teacher."

Therefore, Philip begins to speak about the prophet and Christ and sin and life. And the man now knows that he is a sinner, for Philip is teaching him. Therefore, the man says, "Glory to your God! I want to become a disciple of Christ!" Philip answers and says, "I see a lake. So, I can baptize you in that lake."

And so the man and Philip come to the lake and the man is baptized by Philip. And the man rises out of the lake and becomes a disciple of Christ, but he does not hear [Philip], nor does he see Philip, for God takes Philip and sends him to Azotus.

Story B

(Adapted from Exodus 3–4)

God says to Moses, "I am the God of your father, the God of Abraham and the God of Isaac and the God of Jacob." But Moses does not want to see the face of God. And God says to him, "I see the evil [thing/deed] of Pharaoh against my people in Egypt and their voices are heard by me. Therefore, I want to save them, for I know that they are slaves of Pharaoh. Therefore, I am sending you to Pharaoh, for I want you to say to him that your God is able to destroy his kingdom."

But does Moses listen? And Moses

answers God, "Lord, who am I? I am not able to speak to Pharaoh, because my voice is bad." And God answers him, "I hear you, therefore I want to send another person." Who is sent by God? Aaron the brother of Moses is sent by God with Moses.

And they enter into the land of Egypt. And the brothers see Pharaoh and come to him. And Aaron begins to speak concerning God and the people of God. But does Pharaoh listen to his words?

LESSON 10

ONESIMUS GOES TO ANOTHER LAND

Story A (Concerning Moses and Aaron)

And after these things, Moses and Aaron go in to Pharaoh and say to him, "Thus says the Lord the God of Israel, 'I want to save my people. Therefore, you should send them away from your kingdom and into the desert.'" And Pharaoh says, "Who is your God that I should listen to his voice? I don't know the lord, and I am not sending Israel." And they say to him, "According to the word of God, we must depart into the desert." And Pharaoh says to them, "Why, Moses and Aaron, do you want to take the people from the work(s)? They are bad slaves because they don't want to do the work(s)! Because of this,

I ought to go down and gather them and kill the bad slaves!"

But Moses and Aaron say to him, "God is about to send his angels against your kingdom." And Pharaoh answers them, "Do you see the beautiful temple by the sea/lake? It is a gift from my slaves. For I am able to have these good gifts because I have slaves. Therefore, I cannot send the people into the desert."

After these things, messengers of God are being sent for the sake of his son Israel against Pharaoh and [against] his kingdom. Therefore, Pharaoh comes to Moses and Aaron and says, "Why are these bad [things] happening in my kingdom?" Moses answers, "I was saying to you yesterday that God wants to save his people, but you were not listening to us. But now you should listen, for you cannot rule the people of God." But Pharaoh does not listen to them and says, "You are about to die by my authority, you and your people! For I have authority to judge and to kill!"

After these things, Moses and Aaron depart away from the face of Pharaoh. And God sends the angel of death to Pharaoh and his house. Then, the son of Pharaoh dies.

Therefore, Pharaoh now wants to send the people of God into the desert. And Pharaoh says to Moses, "Why do you remain in my kingdom? You should go out of the land of Egypt." Moses responds, "You were saying that you have authority to judge and to kill, but now you know that the God of our people

has this authority." After these things, Moses and Aaron gather the people of God and depart into the desert with them.

After these things, Moses is beside the land of Canaan with the people and he gathers them around him and speaks to them about the evil days in Egypt.

Moses, "We were dying under the authority of Pharaoh, but God was wanting to save us. Now you are about to enter into the land of Canaan, but I am about to die. Therefore, you should listen to my voice and the words of God! You should believe in God and in Joshua, for Joshua is about to lead you into the land of Canaan."

But do the people listen to the words of God and of Joshua?

Story B (Concerning Philemon and Onesimus)

Philemon was once a bad master of slaves, because he would gather the slaves and would speak bad words to them. And Philemon had in those days a brother and sister, but now they want to kill him. But they are dying because they have sin in their hearts. But Philemon has life and other brothers and sisters in the church in Colossae. Philemon was a bad master before, but now he is a slave of Christ.

And today the brothers [and sisters] are gathered in the church, because they want to hear Philemon. What does he say to them? He speaks about his first life in his house. Philemon says, "In my first life I had gods of stone and I would go up to the temples of my gods. But now I do not go up to those temples, but I come to this church. And I once had a brother and a sister. But they want to lead me to the other assembly in Colossae, for they want to judge and kill me, because I am a disciple of Christ. What should I say to them? What can I say?"

The saints of the church answer, "You yourself cannot save your soul, but God can. You ought therefore to believe him and remain in this church." But Philemon responds, "I was an evil master in my house. I ought therefore to go to my house and speak with the brothers and the slaves about my life, for I want them to receive the love of God." Philemon therefore does not remain in the church, for he has work[s] in his house. Therefore, he departs from the church to his house.

And on the same day, Onesimus is in the house, but he does not see nor does he hear his master. Therefore, he wants to go on the road from the house of the evil master to another land. But in the same hour, Philemon enters the house. So Onesimus finds a not-small [i.e., big] stone and remains behind it. Therefore, Philemon is not able to find him. Therefore, other slaves are being sent by Philemon to find Onesimus. But Onesimus takes bread and departs out of the house.

The slaves of Philemon say, "We can't find him in the house, nor on the road around the house, nor beside the lake behind the house. What then should we do?"

After these things, Onesimus goes through deserts and comes to another land. And Onesimus says, "I was a slave, but now I am not a slave, because I do not have a master!" Then, Onesimus begins to eat the bread of his master and he does not see the crowd around him. And the crowd begins to speak about him.

The crowd says, "Who is this person? This [person] was not in our land before. Therefore, we know that he comes from another land. We ought to take him up and lead him to the assembly. For the assembly has authority to judge and to kill!" The crowd takes up the bread and leads Onesimus into the assembly. Onesimus was about to eat, but now he is not able to eat because the bread is being taken up from him. What is about to happen? Is Onesimus about to be killed?

LESSON 11

AFTER THE DEATH OF MOSES

(This story is about the people of Israel)

After the death of Moses, the people of Israel were beside the land Canaan, for they were not yet in Canaan, but they were about to enter into that place. And Joshua the servant of God was speaking to them,

"Behold! Truly, truly I say to you that Moses was speaking the words from God to the people, but they were not listening to him. For the words and the works of Moses were not being received. And we are the children of those [people]. And our fathers were seeing/saw the works of God both in Egypt and in the desert, but they were still not believing in Moses, nor in God, not even in me. But you were not able to believe, because you were little. But now you are not little. And you are about to see and have the holy land. Therefore, I do not want you to depart from the love of God. But I want you to remain in/on the righteous way/path. For you know that Moses was with us in Egypt and in the desert, but now he is not [with us]. Because of this, I am saying to you that you ought to believe in me, for God was speaking also with me.

God was saying to me, 'Oh, Joshua! Behold! You were going/walking in the desert with Moses and I was going with you. But now Moses is not going with you. But I am still with you. Therefore, I want you to receive the words in the book of the law. And I do not want the book of this law to depart from the hearts of my people.'

Thus God was saying with me. Behold! From this place we can see the land Canaan! Do you see it? That land is beautiful! God is beginning to lead us to the good land."

The people were hearing the word of Joshua, but the eyes of their hearts were looking again toward the evil path/way. For they were about to receive this land,

but their hearts still wanted other gifts. Therefore, even the children of those first people were wicked, because they were receiving gifts of God, but not [receiving] God himself.

LESSON 12

ONESIMUS HEARS PAUL IN PRISON

Story A (Jesus heals a child)

Jesus was with the disciples in a small boat on the sea. Therefore, crowds were coming to the sea and were listening to Jesus from this place, because there was not a place for them in the boat.

Then, a certain person from the crowd says, "Lord! Can you hear me? I have a child and the child has a demon. Because of this I am speaking to you, for I know that you have authority to heal and to save. If you are willing/if you want, I can lead you to her. And if you will heal her, then I will believe you and your disciples."

Jesus hears the voice of this person, but he remains in the boat. And he says thus, "If I go with you and heal the child, will you marvel/wonder? Will you glorify God? Will you have peace? I see your heart; If you see, you will believe. It is not time to see but to believe."

So, the person departs and brings the child to Jesus. The person says, "Teacher! This is the child!" After this, the person throws the child into the sea! And the child is about to die, for she cannot go up from the sea. So Jesus walks/goes on the sea and raises it [the child] out of the sea. And the disciples and the crowds marvel. And Jesus says to the demon in the child, "You will not have a home, neither in the child nor in the sea, for I am sending you into the wilderness."

Then, the demon says, "Lord! I will go into the wilderness."

But the father of the child says, "Now I believe you, teacher!" And Jesus responds, "Not for your sake/on behalf of you do I heal the child, but for the sake of the glory of God."

But the crowds were not accepting this good thing, because it was the sabbath. For they were teachers of the law, but they did not have the law in their hearts.

Story B (Onesimus hears Paul)

"Who are you? If you have something to say, we will listen! If you are a slave, we will bring you to prison because your master is not with you."

The crowds in this assembly marvel/are amazed that Onesimus was thus able to depart from Colossae and come to Philippi. But Onesimus does not answer the assembly, because he does not want to say the truth. He says to himself,

"I was a slave in the house of my master, but now I am not. But if I say the truth, I will become a slave again of that bad master. For the master will come and take me. Then, I will have work in his house. What then should I say to these people? The truth? For they want to bring me to prison. Then will I be able to save my life? I won't be able."

The assembly says, "Why don't you answer? Because you're not answering, we know the truth. You are a bad slave! For we know that you are from Colossae."

Onesimus answers, "I am not a slave, for I don't have a master! Do you see my master? You don't see [him]."

Someone from the crowd responds, "You were a slave and you are a slave and you will be a slave! Oh, Philippians! Why are we still talking to this bad slave? We should lead him into prison with the others! For you know that those other people were preaching about their god. And now there is still a place [still room] in the prison [for Onesimus]."

Then the crowd opens the prison and throws him in it. Onesimus now says, "I should not have departed from my master. I was a slave, but I had bread to eat. But what will I eat now in this place? Who will bring bread for my sake? Will my master come? If he does not come, will I become a slave of another master? Then, my days will be evil/bad. Therefore, I will pray to my gods, for they will save me."

Onesimus hears the voices of people, but he can't see their faces, for it was not day. The people are speaking about truth and love, peace and life. Onesimus recognizes the voice of this person! Onesimus therefore says, "Who are you? [pl.]"

The person responds, "I am Paul and this is Silas. But who are you? Why are you in prison?"

Onesimus can't see the face [of Paul], but he knows the voice! Therefore, he responds and says, "I know you! I was hearing you in the house of my master in Colossae. Weren't you speaking with Philemon in Colossae? I am Onesimus, his slave."

Paul responds, "Hello, Onesimus! Philemon is my brother, for we have the same father in heaven."

Onesimus responds, "Your brother? You have the same father? What are you saying?"

Then, Paul and Silas begin to teach Onesimus about their father.

LESSON 13

THE LAST PROPHET

Do you believe in God? Do you know that God is love? I know, for I have his holy words in the holy book.

The book says, "God sent his only son to save both the wicked and the righteous. For he was wanting to save the whole world. Therefore, God sent his prophets to preach the truth to the world."

Then, the prophets were preaching in those days, but the wicked people of the world were not receiving them. For the prophets were saying, "The Lord will come again! He will send his last prophet! Therefore, he wants you to turn/return to him! Therefore, he sent us to teach about his righteousness. Therefore, it is necessary to prepare your hearts, for he is beginning to prepare his kingdom for your sake/on your behalf.

So, the prophets were [trying to persuade] persuading the people, but did the people of the world listen to them? They did not listen. Therefore, God sent his last prophet, his own son.

Then, God sent his son to release the people from sin and from demons. After this, his son was going through the earth to find good disciples. And Peter was going on the road when he heard Jesus. And Jesus comes to him and says, "It is necessary for you to come with me."

And Peter responds, "Do you have a house?"

And Jesus says, "I don't have a house, because the Son of Man does not have a place for his head. So I do not have a house, but I do have a throne in heaven. If you come with me, I will open your eyes to see these [things]."

So Jesus thus persuaded Peter. And Peter responds, "Are we going up there to your throne? Do you have your own throne? Did you prepare that for me?"

And Jesus says, "It is already time to see these [things]. Therefore, if you go with me, I will teach you about righteousness and about the kingdom of God. Then you will have this throne in heaven after your death."

LESSON 14

SIGNS OF DEATH

Story A (Again concerning Moses and Aaron)

God said to Moses, "I am the God of your father, the God of Abraham and the God of Isaac and the God of Jacob." But Moses was not wanting to see the face of God. And God said to him, "I see the evil of Pharaoh against my people in Egypt and their voices are rising up into heaven. Therefore, I want to save them. For I know that they are slaves of Pharaoh. Now, you will be my messenger, for I am sending you to Pharaoh. For it is necessary for you to say to him that your God is able to destroy his kingdom."

And Moses said to God, "Lord, who am I? I cannot go and speak to Pharaoh, because my voice is bad." And God said to him, "I hear you, therefore I will send your brother, Aaron. And this [one] will be my messenger." And they went into the land of Egypt. And the brothers saw Pharaoh and came to him. And Aaron began to speak about God and about the people of God. And Pharaoh was not listening to him.

And after these things, Moses and Aaron went in again to Pharaoh and said to him, "Thus says the Lord, the God of Israel, 'I want to save my people. Therefore, you ought to send them from your kingdom and into the desert.'" And Pharaoh said, "Who is your god that I should listen to his voice? I don't know the lord, and I will not send Israel." And they said to him, "According to the word of God, it is necessary for us to go into the desert to offer gifts to God." And Pharaoh said to them, "Why, Moses and Aaron, do you want to take my people from the work? Don't they already have bread to eat? Don't they have wine to drink? What will they have in the desert? But the slaves still want to flee? The slaves will not flee, nor will they drink wine, nor will they eat bread! But you will see bad days in my kingdom!" But Moses and Aaron said to him, "If you will not send us into the desert, you will see signs from heaven. And these signs will destroy your kingdom! Do you want to die? Our God has authority to judge and to kill!" And Moses and Aaron were persuading [trying to persuade] Pharaoh, but he did not listen to them, nor did he send the people into the desert. Therefore, God opened the heavens and signs of death came upon the earth. Then, the signs fell upon the Egyptians and upon the son of Pharaoh. Therefore, the son of Pharaoh died.

Then, Pharaoh came to Moses and Aaron and said, "Why did these bad [things] happen in my kingdom? Look! I brought my son to you! Now he is dead! If I send you there into the desert, will your God be able to raise my son? Will I see him again? Moses said to him, "If you pray to him, God can save your son." After these things, Moses and Aaron gathered the people of God and led the people into the desert.

And after these things, Moses was by the land of Canaan with the people and he gathered them around him and spoke to them about the evil days in Egypt. Moses said, "We were dying under the authority of Pharaoh, but God saved us. Now, you are about to enter into the land of Canaan, but I am about to die. Therefore, it is necessary for you to listen to my voice and the words of God. You ought to believe in God and in Joshua. For Joshua is about to lead you into the land of Canaan."

Story B (Onesimus with Paul in prison)

Paul and Silas and Onesimus were in the prison in Philippi. Paul and Silas were teaching Onesimus about the righteousness of God and about Christ, but he was still not believing them, because they did not persuade him. Therefore, he did not become a disciple of Christ.

But God was wanting to release them from prison. Therefore, a sign occurred/happened from heaven. What was the sign? A not-small [i.e., a large]

earthquake occurred in that very hour and God opened the prison. Then, Onesimus fled from the prison because he was not wanting to stay in the prison and become a slave again of another master. But Paul and Silas did not flee.

Then, the jailer entered and did not see the people. Therefore, he was about to kill himself. But Paul cried, "We are still in the prison! It is not necessary for you to die!"

And the jailer marveled and said to Paul and to Silas, "What must I do? Can your God save me?" Paul and Silas said, "If you believe in the Lord Jesus, he will save you and your house."

Then, the jailer and his house believed in the Lord Jesus. And Paul baptized them, and the jailer led Paul and Silas to his own house.

And in his house, he prepared bread to eat and wine to drink. Then, they were eating bread and drinking wine, and they were talking about God and truth and life. And their voices were going up into heaven.

After these things, the jailer brought Paul and Silas to prison. And the people of Philippi came to release them. Therefore, Paul and Silas left and returned to the church in Lydia's house.

Onesimus was not with them, but he was walking/traveling on the road to find bread to eat, but he did not find [it]. Therefore, he was about to die, because he did not have even a good garment/cloak.

Then, he heard voices of people.

Therefore, he approached the voices in the house and again found Paul and Silas. And Onesimus marveled that Paul and the people with him were eating bread and drinking wine. And Paul was saying, "Now, we drink this wine and eat this bread, but the Lord will come and then we will have wine to drink from heaven and bread to eat with the Lord and his saints/holy ones in the kingdom!" Then, Paul started to preach that it was necessary for Jesus to die on their behalf.

And the saints were presenting gifts to Paul, but he did not accept them. But he turned toward Onesimus and said, "Oh, Onesimus! Why do you remain there? We have a place for you in this house. Do you see these gifts? I did not accept the gifts because the gifts are yours!"

And another person said, "Yes, Onesimus. Paul was speaking about you. You don't have a garment? Look. Even this garment is yours. We offer these [things] on your behalf."

And Onesimus marveled, and in that very hour God opened the eyes of his heart. Then, Onesimus believed and became a disciple of Christ. But he became a disciple not on account of the gifts, but on account of the love of the saints/holy ones.

After this, Paul baptized him in a lake and the saints/holy ones glorified God. And Paul said to Onesimus, "Before, you were a slave of Philemon, but now you are a slave of Christ. Before, you were of this world, but now you are of the Way."

LESSON 15

AT THE MARKET

Story A (Onesimus preaches in the market)

After these things, Onesimus was going through the market. What is the market? The market is a place where people sell bread and wine and garments and other [things]. Onesimus was often going/would often go to another market in Colossae. Then, he was taking/would take bread from other people, but now Onesimus is a different person, because he has become a disciple of Christ. Therefore, he does not want to go into the market to find bread, but he wants to preach to the crowds in the market about Christ.

But Lydia had said to Onesimus, "It is not good to enter the market, because bad people are there. Therefore, I want you to remain in my house." But has Onesimus listened to Lydia? He has not listened. Therefore, is he a bad disciple?

So Onesimus was going through the market and saw good bread and beautiful garments, but he said to himself, "You have not come because of bread, but because of the souls of people! Yes, Lydia said that I should not go into the market, but she doesn't know why I have come."

So Onesimus began to preach, "The kingdom of God has drawn near/is at hand! If you do not want to die because of your sins, it is necessary for you to turn to God!"

But a person from the crowd said, "Who are you? Why have you said these [things]? Do you preach another god? We already have gods! We don't need to accept another god. Have you seen the temple of our gods? It is beautiful!"

And another person said, "I know you! Didn't we see you in the assembly? Yes! We saw [you]! We threw you into prison, but have you fled out of prison?"

And the crowd began to approach him. Therefore, Onesimus was not able to flee. And another person said again, "This man has fled from prison! And he has spoken against our gods, because he preaches other gods! Therefore, he has destroyed our peace!"

But Onesimus said, "I have believed in the Lord and have become a disciple. Therefore, I have come to know that God is able to save me even from you. Therefore, you cannot kill me."

Therefore, the crowd threw stones toward him and Onesimus fell to the ground. What will happen to Onesimus? Will Onesimus be able to flee?

Story B (Lydia finds Onesimus)

It became night, but Onesimus had not yet come home. Therefore, Lydia began to believe that something bad happened to Onesimus. And Lydia said to herself, "What has happened? It is already night but Onesimus has not yet come." Then, Lydia picked up her garment and went out, because she wanted to find Onesimus.

Therefore, Lydia was going through the roads of Philippi, but she was not able to find Onesimus. She saw the market. But was Onesimus there? For Lydia had said to Onesimus, "You should not go to the market!" But had he still gone there?

Lydia cried out, "Onesimus! Onesimus!" Then, she saw people and said to them, "Have you seen Onesimus?" And they responded, "We have not seen [him], nor have we heard about him." Therefore, Lydia prayed to God, "Oh God! You must lead me to Onesimus, for I cannot find him."

And Lydia opened the eyes [her eyes] and saw another person on the road. Then, she approached this other person and said, "And you, have you seen him?" And the person responded, "Yes! Yesterday the crowds threw him out of the market. I will lead you to him."

So, this person led Lydia out of the market and to another person beside the road. And Lydia approached this person and saw the face of Onesimus. Therefore, Lydia cried out, "Onesimus! Why do you remain on the road? What happened? Why don't you open your eyes? Have you died?" But Onesimus did not respond, nor did he open [his] eyes. Therefore, Lydia picked him up and carried [him] home. But the person was not with them, for he had left.

After these things, Onesimus and Lydia were in her house. And Onesimus did not die, for Lydia healed him. Then, Onesimus opened [his] eyes and said, "Who are you? Have I died? Am I dead? Have I been raised from death? Are you an angel?"

LESSON 16

ONESIMUS WAS SAVED BY LYDIA

After these things, Onesimus and Lydia were in her house. And Onesimus did not die, for Lydia was healing him. Then, Onesimus opened [his] eyes and said, "Who are you? Have I died? Am I dead? Have I been raised from death? Are you an angel?"

And Lydia answered him, "I am not an angel, oh child, and you have not died, because your hour has not come. I am Lydia, and I found you beside the road. For you were about to die, but a certain person led me to you and I brought you home. But what happened, oh Onesimus? Didn't I say to you that you should not go into the market?"

Onesimus did not answer. Therefore, Lydia said, "Now you must stay in my house and eat this bread." But Onesimus answered, "But who was that person? How was he able to find me?"

Lydia answered, "I believe that he was an angel of God. For I prayed to God and I was heard by him, because I was going on the road when that person appeared to me and I was brought by him to you. Therefore, that person was sent by God! Therefore, I know that the God of heaven hears us!"

But Onesimus answered, "But how do you know that he was an angel?"

And Lydia said, "I already said to you that that person was sent by God. And after this, I turned to speak to him, but I could not see him, for he was taken again into heaven."

After these things, Lydia departed and another person came, his name is Epaphroditus. And Epaphroditus said, "Hello, who are you?"

And Onesimus answered, "Hello, I am Onesimus. And you, who are you?"

Epaphroditus said, "My name is Epaphroditus, and I am a disciple of Christ. I often come to the church in Lydia's house."

And Onesimus said, "I also am a disciple, because I was taught the truth and was baptized by Paul. I became a slave of Christ and of God, but before I was a slave of another person." And Epaphroditus said, "I want to hear. How did you become a disciple of Christ? How were you a slave of another person before? And how were you led to Philippi?"

Then, Onesimus began to speak about his life . . .

LESSON 17

PAUL IN THE SYNAGOGUE

At the same time/hour, Paul was in the synagogue in Philippi, and he was preaching to both the men and the women through the holy spirit. And he was preaching thus,

"Oh, men of Philippi/Philippians! Behold! According to the law and the prophets it was necessary for the Christ to die and be raised on behalf of your sins. For you are dead in your sins, because you are being led by the ruler of this evil age, and you are still under the law of sin and death. *But if you are led by the spirit, you are not under the law,* but you have life in Christ. For *if Christ is in you, the body is dead because of sin, but the spirit is life because of righteousness.*"

The men and the women answered, "What are you saying, oh Paul? We can't receive these words. For how can a person die, and then be raised?"

And Paul answered, "You don't accept my words because you are still in the flesh. But if you pray to God, he can save you. For until the Lord returns, God wants to turn the hearts of men and women to Christ."

The people drew near to him, for they wanted to throw him out. But Paul cried out, "On the last day, the dead will be raised!"

Therefore, the people did not seize/take him, for they started to speak about this word/matter. For Pharisees and Sadducees were there, and Pharisees believe that people will be raised on the last day, but Sadducees do not believe this.

And Paul fled and departed to another place, because he was sent by God as far as the end of the earth.

LESSON 18

PHILEMON AND APPHIA

Philemon was still in Colossae, because he wanted to find his slave. Therefore, he was going through the streets of Colossae. But not being able to find Onesimus [because he couldn't find Onesimus], he returned home. And the wife of Philemon, her name is Apphia, seeing her husband returning home, came to him and said. "Hello, my husband! How are you?"

And Philemon responded, saying, "Hello, my wife. I am not well, not being able to find our slave [because I was not able to find our slave]. What happened to him? Did he flee to another house? Has he died?"

And Apphia responded, saying, "But that Onesimus was a bad slave, because he took our possessions!"

And Philemon said, "What did he take?" And Apphia responded, "He took bread! And you know that the slaves are ours, because we are their masters. Therefore, the whole body of Onesimus is ours, both the head and the mouth and the flesh!"

But Philemon answered, saying, "But because I have a master in heaven, Jesus Christ, I have become a different person. For I was led by Paul to the truth."

And Apphia said, "I want to hear about this. So we should sit." Therefore, Apphia prepared bread and wine, and she led Philemon into the house. While eating and drinking, the wife and the husband began to speak about Paul.

And Philemon said, "Paul was going through the streets of Colossae preaching peace and life. And while going on the road beside our house, he saw me speaking evil against my slave. Therefore, Paul came and preached to me the good news about this Jesus. And I wanted to believe in Christ, but I could not, being a sinner [because I was a sinner]. Therefore, I said to Paul, 'Oh Paul! How can your God save me, being a sinner [while I am a sinner/because I am a sinner]? For I have sinned against my slaves and against [my] wife.' And Paul answered me, saying, 'God can save even you, having authority over life and death [because he has authority over life and death]. Even I was a sinner, because I was persecuting the ones who believe in Christ as far as the end of the earth. But God, having love for sinners, saved even me. For God did not count/consider my sins.'"

But Apphia answered, "And do you now consider Christ your Lord?"

And Philemon said, "Yes! Now I have peace, being a child of God [because I am a child of God]. Do you also want to believe in Christ?"

And Apphia answered, "I am not yet able to believe in Christ, being a Greek woman. But you should not listen to the words of a person going through the streets preaching other gods. For we already have our own gods. Therefore, it is not necessary to receive other gods."

And Philemon said, "I cannot accept our evil gods, because they are not gods, but demons! [not being gods, but demons] But if you believe in Christ, you too will have peace forever. For God is working day and night to gather those who believe in him into the kingdom."

LESSON 19

SYNTYCHE AND EUODIA

Having healed Onesimus, Lydia departed to Euodia's house, for she wanted to talk to her about these things that happened to Onesimus. Who is Euodia? She is a sister of Lydia in Christ.

Having arrived at the house, she found Euodia speaking with Syntyche. Who is Syntyche? Syntyche is also a sister. Then, after greeting them, Lydia entered and sat beside them. What were the sisters saying? Euodia was telling a story about Jesus and Syntyche was listening. And she was speaking thus,

"After Jesus arrived at the house of a woman (her name is Martha), he greeted both her and her mother and father and the whole house. And after they greeted Jesus, they received him into the house. And Martha had a sister (her name is Mary), and Mary sat by the feet of Jesus, and was listening to his word. But Martha was preparing bread and wine and other [things] for the ones in the house.

Therefore, Martha came to Jesus and said to him [having come to Jesus, said to him], 'Lord! My sister is not working! And the one who does not work will not eat bread nor will she drink wine!' But Mary answered, 'But I want to eat and drink!' And Jesus turned to Martha and took her hands and said [And Jesus, having turned and taken her hands, said], 'Martha, Martha. Your sister received something good, by listening to my word. And this will not be taken away from her.'"

And Syntyche said, "I have come to know what the Lord was saying. You are Martha and I am Mary! You often work to prepare bread and wine and other [things] for the ones who have arrived at this house, but I often listen to the words of Paul while sitting. Therefore, I have received something good."

But Euodia answered saying, "I am not Martha! But you speak the truth, because you often come to my house and do not work, nor do you welcome the ones who have arrived. Therefore, you are a bad sister!"

But Lydia, when she heard these things [having heard these things], said to them, "You should not speak thus, because you are sisters in Christ." But the sisters did not listen to Lydia, but having taken up her garment, Syntyche departed to her own home [Syntyche took up her garment and departed to her own home].

LESSON 20

THE THINGS THAT HAPPENED TO ONESIMUS

Story A (Onesimus's first life)

While Lydia was speaking with Euodia, Onesimus was speaking with Epaphroditus about his life in another land. And he was speaking thus,

"You know that I do not have children nor a wife nor a house, but I had these things in another land. For I had a wife, her name was Rhoda, and we had a beautiful house beside the sea, and we had a good son, his name was Titus.

And in those days we often went on the sea in our small boat. Therefore, because we had peace in our hearts, we did not know what was going to/about to happen.

After these things, a bad thing happened to us. For the ruler of another land, because he wanted to seize/

take up even our land, sent evil people upon us. But while I was working in a boat on the sea—for I was the one who created boats for our people—those wicked people came and destroyed our kingdom. But because I was out at sea, I did not know what was happening. But when I heard my wife crying out from the house, I threw my body into the sea and went to the house. And when I arrived at the house, I opened the door and went in. But when I found my son and wife already dead, I fell upon my face and cried out, 'Why has this evil happened? oh, my gods! Were you not able to save them? Therefore, I will not believe in you, who were not able to save [my] wife and son!'

And taking the hands of my wife, I cried out again, 'Oh, my wife! Has your soul already departed? My soul too will depart to you.'

But because the evil people were still in the house, they heard me speaking and pursued me. Therefore, I departed out of the house, but I couldn't flee, for when the evil people found me, I was taken and brought to another land. Therefore, having been carried away from my land, I became a slave of an evil master called Philemon."

Story B (The things that have happened up to now)

Evil and good [things] have happened in our story about Philemon and Onesi-mus. Do you want to hear again about these people? You need to hear the whole story.

First, Philemon was an evil master of his slaves. But after hearing about the grace of God, he became another person, for he believed in Christ. And after this, Philemon wanted to preach the good news to those in his house, but both his brother and sister did not receive his words about the gospel. But while Philemon was preaching, his slave, his name was Onesimus, fled from the house and to another land. And Philemon, when he returned home, could not find Onesimus, for he had already left.

Was Onesimus then saved from evil? Did he find peace in another place? He did not find peace nor was he saved from evil, but he was found by an evil crowd. And when these people approached, they saw that Onesimus was a slave and threw him into prison.

After these things, while Onesimus was sitting in prison, he heard Paul speaking about righteousness and grace and the kingdom of heaven. And because God wanted to save them, a sign occurred in that hour; the doors were opened and Onesimus found a way out of the prison. Onesimus therefore went out from the prison, but Paul remained there with Silas.

After these things, while going through the roads of Philippi, Onesimus saw Paul again in the church [that is] in the house of Lydia. What did Onesimus see? He saw them drinking wine and eating bread. And the saints of this church received him and persuaded [him] to believe in Christ.

But evil happened again to Onesimus, because while he was going through the market, evil people arrived and threw stones at him. Therefore, Onesimus fell to the earth and drew near to death. But Lydia, being a faithful woman of the Lord, prayed to God and was led by God to Onesimus and brought him home. And Onesimus opened his eyes and saw Lydia healing him.

What will happen to Onesimus after these things? I will let you know!

LESSON 21

PHILEMON ENCOURAGES APPHIA

Philemon and his wife Apphia were walking on the road [that is] toward the house of Archippus. And they were going to this house, because the church was often gathered there. Philemon was already following Christ, for after he believed the gospel he was baptized by Paul the apostle, but Apphia did not yet believe, for while fearing her gods [because she feared her gods] she was not able to accept another god.

But Philemon, wanting to persuade her, said: "My wife! Look! The God of heaven who made all things is seeking you! For you know that I was called by him into this salvation and now I walk

in the truth. For you see that now I do not speak evil against our slaves nor do I live for myself but [I live] for my entire household. And God is calling you [God is calling even you]!"

But Apphia answered saying, "Yes! And all these things are good! But I also see that now you do not go up with me to the temple of our gods nor do you pray to them. And you threw out of our house our gods made from stone. Don't you fear our gods who see all things?"

And Philemon answered, "Every god made by the hands of people is not a god but an evil work! My God who has authority over all the earth is now calling all people, because he loves both the wicked and the faithful."

But Apphia answered and said, "But how is your God able to do these things? You said that God having been born of a woman lived on the earth until death. And having been crucified, he was raised from the dead? How can I believe all these things?"

But Philemon was comforting her saying, "We have come to the church. There you will hear all [things] from the saints about these things."

LESSON 22

LISTENING TO YOUR FATHER

Story A (A bad child and a good father)

A certain person had a bad child. Why was the child bad? The child was bad because he often would not listen to [his] father.

It happened that they were walking beside a not-small sea/lake. The child was throwing rocks into the water, and the father was preparing bread to eat. Therefore, the father was good [i.e., a good father], because he loved the child. Because of this, he spoke to the child, saying, "You should not go down by the water! If you do not listen to my word, you will fall into the water!"

Did the child listen? The child listens to himself, but he does not listen to the voice of [his] father. Then, having come to the water, he fell into it and was not able to come up out of the water. But the father, when he saw the child going down into the sea, threw himself into the water. But was the father able to save him? What do you think?

The child cried, "Father! I'm afraid! I'm going down into the sea!" The father came to the child [and] wanted to lift him, but he could not, because the child was not small. Because of this, both the bad child and the good father died in the water. Therefore, every child ought to listen to his father!

Story B (Moses declares the commandments)

The people of Israel saw Moses their leader coming out of a mountain of fire [fiery mountain].

Moses was carrying in his hands two stones that had the commandments of God. And having approached the people he said, "I declare to you all the commandments of our God! Each of you ought to keep every commandment.

And the people answered, "What is the commandment of God?"

And Moses said, "You will love the Lord your God from/with your whole heart and your whole soul . . . and you will love your neighbor as yourself. If you love each other and worship God, the Lord will send bread from heaven to each of you. But if you do not walk in the light and do not keep all the commandments and you worship other gods, fire will fall from heaven on every house of yours [on all your houses]. Then, you all will die in this land and you will not go into the land of Canaan."

LESSON 23

WILL ONESIMUS RETURN TO PHILEMON?

Onesimus and Epaphroditus were speaking with one another in Lydia's house about all the things that happened. When Epaphroditus heard about Philemon the evil master, he marveled at the grace of God. And he said, "What will you do? You must return to your master in Colossae."

But Onesimus answered, "I will never return to that [person]! Having been saved from death, shall I return again to the village of Philemon, so I might be crucified? I am no longer that person's slave."

But Epaphroditus said, "But you fled from him, and the law says that if a slave flees from his master, the master can seek and kill his own slave. Therefore, if Philemon seeks and finds you, what will happen to you?"

Onesimus said, "What do you think? I fear my master Philemon. So let's not talk about him. Let's talk instead about your children. How are they?"

While Onesimus was speaking, Lydia entered the house and greeted the brothers. And she said, "It's already night! It's time to eat! Let's eat and drink!" Then, sitting down, they began to eat. But because she didn't have bread, Lydia asked Onesimus to go to the market to buy bread.

So Onesimus left to the market so that they might have bread to eat.

But there were many people in the market. Therefore, when Onesimus arrived, he was not able to find bread, for others already bought all the bread. So Onesimus said, "I came so I might buy bread, but whenever I come I can't find bread, because there's a crowd."

While Onesimus was speaking, another crowd was forming. And this crowd was gathered in order to hear the words of Paul! Both Paul and Onesimus were in the same market! Therefore, Onesimus sat in order that he might listen.

After these things, Onesimus returned to Lydia and Epaphroditus. But because Onesimus did not have bread,

Lydia's eyes became like fire. But Onesimus answered saying, "Don't you know? The scriptures say that *a person shall not live on bread alone, but on every word that comes through the mouth of God.*"

Then, Lydia cast out Onesimus and said to Epaphroditus, "Let's not send him to the market anymore." But Onesimus departed so that he might find Paul, like a child seeking his father.

LESSON 24

THE CHILD WHO HAD WISDOM

It came to pass in those days when Caesar Augustus was the lord over all the earth, a certain child and his mother and father were traveling to Jerusalem in order that they might worship God. And after these [people] worshiped, they returned home.

But while they were returning, the child remained in Jerusalem and his parents did not know, for when the mother and father were going on the road to Nazareth, the child was not with them. And because there were great crowds on the same road, the parents did not know that [their] son was not with them.

But before the father and mother arrived home, the mother noticed that the child was no longer with them, and she said, "My beloved son! Joseph! We must return to find him!"

Therefore, the parents returned in order to find the child. But while the father and mother were looking [for him], the child was teaching in the temple, so that the people were amazed. For he was teaching not as a child but as a person having wisdom. For he was testifying concerning God in parables. What was he saying? He was speaking thus,

> "Behold, a sower went out to sow. And it happened when [he] was sowing that one fell by the road, and birds came and ate it." (Mark 4:3–4)

While the child was speaking this parable, [his] mother arrived and cried out, "Child! Why have you acted this way to us? Look, your father and I were looking for you."

But the child answered and said, "I remained in this temple because these people don't have wisdom. Therefore, it was necessary to teach them."

And [his] mother and father marveled. But the child followed [his] mother and returned home, in order that he might be a good child.

But the people in the temple said, "We only heard the beginning of the parable. It's not allowed to start to speak a parable and not finish [it]!"

Therefore, they were urging the child to return and finish the parable, but the child did not hear [them] because [he] already left.

LESSON 25

GOING DOWN INTO THE SEA

"Paul! Paul! Look, I'm Onesimus!"

Onesimus had left after talking with Lydia, in order that he might find and follow Paul. Then, having gone through the city of Thessalonica and the city of Berea, he found Paul on a boat about to depart.

And approaching the sea, he saw Silas and said to him, "Silas, where is Paul going? I want to follow." And Silas answered saying, "Oh Onesimus, you can't follow [him], for the boat is about to leave. For both Paul and Luke the brother are traveling to Athens."

Then, Onesimus again cried out, "Paul! I also want to travel with you!"

But because the men were not answering, Onesimus feared that the boat would depart. Therefore, he threw his body into the water! Why did he throw himself into the water? He threw himself in order that he might go up into the boat. For he wanted to go up into the boat, but he was not able, because he was weak. For water was filling his mouth such that he was going down into the heart of the sea.

While Onesimus was going down, his body was becoming full of water. Then, his soul drew near to death. Then, he no longer saw Paul, nor the boat, because the water around him became like night. So he was saying to himself, "It seemed good to me to throw myself into the sea, but now what shall I do?

The end of my life has drawn near. But if I die, I will still say to the Lord my God, you are my God, both now and in the future. Therefore, I will proclaim your name both in my living and in [my] dying [both when I live and when I die]."

After this, no longer seeing the boat, he closed [his] eyes and accepted what was coming.

After Onesimus had thrown himself into the sea, Paul and Luke saw him going down into the water. Therefore, they asked the men on the boat to lift Onesimus out of the water. "Men! Let's lift up this man out of the sea! If we lift him up now, he will yet live."

So because Paul had convinced the others, Onesimus was lifted up, still alive, but having become weak. "Oh Onesimus! Onesimus! I'm Paul. Do you hear my voice?"

Onesimus was not able to open his eyes, nor [his] mouth, because his body was full of water. Therefore, Paul prayed that Onesimus would be healed. And the people on the boat were observing him [to see] whether [his] prayer would be heard.

Because Onesimus still did not open [his] eyes, a certain man approached Paul and said, "I am a priest of Zeus and I testify that this one has fallen under judgment, for he remains dead."

Another priest also said, "I also am a priest of the God of the Jews, who has power to raise the dead. It seems to me that it is the will of God to throw the dead one out of the boat, for it is not lawful to keep a dead body among us."

And Paul answered and said to the priests, "How can we throw this one out, since he is my brother? No way! But let's keep him on the boat until we reach the city."

But the priests were trying to persuade the others on the boat saying, "Men! Let's not listen to this man any longer. If we do not throw out the dead one, God will enact his judgment also against us, as he has done against this dead one. Then, how will we flee from his judgment?"

And the people on the boat were from all nations. And having been persuaded by the priests, they approached Paul with evil in their hearts.

LESSON 26

GIFTS FOR POSEIDON

Having come to himself, Onesimus opened [his] eyes. Hearing the voices of people crying out, he said to himself, "Am I still alive? Have my words entered the ears of the Lord? But what are these voices?" When he opened [his] eyes, Onesimus marveled that the people on the boat were from all nations, for they were talking to each other in their own languages, so that Onesimus did not know what they were saying.

And the people around Paul and Luke, having been persuaded by the priests, approached in order to persuade them too. "Listen! We must throw out the body, so that our ship might be saved. If you don't listen, we'll throw you out, too."

But Paul and Luke answered, "Let the body remain on the boat! Don't throw out the body! Don't be so evil! But have mercy! For he is our brother."

But the people asked saying, "How is this dead person your brother? How is he here on the boat?"

Paul answered, "He is my brother because we have the same father, the God of the Jews and the God of our Lord Jesus Christ."

But the priest of the Jews who was on the boat said, "You're not telling the truth, for you're speaking about a person crucified in Jerusalem. For I heard about this Jesus in Jerusalem." But Luke answered, "Yes! But after being crucified, he was raised in power." But the priest of Zeus said, "If your God is able to raise this Jesus, he will also be able to raise you from the sea! Men! Let's first throw out these [men], then let's throw out the dead one! Let them be our gifts to Poseidon the god of the sea!" And the other priest said, "May the will of God be done. Let them pray to God that they might be saved."

While Onesimus heard and saw all these things, he wanted to speak, but he couldn't, because he was still weak. The people seized Paul by the hand and brought him and Luke to the sea. And Paul, while being carried to the sea, said, "Repent from your sin and you will live!"

And while the people were casting out the men, Onesimus cried out again, "I'm alive! Look here! I'm not dead! Don't do this! Have mercy! Don't throw these men into the sea!"

But after having already thrown out the men, they heard the voice of Onesimus and said, "You're alive? Why didn't you speak until now? We already threw out the men and we can't bring them up." And Onesimus said to himself, "I've come here to follow Paul, but after being saved from the sea, should I go again into it? What must I do?"

LESSON 27

PHILEMON SPEAKS TO HIS DAUGHTER

Story A (Onesimus lives)

One of the people approached and asked, "How are you? We lifted you out of the sea while you were dead, but now you're alive again! How did these things happen?" Someone else said, "Just as that man said, whom we threw out into the sea, his God has raised this one from the dead!" Some others said, "Should we raise up out of the sea those men whom we threw out? If God so listens to them, what judgment will he bring against us?" Another [person] said, "We can't raise the ones we threw out, for they've already died/are already dead."

But while the people were speaking to each other, Onesimus said to himself, "God called me to follow Paul. But now what will I do? Whom will I follow? Shall I remain here with the people who threw out my brothers? I will never stay here! For I do not count my life to be my own, but [to be] God's. For I have hope in God, who saved me and will save me always. Because of this, I will follow my brothers until death." While the people beside Onesimus were talking, they observed him about to throw himself into the water. Therefore, the priest said, "What are you doing? Where are you going?" But Onesimus did not hear, for he threw himself out of the boat. But the people did not know why he did this. Therefore, they approached the water to see what would happen to Onesimus.

Story B (Philemon rejoices and is afraid)

"Onesimus! Onesimus!" Philemon woke from sleep. It was still night, for day did not come. Philemon said to himself, "What was I saying? I saw my beloved slave in danger. Where is he? Oh my God, wherever he is, watch over him! I urge you, save him from all dangers, whatever happens to him!" Because he couldn't sleep, he was walking through the house to find someone with whom he could speak. But when he entered his daughter's room, he found her still sleeping. And because he didn't want

to wake her, he went out into the field to work.

When he got to the field, he saw some seeds on the ground. So having gathered the seeds, as many as he could hold in [his] hands, he spread [them] along the paths that went through the field.

But while he was still working, he heard someone approaching. It was [his] daughter, who was awakened from sleep by the sound of her father working (her name is Thecla). And she said, "Father, what are you doing? It's still night." And Philemon, not answering [his] daughter, picked up some fruit from the ground and said, "Look at these fruits. One is good, the other is bad. I was like this bad fruit, because I did evil against my slaves. But someone taught me that whoever repents and believes in Christ will be saved. So having believed in Christ, I became another person like this good fruit. Do you know what I'm saying, oh daughter?"

And Thecla, not understanding the parable of the fruits, said, "I don't know what you're saying, but now I want to eat some fruit! Father, let's return home so we might eat something!" So Philemon grabbed her hand and returned, rejoicing on the one hand over his daughter, who had a beautiful heart, but still afraid on the other hand over Onesimus, whom he saw while sleeping.

LESSON 28

EVIL FOR EVIL

Philemon and Thecla returned home. They opened the door and saw Apphia already awake. And Thecla said, "Mother! I love you!" And [her] mother [said], "I love you, too. What do you want?" And Thecla [said], "Let's eat!" So Apphia and Philemon prepared bread and fruit to eat and water to drink. When they all sat down, they were about to eat. Philemon said to [his] daughter, "Give me [your] hand." Then, after giving him [her] hand, she observed [her] father and mother praying. And [her] father said,

"You, Lord, give us all that we have to eat.
And whatever we have you gave to us.
I beseech you, oh Lord, give us good days and years full of joy, so that we might give of our possessions to those who do not have.
As you gave to us life and breath and all things, we also will give to others. Amen."

And the daughter marveled at the faith of [her] parents. So she asked [her] father, "Father, why do we pray before eating?" And [her] father answered saying, "We pray to God, who gives us all these things, because he rejoices when we ask of him whatever we wish. You, too, child, ask him whatever you wish and he will give [it] to you!"

So Thecla lifted [her] eyes and said, "Lord, I ask you, wake up my brother, who is still sleeping!"

When Apphia realized [her] son was not with them, she got up to go to him. But Thecla said, "Sit, mother! I will go and wake him." But [her] father said, "Go, daughter, and wake him. But don't act badly [do evil]!"

So Thecla immediately went out to wake [her] brother, whose name is Demas. Then, finding Demas sleeping like a rock, she cried out in a great voice, "Wake up! Wake up! It's time to eat!" But because [her] brother still did not wake up, she cried out again, "Wake up! WAKE UP! WAKE UP!"

Then, when Demas opened his eyes and saw his sister, he answered, "I don't want to wake up! Go away and don't yell like that!" But Thecla was not happy about [her] brother, who often did not listen to her. For the sister was older, for she was five years old, while the brother was four years old.

Then, seeing some rocks on the ground, she knew what she had to do. So she picked up a small rock and threw it at him! And when the stone fell on Demas's head, he woke up and cried, "Ah, ah! What happened? What is this on my face? Is it blood?" But Thecla, because she feared both [her] father and [her] brother, immediately fled out of the house. But Demas got up and followed so that he might seize her. And he cried out, "I will render to you as you rendered to me, evil for evil!"

CARRIED ALONG BY THE SEA

Onesimus was being carried along by the sea, with no hope of salvation. And when the people on the boat saw him, they did not know what they should do. One of them said, "If we leave him like this, he will die. Then, his blood will be on our heads!" But another one said, "Leave him! Whatever happens to him he has done by his own hands. But let's throw him a plank so that he grabs it and doesn't die immediately."

So they threw [him] a plank, which Onesimus grabbed with [his] hand. And the people left him in the sea and departed. And Onesimus cried out in a loud voice, "Paul! Luke! Where are you?" Hearing no one, he prayed, "Oh my God, you saved me once from prison and evil crowds. Therefore, you can save us now from the sea. For what is the sea? It is nothing to you! So I exhort you, do not leave me here, but show me where the brothers are."

And at that very moment/time, he saw something going up and down in the water. It was the hand of Paul! So Onesimus was imploring Paul, "Give me [your] hand!" When Paul did not answer, Onesimus approached and grabbed him by the hand and lifted up his body out of the sea. Then, he placed him on the plank.

Paul was not speaking nor did he open [his] eyes, but he was remaining on the plank, as though dead. So Onesimus said, "Oh Paul. Don't die, for you are adding this too to my misfortunes. For I'm afraid that we are perishing." But Paul said in a weak voice, "Don't be afraid, Onesimus. None of us will perish, because our life is in the hands of God."

They were being carried by the sea night and day. The whole time they ate nothing, nor did they drink [anything]. So they drew near to death. But when it was morning, they were awakened by the voices of people. They opened their eyes and saw a small boat approaching them! They heard a voice from the boat crying out, "Look here! It's Luke! We've come to save you! Stay there!"

So they stayed on the plank until the boat arrived. And after they entered the boat, they rejoiced over Luke, who had found them. And Onesimus said, "Luke! How are you still alive?" And Luke said, "When these good people found me being carried along by the sea, they welcomed me into the boat." But one of the people said, "Don't talk about this, but come! Eat and drink!" Then, the people gave to the brothers bread to eat and wine to drink. So they seemed to them like angels of God.

Then, Paul and Onesimus immediately began to eat whatever they could put into [their] mouth, so that there was nothing left for the others.

LESSON 30

PHILEMON LOSES EVERYTHING

Demas stood up and went out to find and catch [his] sister, who fled from his presence. For he wanted to render to her as she also rendered to him.

And because Demas didn't find Thecla in the house, he went out into the field to look for her outside the house. But Thecla, not wanting to be found, stood beside a large rock. But [her] brother stood on another large rock and said, "Come out! For I know that you are here! Don't flee! I only want to talk about what happened." But because Thecla didn't believe [her] brother, she didn't answer.

So Demas again said, "If you don't come out, you will see fire coming down on you from heaven. Then, you will never escape from my hand." Because Thecla also didn't believe this, she did not get up, but remained where she was.

Then, [her] brother immediately went into the house and returned with fire in [his] hand. And he began to throw the fire into the field so that he might cast Thecla out.

But when Thecla saw the fire she stood up and said, "I urge you, have mercy! Don't do this!" But Demas, rejoicing that he found her, approached so that he might seize [her] and do something bad, but he couldn't, for the fire became large, so that it was about to consume even the house. Then, Demas realized that he did a great evil, for the field was becoming full of fire so that the children couldn't flee. Therefore, the two cried out in loud voices, "FATHER! MOTHER! save us! We're perishing!"

And when Philemon and Apphia heard the children, they came immediately and seized the children and pulled them out of the fire. And Philemon ordered the slaves to throw water into the fire so that he might save both the house and the field and all of his other possessions. So the slaves were throwing a lot of water into the fire, but nothing happened, since [the fire] had already become great. But because he still had hope, Philemon himself brought water and was throwing [it] into the fire. But Apphia cried, "Leave the house! You can't save it, since the fire is already great. But let's flee and save ourselves!"

So the four [of them] fled from the house that they loved. And Philemon's house was being destroyed, so that nothing remained of his possessions. And as Philemon saw the fire consuming the house, he bid it farewell and left behind all that he had.

LESSON 31

PAUL AND ONESIMUS IN ATHENS

After Paul and Onesimus arrived in the city of Athens, they began to preach about Christ in the market, for God opened a door to preach the gospel to the people standing there. While some of the ones standing there didn't accept the message, others said, "We will hear you concerning this again," among whom were both Dionysius the Areopagite and his wife, whose name was Damaris.

So these people invited the brothers to their own house so they might hear again about the faith. And when he entered the house, Paul saw a great crowd gathered. And he said, "What is this?"

So Dionysius answered, "All of us want to hear about this Christ whom you preach!"

And Paul marveled when he saw the people who wanted to hear in this way. And Damaris the wife of Dionysius grabbed his hand and set him before everyone.

So Paul, standing before them said, "I know now that my God truly loves people from every nation under heaven, for you, having come here, wish to hear about this God whom you don't know. For this God is the God of the Jews, who created heaven and earth and the sea and all that is in them, and . . ."

But while Paul was speaking, a certain person spoke up saying, "But is your god stronger than Poseidon the god of the sea?"

And Paul answered, "Yes, my God is stronger than Poseidon."

But another [one] said, "But is he greater than Athena the goddess of our city?"

And Paul said, "Not only is he greater than Athena, but he's also better and greater and stronger than all the gods whom you worship!"

And those who were listening marveled at this word. And Paul said, "My God created not only the earth, but also you all. And after God created all these things, sin entered into the world through one person and through sin, death. Therefore, God sent his own son, Jesus, whom the people in Jerusalem crucified. But after three days he was raised from the dead."

Dionysius said, "But where is he now? He's not still in Jerusalem, is he?"

Paul answered, "Not at all! But he is sitting on a throne of glory in heaven. And he will come on the last day to judge the living and the dead. But whoever repents and believes in him will be saved."

So he was teaching them thus for many days and many received the gospel, having been baptized into the name of Jesus. And after twelve days, Paul and Onesimus prepared to depart.

But before they departed, Dionysius approached and said to them, "If you hadn't come here, we would not have accepted the gospel. So thank you!"

But Onesimus said, "If you hadn't invited us into your house, we would not have preached to you! Thank you!"

And Paul said, "On the contrary, Onesimus, if you hadn't saved me from the sea, I would not still be alive. Thank you!"

But Onesimus said, "On the contrary, oh Paul, if you hadn't taught me the gospel in Philippi, I wouldn't be a disciple of Christ."

But Damaris approached and said, "On the contrary, oh men, if you don't leave now, I myself will throw you all out!"

Then, the brothers immediately went out.

LESSON 32

TIME TO RETURN

So the two brothers were teaching and preaching the gospel in every city into which God sent them. For when they would enter a city, they would preach the gospel first in the synagogues and then in the middle of the city, to both Jews and Gentiles. So Paul and Onesimus and all others who wanted to proclaim the promise of salvation were traveling in this way through the land. But not only good things would happen to them, but also many bad things, for

they were often handed over into the hands of evil people. For this reason, after Paul was handed over into the hands of the Romans, he was sent to Rome.

And now Paul is in Rome with Onesimus and Timothy. While he can't go outside of the house, he can welcome into the house all who want to hear him. And on a certain day, while Paul is walking around the house, Timothy comes and says, "Paul, messengers have come from the church in Colossae, and they want to speak to you."

So Paul, after welcoming them in, prepares something to eat. But the [messengers] say, "Paul, don't prepare anything! For we brought these gifts from Colossae."

And after putting the gifts in the middle of them, they show him fruit and bread, books and clothes, and other such gifts.

And Paul says, "You've come to Rome so that you might give me garments? Don't you know that I can buy all these things also here in Rome?"

And they answer, "Oh Paul, you are the father of us all who have believed in Colossae. But we ourselves never saw you, but we only heard about you from Philemon. Therefore, we came not only because of the gifts, but also so that we might see you face to face."

And Paul, not knowing what he should say, rejoices over their faith and says, "Very well. But how is Philemon?"

And they say, "He's not doing well, for he lost all his possessions in a big fire."

After these things, Onesimus, having returned from the market, comes to Paul. And Paul says, "Where were you?"

"I went down into the market," says Onesimus, "so that I might buy more bread, but what are these? If I knew that you already have so much, I wouldn't have gone."

But Paul says, "Messengers have come from Colossae reporting to me concerning Philemon our brother."

But [Onesimus] says, "*Our* brother? Rather, only *your* brother!"

But Paul says, "Listen, Onesimus! A great evil has happened to him, so that he needs you! For he lost all his possessions in a fire."

But Onesimus says, "But send someone else rather than me. Send Timothy! For if I become his slave again, what then?"

But Paul says, "May it never be! You will never be a slave again, for I am writing a letter to the church in Colossae so that they may not welcome you as a slave, but rather as a brother. And in this way God will show his grace, which he gives to all, for we are all one in Christ. So take this letter and bring it to Philemon."

(What did Paul write in the letter? You will find what he wrote in the letter called "To Philemon.")

After some time, after Onesimus and some others with him get ready, they travel toward Colossae. But before they leave, Paul puts his hands on Onesimus and prays,

"May God show you mercy on the way,
may the Lord lead you with peace toward Philemon,
may the Holy Spirit be with you in every season,
may grace and peace be with you all now and forever. Amen."